BUTTERTEA
AT SUNRISE

A Year in the Bhutan Himalaya

BRITTA DAS

Summersdale Publishers Ltd
46 West Street
Chichester
West Sussex
PO19 1RP
UK

www.summersdale.com

Printed and bound in Great Britain

ISBN 1 84024 498 4
ISBN 13: 978 1 84024 498 4

ACKNOWLEDGEMENTS

At first the idea of working in Bhutan seemed like a dream, but some practical-minded miracle workers nudged me in the right direction. While it would be impossible to mention everyone who lent a hand or gave me valuable advice, the following people were my pillars: my parents, who had the courage to let me go and support my wild ideas without hesitation; Wangdi and Gaki Gyaltshen, who opened their home to me in Thimphu; Marion and David Young, who saw a way where no one else did, who stood up for me, and whose friendship surpassed and outlasted my placement with VSO; Andreas Guggemos, who believed in me more than I did in myself. To my expatriate friends in Thimphu, thank you for your hospitality while I waited for my placement, and even more so when I came back sick and scared.

In Mongar: to my friends and patients in the villages, thank you for welcoming a blonde, blue-eyed girl and opening her eyes to the true wonders of Bhutan, for your unlimited hospitality, deep faith and most astonishing sincerity. Beda, you are a true friend who helped me to understand so much more than the language; and Dechen, thank you for standing faithfully by my side.

I never thought that I could write a book, so I am indebted to those who convinced me otherwise: first and foremost Bikul, my guiding light and inspiration; Charlotte Hale, who travelled across the continent to provide counsel and encouragement; Jamie Zeppa, a cheering admirer of my photographs who was convinced that there would be room for another Bhutan book.

When I turned my sights from publishing mainly photos to writing a travel memoir, I am deeply thankful to many people for their good advice or critical reviews of earlier drafts of the book; among them are Bruce Kirkby, Don Watt, Marjorie Green, Tej Hazarika, Stephen Schettini and Sandra Chong.

In deciphering Bikul's complicated explanations about Buddhism and religious customs in Bhutan, I often relied on Françoise Pommaret's *An Illustrated Guide to Bhutan*.

Frederking & Thaler took the first leap of faith by publishing *Königreich in den Wolken* in Germany.

With Jennifer Barclay, my English language publishing began and now came full circle. Jennifer, without you, this book would not exist! At the agency, Hilary McMahon and Nicole Winstanley, thank you for believing in my prose. To everyone at Summersdale, I am immensely grateful for your enthusiasm, with a special mention to Carol Baker for her discerning edits.

Once again, thank you to Bikul, in more ways than I can count.

CONTENTS

For Mutti and Hardy, who encouraged me to explore the world and for Bikul, who waited to share the way with me

If you blow on a conch, guiding your breath deep into the twists of its pearly coil, it produces the sound of Om. Some say that this is the beginning of all things.

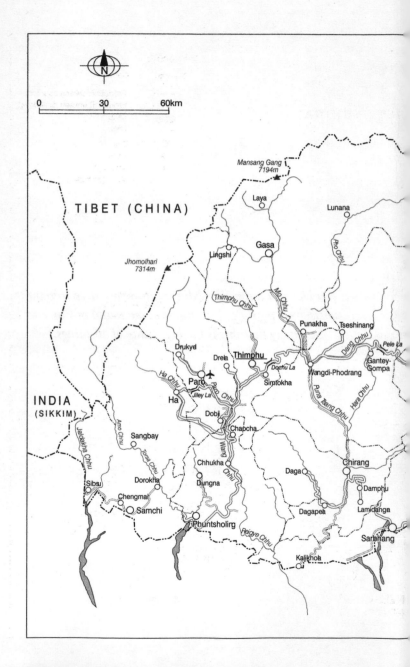

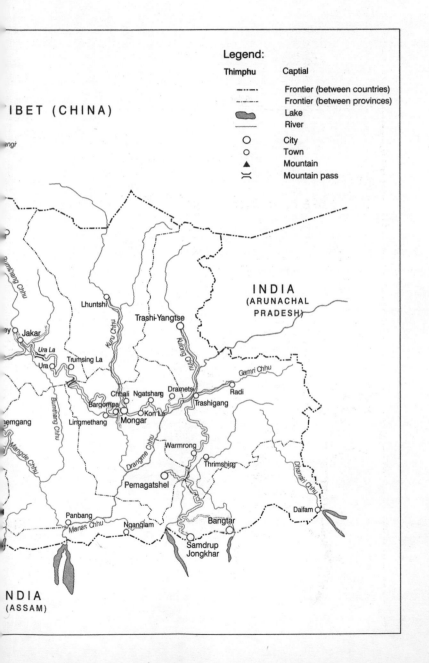

PROLOGUE

Somewhere in the valley, a conch signalled the start of a new day. The deep echo bounced off the cliffs of a magnificent mountain range and, faithfully, the sheer walls repeated the ancient message until it faded in the thickness of the jungle.

Two red-robed figures sat motionless under the long thin branches of a cypress tree. Only a wispy beard danced on the chin of the old lama as he solemnly murmured a prayer. His eyes were closed. He did not need to see the script written on a page to follow its rhythm and intonations. After a few moments, the other monk joined the recitation. His young voice was strong and confident, and the old lama quieted, only his body continued to sway back and forth to the ebb and swell of the holy words.

In the distance, the softly rounded Himalayan foothills were flushed in pink while morning sun flooded the Indian plains. Gradually, the bright yellow fireball climbed in the eastern sky. When the first sunrays reached over the ascending height of a mountain range culminating in the highest peaks on earth, the last lines of the prayer were completed. The old lama stacked the sacred pages back between their wooden covers and wrapped them with a yellow cloth. He nodded and heaved his body from the seated position. Then he turned to face the young monk by his side.

'Today we will see if you are ready for your lessons,' he said. 'You have grown up, Sangay.'

The young monk also stood, but he did not meet the eyes of his elder.

'I hope that I will not disappoint you, la,' he replied. 'I am still small and ignorant.' With these words, he bowed deeply and offered a white silken scarf to the old lama. The teacher accepted the respectful gesture and then motioned to a narrow muddy path.

'We will go now,' he said and turned towards the mountain.

Sangay followed his teacher without comment. His mind wandered ahead to the test that he must pass, an initiation rite, which many had failed before him. An enormous cliff stood above the monastery of Larjap. He used to come here as a little boy, when the red robes he wore were the only thing he knew about being a monk. His mother had always warned him to stay away from the deadly drop-off that plunged hundreds of metres into the forest below. When he was a child, he used to turn from the ledge in tears. Today, however, he must face it.

A group of long white prayer flags rippled lazily from their wooden poles on top of the crest. A few feet from the edge of the cliff, the lama stopped. Hesitantly, Sangay approached.

'Go now, Sangay,' the old man urged. 'Do not be afraid. Believe in yourself and the teachings you have learned. Show me if you are ready for the true meaning of the dharma.'

Sangay nodded. Bravely keeping his gaze fixed on the line of earth separating solid ground from the airy void beyond, he placed one foot in front of the other until he stood only centimetres from the abrupt ledge. There, paralysed with fear, he choked on his breath and quickly averted his eyes to the soft blue of the morning sky.

'What do you see?' He heard the old lama's words drifting to him through the haze in his mind. Forcing his body to remain fixed at the very edge, Sangay lowered his gaze slightly. Immediately, he began to sway.

'I see clouds,' he stuttered truthfully. Perspiration began to collect on his forehead. With each passing second, the cliff seemed to draw him farther off his carefully balanced inner strength.

'Everyone sees clouds,' the old lama replied. 'Look down!'

In the distance, a silvery band snaked its course through the valleys to disappear in the mist, and Sangay stammered, 'I see a river.'

Again the lama corrected him; 'You are looking too far ahead, Sangay. Look down!'

Trembling with fear, Sangay let his view span the land from the bluish hills in the distance to the green of the forest below. Suddenly, a sea of spiky treetops rose out of the bleary landscape. Again, the lama's voice travelled to him from afar.

'What do you see now?'

Sangay refocused and let his gaze settle on his feet. Dizziness and nausea fought within him. His toes gripped onto grass and rocks, and he wondered almost passively if he would now fall and tumble into the great emptiness.

As if the lama could read his mind, the old man walked up closely behind his student. 'Look beyond your toes, Sangay. Believe in your teachings. Find your strength.'

Sangay's sight blurred and his body swayed dangerously close to the edge. A shiver ran down his spine, and he failed to notice how the old lama stretched his hand protectively towards him.

Closing his eyes for a fraction of a second, Sangay took a deep breath. Then, at first faltering, but slowly increasing in strength and conviction, he started to murmur the syllables of his mantra, the secret formula given to him by his guru. As he spoke the precious words again and again and let his mind open to the image of the guru, the young monk could feel his body relax. After a while, the features of the guru's face became strong and clear and finally Sangay allowed his sight to shift to the awesome splendour of the morning before him.

This time, unhurried, he took another deep breath and tilted his head and body forward. Below him, beyond the edge of the rugged cliff and the outline of his big round toes, he saw the gleaming light of the golden pinnacle of a monastery. At that moment, Sangay felt the gentle pressure of the lama's hand on his shoulder.

'Yes, Sangay, you are ready.'

For a long time, the teacher and the student stood in that same spot, watching the morning climb over the giants of earth around them. Then, after a deep silence, the old lama spoke again.

'Sangay, you have travelled far in your young life. You have received an education outside of our world in the mountains. You have seen places that I have never journeyed to. Tell me what you saw.'

Quietly Sangay described the Buddhist college in Bangalore, and the lessons he received in southern India. The old lama did not interrupt. Finally, Sangay pointed to the faint line of the horizon where the kingdom of Bhutan bordered its giant southern neighbour. 'Life is different there,' he said.

The old lama nodded. He himself had made a pilgrimage to the temple of Bodh Gaya in his younger days, and had seen that the world beyond the Himalaya was a different one.

'It is not that,' Sangay tried to explain. 'Things are changing.'

Again, the old lama studied his student with fondness. 'Of course, there is always change,' he said. Then he shook his head. 'But we are happy to live in this ancient country with a good king who knows how to protect his people. I do not think that for us life will ever change.'

For the first time, Sangay met the eyes of his teacher. He did not want to oppose the old man's words. He did not even know what it was that made him question the future. Coming home to his village in the mountains, nothing had appeared different, and yet it was. Without understanding the rising feeling of sadness, Sangay could sense that even here in his isolated home, the tiny Himalayan kingdom of Bhutan, old traditions and customs were dying. No one could prevent the flow of the years. Bhutan was changing, too.

ONE

A ROAD LEADING EAST

Massive monsoon clouds loom before us, barring the path and drowning our sight. The air is a heavy white curtain, dripping with moisture. Thick mist is hanging low in the crooks and crevasses of the mountain ridges, filling the valleys and blanketing the plateaus. Although no rain is falling, the windshield wipers squeak on, busying themselves with the endless task of providing the driver with a small, dirty window into the morning wetness. Everything is cold and dank. At almost 4,000 metres, we are not only driving in the clouds, we are breathing them, feeling them, living within them.

The pickup truck is heavily loaded, its weight pushing it on as the brakes squeal and the car skids around the tight, steep curves. Some corners seem to warrant a loud boast of the horn; others are left to silence and destiny.

Huddled in the front passenger seat, with two people in the back and surrounded by laboratory equipment, my radio and a handful of valuable items that must stay dry, I stare into the illusive milky blankness ahead. Most of my gear and household wares for the forthcoming year are tied onto the loading surface, stacked and stuffed under a brown tarp whose edges and corners are angrily flapping in the wind. The rest of the truck's load consists of several huge laboratory machines and some boxes containing test tubes and reactants with the same destination as mine: Mongar Hospital in Eastern Bhutan.

The solemn quiet of my fellow passengers lets me contemplate my journey to the East. Bhutan has been my dream since the fall of 1995, less than two years ago. I was 24, and my father, the world traveller, wanted to show me his beloved Himalaya. He had been to Bhutan six times already, and each time he had returned full of enthusiasm – but also with a new worry line on his forehead. 'What an incredible country!' he would exclaim, and then invariably update me on the most recent changes he had observed. 'The traffic in the capital Thimphu must have doubled. They even put up a traffic light,' he said one year. The next time, he had different concerns. 'Well, the traffic light is gone again. But the number of tourists I saw in Thimphu! Minibuses full of tourists! You really should see it before it's too late. I want to show you Bhutan. This is one of the last untouched cultures in the world. And it is bound to change soon. Look at its neighbour Nepal, or even

Thailand. They were so different twenty years ago. Why don't you come with me?'

For a long time, I was sceptical. I was busy establishing my career in physiotherapy, taking postgraduate courses and trying to climb the ladder of success. I looked at my father's pictures of the Himalaya with interest and studied the map long enough to know that Bhutan was a tiny kingdom south of Tibet and east of Nepal, but it was not until internal problems at my workplace forced me to think about changing jobs that I seriously considered my father's offer. On his sixtieth birthday, when he again talked about his need for a travel companion, in a sudden flash of daring I said 'OK, let's go.'

We packed our bags and off we went, first to India and Nepal, then to Bhutan. My father took me on the trip of a lifetime and indulged me with the sights of a world unknown to me. He opened my eyes, and I opened my heart. Bhutan mesmerised me. The mountains loomed to spectacular heights, a cheerful people welcomed us with sincere generosity, and I felt an undeniable peace in the gentle philosophies of Buddhism.

Suddenly, my ambitions changed.

From the window of a monastery perched on the rocky outcrop of a mountain, my world of materialism and fashionable stress in Canada seemed absurd. I realised that now was the time for me to travel, to experience different cultures, to discover if our globe has more fascinating places to offer. I would go to a place where living still made sense. I wanted to learn and I longed for adventure. In return, I would do something worthwhile, something meaningful, I would offer whatever skills I had to people who were less fortunate – I would become a volunteer. The three weeks travelling with my father had drawn an enormous line between our wealth and the poverty we encountered, and my first exposure to the Haves and Have-nots of a developing country had shocked me deeply. I had always known that my life had been pampered, but now I felt over-privileged. All at once, treating sports injuries in a modern, well-equipped clinic was no longer enough. I wanted to give back, to share what I could. In my imagination, I saw myself surrounded by little dark-skinned children who knew that I had come to help. For the first time ever, I contemplated the possibility of fate. Someone in Bhutan was calling my name.

Back in Canada, my parents were less than enthusiastic about my ideas and plans.

'But you don't have to go for a whole year,' my father tried to caution me. 'That's such a long time. Have you really thought about it?'

I had. I had contacted the Bhutanese Ministry of Health and had been told that if I wanted to volunteer, I would have to commit for an entire year. I was 26, bursting with energy, and full of ideals. I said yes.

My father tried another approach: 'Now you are a young woman, this is the best time of your life. You should go on dates, fall in love, look for a husband. Who are you going to meet over there?'

I was not worried. After a painful split from the man I had thought I would marry, a serious romance was not what I yearned for.

'Please don't think that you have to stay there for the whole year, just because you are too proud to come back if things don't work out,' were my father's departing words. I realised that my parents were worried beyond measure, and yet I was determined to go. So, in February of 1997, after months of preparation and tearful goodbyes from my family, I stuffed my two hockey bags full of clothing, thermal underwear, physiotherapy books, spare batteries and a year's supply of female hygiene products, took a plane to Bangkok and bought a one-way ticket to Bhutan.

In Bhutan's capital Thimphu, Voluntary Services Overseas, a non-governmental organisation that places volunteers in developing countries, recruited me, giving me the chance to live and work in this mystical country. Through them, the Royal Government of Bhutan considered my enthusiasm and skills and found an opening for me in the physiotherapy sector of the country's health care system.

During my orientation in Thimphu, I learned that over the last 25 years, Bhutan had worked hard to develop a new and surprisingly active health care network. In the past, this landlocked Himalayan kingdom relied mainly on traditional medicine and village healers. In the mid 1970s, leprosy missions came and set up permanent buildings for admitting and treating patients. Now there were hospitals in most major towns in the country, and many small villages were served by little outposts called Basic Health Units, which offered rudimentary treatments, basic medications and vaccinations.

Although the first physiotherapists came together with the leprosy missions, most of the mission staff have now retreated, leprosy being more or less under control. Physiotherapy for non-leprosy cases is a relatively new idea in Bhutan and far from universally recognised.

When I arrived, there were three qualified physiotherapists working in the country. Two of them, one Bhutanese and one American UN volunteer, worked in the large national referral hospital in Thimphu. One Finnish therapist still works with the Leprosy Mission in Gidakom, a tiny village only about a 45-minute drive from the capital. In addition, eight trained physiotherapy assistants (or 'technicians' as they are called here) were spread throughout the country. Three worked in Thimphu and one with the mission in Gidakom, while four of them were posted in Eastern Bhutan; one in Mongar, one in Yebilapsa near Zhemgang, one in Trashigang, and one in Rizerboo near Pemagatsel.

The Royal Government's Ministry of Health determined that my responsibility would consist of training the four physiotherapy technicians in the eastern districts. I was to teach them more independent assessment and treatment skills.

Spending several weeks training at their Thimpu base, VSO prepared me for my posting in the more remote regions of Eastern Bhutan. Cooking lessons focused on dishes using locally available foods, while discussions about health and hygiene pointed out the dangers of improper meal preparation, poor water quality, and the possibilities of vitamin deficiencies and malnutrition due to a limited diet. Confident that I was prepared for even the remotest of relocations, I went shopping for luxury items such as peanut butter and chocolate bars, read up on the local traditions and customs, and received my first rabies vaccination.

During several days spent in the physiotherapy department of Thimphu hospital, I learned that everyone who works in nursing, physiotherapy or medicine had received their training in English, which would make my communication with hospital staff easy. Understanding my patients would be an entirely different issue. Several different languages are spoken in Eastern Bhutan, corresponding to different geographical regions within the country as well as dialects that have evolved in isolated valleys. VSO gave me a booklet on Sharchhopkha (also called *Tshangla)*, the language spoken most commonly in the region of Mongar and Tashigang. Even some of the simplest words seemed tongue twisters, and since I was eager to start my new job, I convinced VSO that I should skip the language course offered in the capital and instead pick it up once I was immersed in my work and confronted with patients.

I was overjoyed at the prospect of my new job and packed my bags in Thimphu to start my long journey eastwards.

After fifteen hours crammed into the car, feeling wrinkled and edgy, now more than ever I question my wisdom. My only overseas working experience is a three-month locum at a regional hospital in Australia, and yet here I am travelling towards one of the most remote corners of the inhabited globe. 'I would like to help wherever it is most needed,' I had told my parents heroically. Mongar

Hospital was the place which the Health division of the Royal Government of Bhutan deemed worthy for my cause.

Suddenly, the question of accommodation torments me. I was told that it would be basic. But how basic? Will it be bright? Or dark? Running water? Hot water? No water? I recall terrible stories about Mongar, the construction site around the hospital, the overcrowded housing.

The journey seems to offer a taste of what is to come, and the arduous two-day car ride from Thimphu to the eastern district of Mongar takes me farther and farther into the unknown world of the Himalaya. Our speed never exceeds 20 miles an hour, but we are flying. To my left, rocky cliffs rise steeply out of sight. Short stumpy trees grow from overhanging boulders and cling onto their narrow crags. To the right, too close for comfort, the edge of the road drops hundreds of metres into bottomless gorges. The narrow strip of tarmac is flooded with water, rivulets turning into little streams, waves of rainwater washing the road ahead. The occasional swollen creek, which has overgrown its drainpipe and escaped onto the road, blends in completely, only announced by the splattering and gurgling of its waterfall at the road side. To quiet my nerves, I trick myself into believing that this is an ordinary road in the mountains, simply boasting a lot of bends. The Gravol I took earlier helps. Fear makes the fog a welcome obstacle to the view, obliterating the spectacle of what otherwise must be one of the world's most awesome roads.

A little white chorten, a religious stone monument, protects the tip of one particularly tight curve. It must be a good luck sign, a protector of the wary traveller. Behind it, only some trees and grasses obstruct the near vertical tumble into the valley.

We have left Trumsing La, at 3,800 metres (12,400 ft) the highest pass on the road traversing Bhutan from Thimphu to Mongar, and continue our descent, spanning one and a half kilometers in altitude over several hours. Rocks and shrubs change into a deciduous forest. After the cold climate of the higher elevations, the thermometer now rises until we are surrounded by hot and sticky tropics. Huge vines cover the jagged edges of the road. Bamboo, banana trees and cacti dominate the scenery. The dampness becomes almost oppressive. I open my window all the way but the air seems to hang motionless.

In Lingmithang, our descent bottoms out at 650 metres before we immediately resume our climb, and the truck huffs and puffs its way up the opposite mountain. The road is uneven at the best of times, and often spiked with potholes. At every jolt of the truck, a dull headache thuds at my nerves and makes coherent thinking impossible. I am tired and hungry, and a little bit afraid.

The clouds refuse to budge, and we continue to plough through them, one bend after another. Several times we nearly collide with the huge orange, Indian-made TATA trucks, fully loaded with logs or stones or sometimes people. The result is always much honking and manoeuvring; then somehow we manage to squeeze by.

Oddly enough, over these last few hours of the journey the traffic has increased and I wonder where everyone is going. As far as I can tell, there are only a few houses scattered along the slopes, and we left the last town of any size eight or more hours behind in Bumthang, where we spent the night in a tiny guesthouse.

Perhaps the fog is hiding glorious old settlements and picturesque villages, which I will soon discover and explore. My imagination paints colourful pictures to pass the time.

'Here Mongar,' the driver gleefully announces, and I squint into the mist to take in the first impression of my new home. I imagine a vibrant market to meet plenty of friendly villagers, a quaint hospital, and perhaps even a small house for myself.

Eagerly I peer out the window – but there is nothing. All I see is a little stretch of road in front of us, a few trees on both sides, and clouds. The driver points ahead and to the left. Again I squint and strain – nothing.

Then suddenly, out of nowhere, a large façade of three-storey houses rises beside the road. There must be eight or ten impressive buildings, their wooden exteriors artfully painted and decorated with carvings. I rejoice at the prospect of such a pretty town, but already the mirage disappears. We take a hairpin turn to the left, and bump and rattle down a cracked, gullied side road, leaving all signs of habitation behind us.

The path continues to curve steeply through a treed incline and finally stops in front of a long, white building with a wooden sign: Mongar Hospital, Referral Hospital of Eastern Bhutan.

TWO

FROM A
DISTANCE

My house turns out to be a classroom adjacent to the Mother and Child Health Clinic. Standing amidst the clutter of my boxes and bags, I take a first look around. The room is bare and uninviting. On one wall, stacked neatly, are six chairs, a large table and a white drawing board depicting a chart of various modes of contraception. An X-ray viewer along with two posters of Buddha and a picture of the king of Bhutan decorate the far wall of the room. Beside it, an old bowed metal shelf holds a collection of dusty books. In the opposite corner, a lonely bed awaits my arrival. The hospital's administrator assures me that I will be moving into my permanent quarters within ten days. Most regrettably, though, at the moment, this modest room is the only available accommodation.

His English is somewhat stiff with a strong accent. He asks me to use the weekend to get settled in and begin my hospital duties on Monday. After introductions to some of the other staff of the hospital, and a quiet 'We hope you like it here,' I am left alone.

Tired, my whole body aching as if I had hiked and not driven the 480 kilometres from Thimphu to Mongar, I survey the situation. Outside, the rain pours steadily, drumming on the corrugated iron roof in a monotonous beat. I cannot see more than a few yards into the distance; my world is wrapped in white oblivion. From somewhere below my window drones an insistent clunking of hammers on stones. The fog muffles the sounds, yet the continuous vibration under my feet tells me that the construction cannot be more than a few metres from my doorstep. Behind me, the refrigerator which holds the hospital's supply of vaccinations is humming like a motor engine. A large black beetle propels itself through the room, crashing into the walls with full force, then resuming its noisy flight.

It is nearly five o'clock, and dusk is creeping through the cracks. I open the door to let the last light into my abode, but instead an impenetrable wall of cloud rolls in and settles on my belongings. The air inside and out is cold and clammy, and I wrap my jacket tightly around me. I ensure that my flashlight is safely stored in my pocket and start digging through my boxes to find a candle and some matches.

There is a knock on the door and two petite women with boyish short haircuts smile at me.

'*Kuzuzang po la!*' The younger woman introduces herself as Pema Dorji and the other as her cousin Wangmo Dorji.

'I will be working with you, madam. I am physiotechnician. How you like Mongar?'

I am at a loss for words. What might be considered polite conversation in this country? Unprepared to offer premature flattery, I mutter something about 'very nice'. Then, just to be on the safe side, I add, 'I love Bhutan.' Next I enquire, 'Do you live on the hospital campus, too?'

Pema shakes her head. 'No. My husband is administrative officer in dzong. We are staying a little bit in town.'

'Have you been in Mongar for a long time?'

Pema tilts her head from side to side in a strange wagging motion. Not the same as the definite negative shake of the head that accompanied her previous 'no', instead it seems to imply agreement.

'My family is living in Bargompa, not far from here,' she affirms.

My visitors look at me quizzically, but there seems to be no need for further formalities. Together the two women seat themselves on my bed and simply admire my packed belongings. They praise my big red hockey bag, my new mattress, my shiny blue plastic 'bathtub-bucket', and my *two* gas cylinders.

'In Mongar, it is too difficult to get gas! We have terrible waiting list, just to get a cylinder. At least six months,' Pema exclaims. 'You are very lucky – you have *two* cylinders! Sister, when you leave, we may have one of your cylinders?'

I nod and suddenly feel extremely privileged.

After informing me that I need to buy a kerosene lamp as soon as possible and that I should not forget to go to the vegetable market on Sunday morning, Pema starts rearranging the room. She pulls out three of the stacked library chairs and lines them up below the window. Then she advises me to lift up all of my bags and to balance the load on the armrests in order to protect my things from the rats overnight.

The rats! I must indeed be privileged.

'You are hungry, sister?' Pema asks while examining my taped boxes of kitchenware. 'You please come to my house.' Abruptly, the two women move towards the door.

'I'll be OK, thanks,' I stammer – which earns me a disapproving look.

'You must be tired. We are thinking of calling you for dinner. Do you have torch?'

I nod and show them my little flashlight, a Maglite.

'This is torch?' Pema asks with obvious disbelief. 'You must have big torch! But no problem. I have one.' She settles the matter by waving an enormous steel flashlight in front of me.

A little later, wrapped in a raincoat and gripping my umbrella like a shield, I trudge behind Pema and her silent cousin along a muddy road that leads past the hospital to a small settlement of cement houses.

'Careful here!'

We clamber up a precarious staircase cut into the hillside. At its top, we reach a square building with several entrance doors and a row of dilapidated windows, the shutters of which have been closed tightly. Pema opens a door leading to a dark and crammed hallway. We duck into dry warmth. My host disappears behind a blue and green checkered woollen curtain beside a pile of cast-off plastic slippers and rubber boots. Her cousin vanishes.

I pull off my soggy shoes to add to the remarkable pile of plastic, rubber and leather and search for a place for my dripping umbrella.

'I will take. Please come.' Pema peeps back around the curtain and pulls me into a dimly lit, narrow room, dominated by a rusty woodstove at its centre.

'*Kuzuzang po la!*' From a bed along the far side of the room, a man with a little boy in his arms unfolds his legs and rises to greet me. Pema introduces us. 'This is Karma. My husband.'

'We were waiting for you!' Karma's soft smile brightens. He bows as far as the toddler in his arms will allow.

'Welcome!'

Pema prods a little girl of about five towards me.

'This is Chimmi. Chimmi say hello.'

'Good evening, auntie!' Chimmi beams.

'And this is Nima.' Pema takes the toddler from Karma and places him on her hips.

I smile at the cute little boy who almost disappears within his loosely crocheted blue jacket. Long lashes frame his beautiful brown eyes, his gaze is focused on something behind me. A small gurgling sound escapes from his throat, and his lips pull into a distraught whimper. Pema lovingly strokes the thin black curls and coos reassuringly.

'Nima needs much care. We are always worried about him.' Without any other explanation, Pema smoothes out the blanket on the bed and places Nima in her daughter's charge.

'Please sit.' Karma offers. Then both parents leave through the curtained door.

Feeling exhausted, I slouch on the bed and study the two children beside me. Chimmi has started to sing in her little girl's voice, but Nima is oddly quiet. Hands raised to his face, he busies himself by rolling his lower lip between thumb and index finger. Affectionately, Chimmi takes Nima's tiny hands in her own, pulls him towards her and leans over to kiss his cheek. Then she reaches for a tattered teddy bear and parades it up and down on the bed. Still, Nima only rocks himself rhythmically, staring at the wall behind us and rolling his lower lip ceaselessly between his fingers.

Pema returns only long enough to place an assortment of steaming bowls on a wooden stool beside the bed. 'Please eat,' she says and disappears again.

Uncomfortably I stare at the dishes and the spoon placed in front of me while Chimmi continues to play with Nima. Am I supposed to eat on my own? I wait until the rising steam dissipates from the bowls, then I tentatively push the rice around on my plate.

Pema slips back around the curtain with a cup of tea in her hand. In surprise, she looks at my untouched food.

'Please eat. We will eat later.'

I nibble at the curry that stings my throat and makes my eyes water. Nima begins to gurgle and startled I let my spoon drop back. Nima's sounds are identical to someone choking, yet the boy continues to make his noises without any signs of being upset. Neither Chimmi nor her mother are paying any attention. Over the rim of my plate, I study Nima. His eyes are glazed and his gaze is fixed into the distance. His movements seem slow and mechanical.

Pema squats in front of the open woodstove.

'We have to make fire in the summer, too,' she explains and gently blows into the sooty opening. 'It gets hot, but at least it is dry. We have to keep everything dry because of Nima.' Pema points at her son and frowns.

I want to ask her about Nima. Maybe she will bring him to physio. A little excited, I wonder if he will be my first patient in Mongar, but I decide to wait with my enquiries until Pema volunteers some information. Meanwhile the curry burns its way down my throat and my eyes brim with tears.

'Too hot for you?' Pema asks with a concerned look.

'No. No, it's great.' I shake my head and manage a smile. I would rather eat the entire bowl of curry than disappoint this kind woman with her silent child.

'You'll come again soon, isn't it?' Pema asks when we say goodbye.

I nod and wave to the children. 'Of course – thank you so much.' Chimmi follows me with huge bright eyes and cries, 'Goodbye auntie!'

33

I put on my shoes and fumble for the umbrella. Truthfully, I am not at all ready to leave, not yet. Karma darts outside to show me the way, but the beam of his flashlight is swallowed by the fog and the rain. The dark night looms before me like the entrance to a haunted house.

So, this is it; I am about to face my first night alone in my new home. The prospect is terrifying and suddenly I wonder why I only ever imagined what Mongar would *look* like, never how it would *feel*. Pema adjusts the raincoat on my shoulder and I quickly pull up the zipper. When I turn around once more, the silhouettes of Chimmi and her mother are outlined in the lighted door frame.

'You come again,' Pema repeats, and as I head into the wet murkiness of the monsoon night, I clutch her words like a lifeline.

Back in my classroom, alone and tucked under my mosquito net, the cheerful voices and reassurance of Pema's home are quickly replaced by a miserable emptiness. Images of my room at home, the comfort of my bed in the corner below the slanted wood ceiling, and the honking of Canada geese drifting in through the window start circling in my mind. Suddenly, I feel the barren silence of Mongar's cement walls as acutely as if they were touching me. The candle flickers tenuously while a squad of flies, mosquitoes and who knows what swirls around my head. I blow out the candle and crawl deeper into my sleeping bag. In the darkness, I listen to the mosquitoes' concert and wonder if the fleas are already marching in.

I wake up in the middle of the night. A loud alarm is going off right beside my ear. I reach for the flashlight but still see nothing. The threatening, shrill buzzing sound continues, and I clamber from underneath my mosquito net to investigate the state of emergency. Ready to grab my passport and my diary, I plan my escape. Then as abruptly as it began, the noise disappears.

I light a candle and stare at the ceiling. Immediately the black beetle I noticed earlier resumes its mission, throwing itself headlong into the walls. The rain continues to play drums on the roof, and eventually I fade off into a restless sleep.

The next morning, the rain continues. It is the middle of June, and the monsoon has just begun. I was told to expect it to last for at least three months.

My quarters smell musty and mouldy, and within a few hours, my belongings feel damp. My hair hangs limply in my face, and my skin itches all over.

Outside, the noise of the construction site fills the air. Most insistent of all is an endless cacophony of hammers. It is not a noise one gets used to and ignores. The uneven racket pierces the ears, and sets up a disturbing vibration in the skull, hitting on the most sensitive nerve.

Now and then, there are loud shouts in Bengali or Hindi. I guess they are orders, instructions, or perhaps even a greeting. Then, somewhere in the mist, a generator springs to life, roaring and sputtering as the diesel fuel fills the chambers.

When the rain eases, I slide a few steps towards the hospital. A huge scar of bare soil gapes to the right of the main building. In its middle, waving metal rods pierce the concrete foundations of two new buildings. Amongst an apparent chaos of heaps of stones, old oil drums and piles of sand sit women, children and old men, hunched on the ground, patiently beating heavy axe-size hammers onto blocks of stone. Clunk, clunk… clunk, clunk… the sound reverberates between sheets of mist. Mechanically, driven by a force astounding for such skinny arms and slender shoulders, they turn boulders into rocks, then stones and then pebbles. One huge piece successfully crumbled, the next one is rolled forward and thrashed with the same unremitting stubbornness, until all that is left is a pile of gravel.

One of the women turns her head and stares at me long and hard. Her simple, orange sari is mud-caked. The loose end is wrapped over her head as if to protect her from the wetness and misery all around. On her arms a few bangles clink together, singing a cheerless tune. Beside her, a boy of maybe twelve years does not bother to look up. He feverishly attacks his rocks; perhaps his speed interrupts the monotony. Feeling sad and guilty for my own idleness, I turn to follow the 'new' road leading to the bazaar.

The muddy lane snakes up and to the left around a hilltop, and having reached its highest point, abruptly ends in the middle of a huge green field – a football field. Maybe a hundred metres ahead and raised up on an embankment five or six metres high, Mongar's bazaar oversees the valley behind me. The far edge of the football field also offers an unobstructed outlook over Mongar Hospital. Below a protruding hilltop, which serves as an emergency helicopter pad, the green roof of the hospital is sheltered amongst big leafy trees. The building is designed in a square, hollowed by an enclosed courtyard, with the glassy dome of the operation theatre sticking up in the far corner. Behind the hospital, the road disappears in the trees and emerges further down at an open space, lined with many separate staff buildings. Construction noise fills the air.

I cross the field and arrive at a set of steep steps at the base of the bazaar's fortification. The houses of the bazaar line a muddy road cut into the hillside. There are three 'hotels' for 'Fooding and Lodging', and shops open their doors on the ground floors of the remaining buildings. Every shop has a number and a name printed in bold white letters on a blue sign. The upper words must be written in Dzongkha, the beautiful Bhutanese script. Underneath English translations inform me about the shop and its owner: Shop No. 4, Dechen Lhendrup; Shop No. 6, Karma Yeshey; Shop No. 7, Dorji Choden. Unsure of whether to turn to Dechen, Karma or Dorji, I postpone my shopping for a closer inspection.

The buildings are magnificent works of art. Wooden beams frame white stones, and the second floor projects like a gallery, supported on wooden pillars. Trefoil-style window frames are carved in smooth arches, painted with flowers, jewels and other auspicious designs. The walls leading up to overhanging roofs are also carefully carved in intricate trims and painted in joyous colours and patterns. A few windows have iron grids shaped in a traditional endless knot or a wheel.

Cautiously stepping over the threshold into the first shop, I find myself in a dark room with one naked bulb throwing a gloomy light on shelves of non-perishable items, cheap reproduction clothes, plastic ware, flashlights, pots, matches, coke bottles, boxes with nails and other hardware. Wire baskets hanging from the ceiling are filled with spicy potato chips, sandals, Tupperware, soap containers, string and packets of Maggi noodles. A big barrel with lentils stands on the floor, the one beside it contains dried beans. Huge sacks of rice and flour are opened, but no sign indicates the cost. A basket contains some bruised bananas and green, pear-like fruit.

'*Kuzuzang po la!*'

The man behind the counter speaks in a heavy slur and seems to suck on something in his mouth. Then his lips part and reveal black-stained teeth between dark red gums. He looks at me with interest, continuing to wrap a broad green leaf into a tiny package.

'*Kuzuzang po la!*' he repeats loudly and waves me with a huge hand towards him. His lips part even further and dark red juice collects in a little pool on his lower lip. His greying beard is patchy and equally stained, and the stare of his small eyes is disconcerting even if friendly. Suddenly he coughs and in one unexpected agile movement, turns and spits noisily into the darkness behind the counter. Too intimidated to even offer a courteous greeting, I flee the store.

THREE

FIRST ENCOUNTERS

My third day in Mongar begins with a visit to the weekly Sunday 'subjee bazaar', the vegetable market. As Pema had advised me, at 8 a.m. sharp I head up the road to the 'market' – a fancy name for a muddy patch of grass where farmers unload their crops on the ground. To me, it looks like a stampede. Villagers sit or stand behind their goods, and a huge crowd of people rushes around, trying to buy as much as possible as fast as possible. The supply is limited and not particularly diverse: piles of chillies – red and green and of various sizes; spinach leaves bound with dried grass into bushy bundles; a basket full of sugar cane; some green beans; a few tins filled with colourful powders that smell rather pungent; tennis-ball-size white cakes of stinking cheese wrapped in banana leaves; and a few brown eggs packaged carefully into cans filled with cracked corn.

I stand helplessly and watch the chaos. Pieces of conversation in a foreign language whirl all around me. In some areas, heavy bargaining raises an argument. An old lady shouts furiously at a thin Indian man who is busy filling an entire load of potatoes into a heavy hemp bag. Beside me, three different people are thrusting their well-worn plastic bags at an old man selling gnarly carrots.

Intimidated, I try to figure out the cost of all these delicacies. It seems that for everything, some one-ngultrum and maybe five-ngultrum notes are the highest value needed. Even if not plentiful, food is definitely cheap (twenty ngultrums are not even one dollar). But how do I ask for anything? Desperately I look around for a sign of Pema or Karma.

A young woman, carrying a woven bamboo basket on her back, pushes past me. She is barefoot, and her dress is carelessly wrapped and hitched up above her ankles. Like all the women at the market, she wears a *kira*, a long piece of rectangular cloth wrapped around the body and fastened by two buckles over the shoulders. A belt around the waist keeps everything in place. Her jacket, the *toego*, is flung over her basket. She stoops to pick through a pile of beans.

Ever-increasing floods of people push through the undesignated aisles and elbow their way to the preferred sellers. I can hardly see what is displayed on the ground. Young lads, fat women, little girls and endless numbers of thin, wiry Indian men equipped with huge sacks stoop

40

to the best bargains. Like a frozen statue, I am fixed to my patch of mud and stare at the turmoil. Everyone is moving fast, talking loudly and filling their shopping bags. Everyone except me.

A steady, warm rain continues to soak sellers, buyers and the earth-smeared goods. I start to wander aimlessly between piles of vegetables and fruits, trying not to step on anything, trying not to get pushed over. Soon I realise that the amount of food for sale is dwindling fast and further dallying will cost me my vegetables for the coming week. Yet, how do I get the stuff laid out on the ground to end up in my backpack? There is no one to ask. I wait to see a familiar face, but receive only a few stares of old, wrinkled women, sitting beside their daughters who are busy bartering. '*Nigzing, nigzing!*' someone cries. '*Mangi, meme, sam!*' '*Sam mala!*' '*Gila, meme! Sam!*' the shouting continues. By the time I am ready to choose something, all is sold out. Gone. Finished. Everyone is packing up.

Frustrated and drenched, I shoulder my empty backpack. On the way home, I meet one of the hospital employees, fully loaded with two woven bags overflowing with vegetables.

'You must go to bazaar,' he advises, pointing at the façade of houses along the main street. 'You will get things in shop there. All foreign things. You will like.'

I am lucky. In one of the shops, I discover a man who speaks English, and I recite my shopping list. He nods cheerfully and immediately shows me an assortment of tea, all in its original leaf form, which causes

41

more confusion. I manage to choose a packet of Red Label and acquire a tiny strainer, a bag of powdered milk, and some not so clean and not so white sugar. As a special treat, I ask for some cookies. Then the shopkeeper climbs onto a shaky stool and, from a rope suspended from the ceiling, unties two rolls of toilet paper wrapped in foil. He scribbles some numbers on an old piece of newspaper and smiles. We look at each other in mutual sympathy.

His name is Rinzin Tshockey, and he owns and runs this little shop. A short man, almost disappearing behind his counter, he seems in full control of his dominion. The shop is brighter than the ones I had been to earlier, lit quite efficiently by a huge gas lamp on the counter between several jars of sweets. There seems to be more variety in the goods on the shelves. I notice it especially in the cookie section.

'All coming from India,' he explains. 'Samdruk Jongkhar bus is arriving every week, but during monsoon, there is often road block. These days we are needing many food for people. So many people in Mongar. Good business now, only power is always going off.'

Rinzin Tshockey points at the hissing gas lamp. 'Many Indians coming here for Kuruchu power project. In some years, we have good electricity.'

'Do you bring all of this food from India?' I ask.

'Not all, madam. But every month I take a truck to Samdruk Jongkhar, you know, to our border with India. I am thinking to expand this store. Last time I was buying some Coke. Do you want?

Rinzin Tshockey points at a lone bottle of Coca Cola amongst a dusty shelf full of canned fruit juices that announce their Bhutanese origin with the label 'Druk'.

Amused I shake my head. I am not yet desperate enough to buy Coke.

'Please let me know what you need. I will bring from Samdruk Jongkhar,' the eager shopkeeper offers.

'Thank you.' I nod and inspect the other opened bags and baskets in front of the counter. There is a basket with potatoes and, miraculously, another one with broccoli.

'I will get for you, madam. How many you need?'

Rinzin Tshockey picks up several potatoes, turns them in his hand, checks them for bad spots, and drops only the most satisfactory ones into another plastic bag for me. He adds a head of broccoli.

'Please doctor…' Already the word has spread throughout town that the blond foreigner is a doctor. I have no idea who anyone is, and yet everyone else seems to be well informed about my identity. Doctor is a word they know. 'Physiotherapist' will certainly take a while to be remembered. Doctor. I try the title on and find that it sits comfortably. All of a sudden, I feel more respected, more of a somebody than just an odd foreigner.

'Please doctor,' Rinzin Tshockey repeats. 'Please, you come again.'

He bids me farewell with another impish smile, and I, Madam Doctor, turn back to the road.

Mongar does not claim any flat land, other than the football field. Everywhere else houses cling to slopes of varying degrees, fields are terraced, walkways snake along inclines, and the road is cut into the mountain. Life seems to balance on the verge of sliding down the hillside.

I take the long way back to the hospital, following the road as it curves in a U-shape away from the bazaar towards the dzong. Dzongs are fortresses built during Bhutan's unification in the seventeenth century in an attempt to repel Tibetan invaders. Today they house both the governing administration as well as a monastery for the monk body. Huge, impressive buildings with Tibetan-style inward slanting walls, they dominate the view of most Bhutanese towns of any size.

Following an inconspicuous footpath up the slope, I pass a few large houses and find myself suddenly standing beside the upturned cone of a white stone chorten, poised at the edge of a rather steep cliff. A soft lapping sound, somewhat like clothes fluttering on a line in the yard, draws my attention and I notice a few scattered flags on the hilltop. Suspended from long wooden poles, the white bands of cotton cloth are flapping idly back and forth. Like their neighbour the chorten, the prayer flags have aged considerably. The material is torn in places, badly beaten by wind and weather. From close up, I can barely identify the print. All that is visible are row upon row of symbols in a foreign script. Throughout the length of the cloth, a square box with texts and pictures is repeated several times without variation. The same prayer?

Though bleached and faded through time, the flags charm me into staying. I imagine the wind, how it breathes by my little outlook and picks up a prayer; how the devout petition is carried over the ridge, down into the next valley and up a mountain where more prayer flags join the chorus. It waltzes around every house, over every pass in the country. Far and wide, like a faithful servant, the wind collects and strengthens the softly sung lyric, and then carries it up, up, up...

My dreamy contemplation is interrupted by the figure of a man emerging from the bushes. He throws me an expressionless glance and disappears. Soon after, a young boy surfaces out of the thicket. He, too, stares at me and then walks on without a word. I am intrigued.

Where did these two come from? Carefully, I retrace the footprints which my two silent visitors have left to a trampled patch of grass, surrounded by thick shrubs. A penetrating smell prevails. I turn on my heels and contemplate the two new vistas: a lovely chorten on the edge of a cliff, and the public toilet.

My organised, compartmentalised western mind rears at the association of the two contradicting localities. Do the people not bestow honour upon this sacred site through prayer, rituals and, above all, the erection of a chorten? Chortens are supposed to be guardians of treasures and relics, as well as memorials of great saints and priests. Is the very act of building a chorten not witness to devout belief, which is pure and clean?

Murmuring a soft prayer, an old woman approaches. Her figure is stooped. The sinewy muscles of her neck stand out and it appears that the cane she clutches keeps her from toppling over. When she stops and rests, the thumb of her right hand stays in motion, methodically moving the beads on her rosary. For a brief moment she takes notice of me and lifts her head, squints at me, then smiles and shuffles past. At the chorten, she extends a shaking hand, reaches out to place her fingers on the rough white stones, turns to her left and walks slowly three times around the monument. Finally, apparently satisfied, she carefully lowers herself onto the bottom step and rests, her head supported on her cane, her hand still clutching the rosary. As I turn to go, the old woman gets up and shuffles past the thicket of bushes, apparently oblivious of the offending smells.

FOUR

WHERE YOU GOING, MISS?

Like a grand theatre enrapturing its audience with magnificent drama, the monsoon continues to dominate the sky. Sometimes playful, sometimes foreboding, the grey masses of moisture change shape and form in an everlasting masquerade.

On Sunday afternoon, inspired by the clouds floating through the lowland and climbing the ridges in dreamy white patches, I wander along the road following my nose. No immediate intent guides my way, only the urge to explore this land of which I know so little. I am impatient to broaden my horizon beyond the borders of this valley. Walking is the only transportation among these people of steep mountains and rounded hills, and so my feet are becoming the only limit to my travels.

I had imagined a walk in solitude, but instead I find myself surrounded by happily chatting villagers, some shouldering heavy loads, others gaining ground with long strides. The paved main road leading through Mongar is well worn by many thousands of footsteps. Villagers carrying goods to the market, or patients to the hospital, schoolchildren on their daily walk to class, farmers moving cattle from one field to the next, or people on their way to visit relatives or friends in the next village. The road is a welcome break from the steep, winding foot tracks along bevelled grades. In fact, this road belongs to the people, and the odd vehicle that wants to get by has to obey the speed and willingness of men, women, children and animals to clear its path.

A group of girls giggle and nudge each other as they pass by some boys sitting beside the road. The scene is familiar, much like at home; shy teasing, brave haughtiness and a flirtatious jiggle of the hip. The boys seem pleased, but pretending not to notice, they only steal a few sidelong glances at the shiny black hair and the soft curves hidden by a kira.

From the bazaar, the road in the direction of Thimphu leads down, and I follow it with easy steps. At a tight bend, a creek slows its rush and meanders through the trees. A group of Indian women is squatting by its side, rinsing their laundry and slapping the clothes on the flat stones around them.

A little further on, a steep path leads almost vertically up to a small cluster of houses. I decide to stray and start climbing. The track is wet and slippery, and my running shoes fail miserably to grip the ground.

Within minutes I am winded and sweaty, and without much courage, I consider the folly of my adventure. The path divides into three, and there is no indication which one might lead me to the most rewarding destination. Three tiny mudslides polished by the tread of bare feet, each begging for a decision. The answer comes in the form of four girls who clamber up the path behind me. Giggling, they stop and stare at me. Then the smallest one, maybe ten years old, looks up at me with a saucy smile. 'Where you going, miss?'

'I am just walking,' I answer.

'You going to Barpang, miss?' The girl wrinkles her forehead. Just walking must seem like an absurd idea to her.

'I don't know, actually,' I stutter.

Where is Barpang?

The other three girls push on, but my little inquisitor is not yet satisfied.

'Where you from, miss?'

'I am from Canada.'

'My name is Jamtsho, and this is my sister Kesang.' She points at the oldest of the three girls, and then looks at me expectantly.

'I am Britta,' I answer, and search for something else to say.

Jamtsho flashes me a winning smile. 'Please come to my house. Will you be coming?'

A little suspicious of the muddy incline, I ask where her house is.

'There!' Jamtsho says and points at a line someplace where the clouds meet the mountain.

I debate with myself. What do I have to lose? Jamtsho is the first English-speaking friend that I have made on my walk. Having a conversation with the older generation of villagers will be a problem until I pick up more Sharchhopkha. Schoolchildren, on the other hand, all have to learn English and, for now, will probably be the only ones who can teach me a little about the culture. I agree.

The girls respectfully let me lead, slowing their quick steps enough to pace themselves with me. I feel clumsy and utterly unfit as I try to hurry up the hill. We pass a big old farmhouse with a wooden water trough out front. A big black dog growls at us, and immediately, the four girls start yelling and throwing stones. Still baring its teeth, the dog retreats.

We continue climbing. Suddenly Jamtsho's sister rushes ahead and hollers something up the mountain. A voice answers. She hollers again. Now the other girls shout something as well, and then instantaneously they vanish in the trees ahead. Only Jamtsho and I lag behind.

After half an eternity, we climb over a small wooden gate and reach Jamtsho's house. Adorned with a few banana trees and a dusty yard with some clucking chickens, the wooden and stone-set building fits perfectly into the surroundings. Wild grasses and shrubs encroach on the yard, and there is no precise distinction between cultivated and untamed nature. It looks almost as if one day the jungle might reclaim what is now a peaceful human dwelling.

A set of stairs lead up to a tiny platform that connects the main house on my right to a separate kitchen room on the left. Jamtsho leads me through the large, wooden entrance doors into the main building. To my left, there are two smaller rooms, both without any kind of furniture or decoration. Straight ahead, I can see a huge empty room, apparently not inhabited. It is to this parlour that Jamtsho leads me. Quickly she shakes out a small, woollen carpet, and places it in front of a half open window. Then she asks me to seat myself and immediately disappears. Left to myself, I twist my legs into what I think is an acceptable position, careful not to point my feet at anything that might be sacred, and take a closer look around me.

Heavy wooden beams frame the whitewashed walls, giving the impression of a half-timbered Tudor house. The floor consists of wooden planks, smooth and polished. The wall behind me and the one adjacent to it are lined with wooden framework windows, each having a solid sliding shutter on the inside. A light breeze enters through the openings, leaving the room cool and pleasant.

A cat jumps out from behind two thin mattresses, neatly rolled up in a corner. On the wall above that, some nails are occupied by ghos, the large robe-like garments of Bhutanese men. Beside them, a long thin wooden tube is fastened by a leather strap. To the right of the door leading to the hallway, a weaving stool is anchored to the wall, with a beautiful, half-finished piece of weaving strung into the frame.

The minutes tick by. Wondering what happened to Jamtsho, and not quite sure of what a guest's proper behaviour might be, I wait for a sign from somewhere.

The cat returns and curls up in its corner on a pile of kiras. Through my window, I can hear a cow munching on grass and the distant bark of a dog.

Smoke starts to emanate out of the adjacent kitchen, and I get up to investigate. Inside the little room of packed mud walls, Jamtsho is squatting in front of an earthen fireplace, blowing through a bamboo stick into the embers of the fire. A blackened kettle sits amidst the cinders. Two cats lazily clean themselves by the hearth. The walls are lined with wooden shelves. Pots, pans, jars and empty bottles are neatly arranged, and a couple of aluminium ladles shimmer in the otherwise sooty surroundings. There are two plastic storage drums and a can of tuna fish. Dust and cobwebs cover the windowsill, and ashes and soot have given everything a powdering of black.

Satisfied with the flickering flame at the end of a piece of wood in the embers, Jamtsho reaches for a black tin and produces some tea leaves. 'Tea coming,' she announces, and I detect a polite request to return to my assigned seat.

Finally, I hear dishes rattling and Jamtsho reappears in the door. Without a word, she serves me and vanishes once more. I look at the bowl of tiny roasted rice kernels beside my cup. Tentatively, I taste some. To my surprise, the rice is light and crisp, even a little sweet with the faint aroma of butter, and it crunches wonderfully – a superb complement to the milky tea.

Jamtsho returns with a plate of cookies that look stale and have a rather unsavoury pink filling. Obligingly I eat one but quickly revert to my tea and the rice, which

Jamtsho calls *zao*. My generous host keeps darting out of the room, reappearing only to refill my cup and bowl. Finally when I am finished with thirds of tea and zao, she sits beside me and inspects my rain jacket. As if it had just occurred to her, she tilts her head slightly to the side and asks, 'You sing a song, ma'am?'

'A song?' I double-check the request.

'You know any song?' Jamtsho repeats, adjusting her kira to get comfortable. Obviously, this is my expected contribution to this social get together, which, so far, I have enjoyed alone by stuffing my stomach.

'I don't sing very well,' I try to excuse myself.

'You sing, OK?' Jamtsho is relentless.

Hesitantly, I launch into the first line of an old German folk song. Somehow, singing in a language which I am sure Jamtsho cannot understand eases the embarrassment.

No sooner have I started to sing than my audience multiplies. Out of nowhere Kesang, Jamtsho's older sister, and a stooped little grandmother join us. All three listen attentively to my quavering voice. Mercifully no one laughs, and encouraged by eager nods, I venture into the second line.

Finally finished, I sit in embarrassed silence. Grinning, Kesang and the old lady retreat. Jamtsho claps her hands in what I presume to be applause, and I ask if she would now sing something for me. Jamtsho nods and starts humming. With her hands, she draws curvy lines in the air. Then she begins to sing, and her voice is light and soft, but the rhythm of her tune sounds sad, melancholic. Fascinated, I watch as she lowers her eyelids and slowly starts swaying her body from side to side – in somewhat suggestive movements.

'Was that a Sharchhop song?' I ask later.

'No, madam, this is Hindi song.'

'Hindi?'

'I learn from watching movie, madam. Hindi movies is so nice.'

'Ah. And do you also know Sharchhop songs?'

Jamtsho nods. 'Yes, madam, but they not good. Hindi song much better. Now you sing again.'

What can I do but agree to her wish? I am the guest after all, and this seems to be the expected behaviour. After two more song requests, though, the dimming light of dusk reminds me that it is time to go. It would be a nightmare to be caught by darkness on the unfamiliar path back to town. Apologetically I explain my predicament to Jamtsho, but just when I think that she understands me, the girl gets up and vanishes without a word.

Unwilling to leave before I have at least thanked my young host, I set out to search for her. I find her beside the barn, washing something over a small bucket. Apparently she is not interested in my gratitude speech.

'I am so sorry. We have nothing to offer,' she says instead, and then slips two clean brown eggs into my hands. 'Please come back next week, OK?'

I am touched and promise to come as soon as I can. Then, carefully balancing my precious gifts in my pocket, I slide and tumble down the muddy path towards Mongar.

I spend the rest of the day puttering around my 'house'. Somehow, I have to make the most of the little space available, without crowding my rat-combatting chairs, or my all-purpose table. I arrange my bags, furnish my kitchen with the necessary utensils and cooking ware, scrub the toilet, and fasten curtains on the window.

Just when I think how amazingly quickly I have adapted to completing all important tasks while the lamps are still on, the power vanishes. Thankfully, the light in the bulb lingers for a few seconds, dimming slowly, and allowing a grace period to scramble for the flashlight. I scold myself for not filling my kerosene lamp.

Next door, the shrill alarm goes off again, but this time I ignore it. I have concluded that it must be a warning device on the refrigerator for the vaccines, indicating that there is no electricity. I do wonder, though, what happens to all the little vials that say 'Store at 4–6° C'.

While I stare at the gentle flicker of my candle, images of the past day lodge themselves in my mind: the market and its circus of impatient customers rushing in a frenzy to bargain for the best buys... the thin Indian woman in her orange sari, breaking stones for a living... Jamtsho, as she crouches beside the glowing embers of the kitchen fire... the villagers at the market, barefoot in their grimy worn kiras – I have landed in a peculiar old world.

What do they think when they see me? I guess, to the Bhutanese, I am as strange as they are to me. They gawk at my clothes as I stare at their poverty. Reluctantly, I picture myself wearing jeans and a T-shirt amongst women dressed in ankle length dresses. Somewhere in that contemplation of *me* versus *them*, the seed of a feeling of strangeness is planted inside me.

FIVE

DON'T CLOSE YOUR EYES

With a loud whack, the mosquito-screened door slams shut behind me. A cat scurries through the hallway and disappears out of sight. Before me lies a wide corridor, empty but for a few cushionless iron wheelchairs. A couple of bright yellow doors bear the label 'Operation Theatre DO NOT ENTER'. From somewhere beyond a small passageway, I can hear voices. Bewildered, I wait for someone to discover me.

The smell is what strikes me most. It overwhelms me like a heavy blow in the stomach; a biting reek of urine, unwashed skin, waste and strong disinfectant. It is nauseating. To my left lies a small, rectangular inner courtyard, enclosed by the main hospital building. I walk closer to the dusty, punctured fly screen, and take a breath of fresh air. Across the yard, I can peep into the windows of the duty room. The hospital is still quiet. A few nurses shuffle past and stare at me, but no one seems to pay particular attention. It is 9 a.m. and official duty time has just started. I wonder where I will find Pema, my assistant.

The administrative officer (addressed as 'ADM') arrives and shows me to the physiotherapy room. We follow the courtyard on our left and reach the last door before the hallway splits at a T-junction. A sign announces the 'Treatment Room'. The ADM opens the door to my department; two connected rooms with an adjoining toilet. Until recently, the first chamber was used as a dressing room. A table covered with a dirty rubber sheet still tells its stories of blood and bandages.

The officiating head of the hospital, the District Medical Officer (known as the DMO) joins us. 'Welcome to Mongar.' The DMO assures me that they are happy to have me here. 'Unfortunately,' he adds with an apologetic smile, 'we have only recently found out about your coming. We did not have much time to prepare.' He points at the many scattered instruments and furniture of definite dressing room status.

'I will send the wardboy to clean up,' the ADM promises. The DMO adds that it will be my responsibility to design a plan of action for the coming year. By the end of the week, I should hand him my official goals and objectives, which he will evaluate and then pass on to the headquarters in Thimphu.

The polite and somewhat stiff conversation continues for a few more minutes before the two men return to their respective duties. I watch them leave. One, thin with a nervous yet controlled step, the other rather hefty, walking along dignified, fully aware of his distinguished rank.

Gradually I take in the details of my new domain. The rooms are far better than I had expected. In my mind, I have already designated the first one as the exercise room and the second as the treatment room.

The exercise room is square and bright. In synchrony with the rest of the hospital, the walls are yellow up to shoulder level, coated with a thick, washable latex paint. Above that, the remainder of the wall is whitewashed. There is a set of double doors and, on the opposite side, the entry to a little storage room with the toilet. From there, tinted windows communicate with the laundry room.

The treatment room is dark, with blue painted walls above the standard yellow. A huge iron frame with a set of pulleys and a suspended rope towers over a bed. Partly above the bed and immediately to the right are a couple of frosted windows that open into the hallway, allowing a view of the inner courtyard. They must have been designed to function as a light source during Mongar's power outages, which occur almost daily and can last for hours or even the entire day. The length of the opposite side of the room consists of a door and frosted windows leading to the operation theatre. An enormous wooden cupboard occupies most of the wall space beside the door. Pushed into the corner are a heat lamp, an ultrasound and a short wave diathermy machine. One wall displays a colourful calendar with advice on how to prevent AIDS. The room is not dirty but years of use and wear have left their marks. Everything droops a little, tilts a few degrees, or grows some cobwebs.

I grimace, thinking of our private sports clinic back home. We were six therapists working together in the same building with several orthopaedic surgeons. Our huge treatment room was bright and always spotless, with different types of gym equipment and twelve beds. Our patients were either athletes or very active students and professionals, mostly fit and trim, popping by for their treatments before or after work. Our equipment was state of the art, with distributors coming regularly, trying to sell us the very latest machines.

Again I look at the prehistoric ultrasound machine. Here, I cannot even count on steady electricity to make whatever we have work.

Yet the heavy reference textbook I have brought with me from Canada reminds me that the biggest difference will be my role as educator here. At home I was considered more of a junior therapist, having had only two years of work experience. During assessments and treatments, I used to confer regularly with my colleagues. Now I am the one who is supposed to be giving advice. Was I overconfident in coming?

Pema arrives at 9.30 a.m. with a shy, apologetic greeting.

'Good morning,' she smiles. 'When did you reach?'

I have to chuckle. 'At nine a.m. when our duty time started.'

My innocent hint is gracefully overlooked, but Pema offers an explanation. 'Nima is sick, and so I am late.' Obviously, the topic of tardiness is of little concern.

I decide to press a little about her son's illness. 'What is wrong with Nima?'

'I think he has a cough. He didn't sleep last night.' Now I notice that Pema herself has dark rings under her eyes. 'Actually, he never sleeps at night. He always wakes up, then I have to play with him. Otherwise he will cry. Sometimes, he doesn't sleep until morning.'

'How old is Nima?'

'He is almost one,' Pema replies proudly, but then a shadow seems to settle on her face. 'But he does not know how to crawl or stand. Sister, what do you think?'

'I – did any of the doctors look at him?' Thinking about Nima's slow, writhing hand motions, the first thing that comes to mind is cerebral palsy, but I am afraid to pronounce the name of such a dire long-term prognosis. 'Did something happen to him?' I ask instead.

'He was OK at birth, I am sure. But we had a very bad babysitter, you see. Maybe she let Nima fall. I am always so worried when I leave him at home.'

Absent-mindedly, Pema strokes the blue sheet on the treatment bed. 'I want to take him to Vellore,' she says, turning to me with a desperate look in her eyes.

I nod. I have no idea where or what Vellore is, but it seems to mean a lot to Pema.

'Do you think he will walk?' Pema's question is hesitant, yet lined with a trace of hope.

'I don't know,' I answer honestly. 'Why don't you bring him here some time?'

Pema seems to consider my question but then shakes her head. 'Actually, I want to bring him. But Nima is so heavy. And now, in the rain, he will get wet. And who will look after him all day? I cannot take him back in the middle of the day.'

Now I feel guilty for my thoughtlessness, but Pema smiles at me. 'I think now you are here, we will make many changes in physiotherapy. It will be good. So long I was asking for two rooms. Now you are here, and already we are getting an exercise room. That will be very good for patients, isn't it?'

A couple of nurses stick their heads through the door and exchange a few words with Pema in a foreign tongue.

'Welcome sister!' they greet me and immediately the now familiar question follows: 'How do you like Mongar?'

I smile and nod, still searching for an appropriate answer. 'Please come for tea, sister,' they invite, and in leaving call a few more words to Pema. Grateful for Pema's fluent English, I turn to my new assistant and ally.

'How many languages do you speak?'

'Sharchhopkha, Dzongkha, Nepali and Hindi. At home with my parents, I speak Sharchhopkha. Most of our patients also speak Sharchhopkha. I will teach you. And we will go to see my parents in Bargompa. You will like it there. It is like real village. But you must speak Sharchhopkha. You know "*Kuzuzang po la*", isn't it?

'Ku zoo zang poo la!' I repeat and we both laugh.

Together we continue the survey of our room. The cupboard resists all attempts at opening until we fiercely bang against the sliding door. Once open, we are greeted by a wild mess of blankets, corset-shaped elastic back supports, various slings, a tub with black grease, a new white bed sheet, another supposedly temperamental ultrasound machine, a box with all kinds of screws, toothpicks, clasps, spare parts for machines that are long gone, and a pile of telltale mouse droppings. Most of the supplies look ancient and must date back to a time when Mongar Hospital was established and then run for twenty odd years by the Norwegian leprosy mission.

Pema explains that a few years ago the mission left, and Mongar Hospital was turned into a general hospital managed by the Bhutanese government. In January of this year, it was officially upgraded to become the Referral Hospital for Eastern Bhutan.

We examine a decrepit exercise bicycle and a pair of crutches with missing rubber tips.

'We have many more crutches, but I cannot use them. They are in storage room. When the mission goes, they leave us all crutches.' Pema points in the direction of a building above my classroom. She then proudly shows me her collection of bandages that have been given to her by the operating nurses. 'I keep them here, just in case,' she explains.

Our tour ends with a close inspection of the appointment book in which she records who the patient is, whether he was an in or outpatient, and what the diagnosis and treatment were. Overall, her records are meticulous and I am well satisfied.

One thing that begins to bother me immediately is the number of spectators that soon assemble in front of the physiotherapy rooms. Judging from the number of faces staring through the open windows into our physio room, I must be a rare species of *Homo sapiens*. Feeling none too self-conscious, patients and visitors who are on their walkabouts of the courtyard stop and gawk at me intently. Every inch of me is scrutinised. They study my blond hair, my pale skin, my skirt, my shoes, my gestures, my speech. They nod in my direction, or point at something. A few talk to Pema, others just silently stare. I would not be surprised if someone said that they were counting my breaths per minute.

Clusters of schoolgirls whisper and giggle, turning away shyly if I return their gaze. Occasionally, I hear the word '*phillingpa*' (foreigner) and 'doctor'. Pema takes pity on me and asks them to leave. Still giggling they retreat, only to be replaced minutes later by another group of curious spectators.

After a couple of hours, I crave anonymity. I want to have black hair and dark skin. I promise myself that from now on I will wear only kiras. I will learn Sharchhopkha and I will fit in. Soon. Nevertheless, for now, I want to shut the doors and windows, and I want the patients in the hallway to stop staring. With much difficulty, I continue smiling.

At the end of the day, the room has received a facelift. All surplus furniture and equipment are shoved into the hallway for removal, and the exercise room shines with a fresh coat of paint. The floor is swept and mopped, the dirt having been effectively wiped from one corner into a new one.

The windows remain open; I try not to notice. By three o'clock I am exhausted. Pema, in a hurry to get back to Nima, leaves me to close up the department. The crowds in the hallway have not yet dwindled and, without Pema, I feel stripped of all self-confidence and fully conscious of my every move. Like a model on the runway, I slowly tiptoe home.

The next morning, when the monsoon rain pelts down in heavy downpours, and Pema again fails to arrive at nine o'clock, I join the doctors on their morning rounds. Dr. Lhendup, a general doctor in charge mostly of outpatients, seems like a jolly fellow. He looks sincere and is full of conversation. Reviewing the patient's chart, he wrinkles his forehead in concentration and then talks rapidly in Sharchhopkha.

Dr. Kalita, the orthopaedic surgeon, is a newcomer to Mongar, having been transferred here shortly before I arrived. Originally from the state of Assam in India, he completed his medical education in Scotland, and is now one of the leading orthopaedic surgeons in Bhutan.

Dr. Shetri, the dentist, is a short energetic man. His mastery of the local language seems to be in its infancy, but while constantly cracking jokes, he tries his best to communicate with his own mixture of Nepali, Dzongkha and Sharchhopkha. Surprisingly, he also takes a very active role in the diagnosis and evaluation of the patients. Obviously, his medical knowledge is not limited to teeth alone.

The DMO is an eye specialist and, when not called away by administrative duties, joins our little team off and on.

Dr. Bikul, a young Indian general doctor, seems preoccupied with his cases and keeps disappearing to his outpatient chamber.

I am told that there is also a medical specialist, Dr. Pradhan, and a gynaecologist from Cameroon, Dr. Robert, both of whom are on leave at present.

The matron of the hospital, a short, compact woman with a determined attitude, pushes a little yellow cart containing all of the patient charts through the wards. There are other nurses as well, all dressed in white kiras with little caps on their heads. They take off bandages, comment on the patients' condition and get the necessary charts ready. One round of the hospital includes five main wards and a few private or semi-private cabins. Ward A and B are for females and children, C and D for males, and there is a separate ward for active TB and leprosy. In total there must be about sixty beds, give or take a few; overflow patients are bedded on mattresses on the floor as needed.

Quietly, I follow the little procession of doctors as they make their way through the wards. Most of the diseases presented here are unknown to me, and I am unsure of the patient's source of suffering. In addition, none of the patients are addressed in English, and my grasp of the local language is far too sparse to understand anything. Yesterday I learned that *lekpu* means good or better; *mangi* or *mala* are forms of no; *phaiga*, at your home; and *pholang* means abdomen, a word I hear frequently used. It seems that a large number of patients suffer from some sort of stomach trouble. On the charts, I read other foreign sounding diagnoses: osteomyclitis, viral encephalitis, chronic malaria, typhoid, abdominal tuberculosis, leprotic ulcers, grade three malnourished... I have entered a world of medicine unknown to me.

In the wards, I have difficulty separating patients from attending family members. More often than not, two or three people sit on one bed. Like their attendants, patients are dressed in everyday clothes. There is no sign of pyjamas or hospital gowns.

The thick hair of both men and women is short, at times spiky, dust and oil turning into a natural hairspray. Everyone wears a certain amount of grease and grime. Many lips and teeth look as if they were bleeding, permanently stained by the juices of betelnuts mixed with lime. Clothes are smudged and tied carelessly, often well worn to the point where the material is hanging on by merely a few thin threads. By far the most remarkable attribute is the patients' feet. Disproportionate to their short stature, their feet are huge, with round stubby toes and unkempt nails. The soles are covered by a thick layer of dirt which has grown deep into the chaps and cracks of a lifetime of barefoot walking.

The general lack of cleanliness has rubbed off onto the surroundings. The blue hospital sheets are stained, and often a kira is used instead of a blanket. The yellow and white walls are spotted with mud and mildew, and the windows are faintly tinted by a covering of dust. Despite the screens, thousands of flies populate the hospital, crawling over beds, people and food. Although I had mentally prepared myself for a certain lack of hygiene, what I see worries me deeply. Garbage litters the corners, and patients readily dispose of bloodied bandages, plastic bags or food scraps under the beds. I think of the flies crawling over everything and then looking for a hatching place for their eggs. As we continue along the rows of beds, my stomach twists into a tight knot, and my knees begin to wobble. Shocked, I try hard not to avert my eyes.

Privacy is not a concept practised or valued, and the metre of space between beds is hardly enough to keep neighbours from actively observing every detail of an examination. Many patients wear a look of dull surrender, a blank stare that seems to reach beyond the hospital walls, yearning for the world outside in the hills. Yet it is not an expression of suffering, but rather of resignation or disbelief. There is no questioning and often no response. What goes on inside their minds is hidden to me.

How would I feel if I had to lie in one these beds, lined up in a row, no curtains and no dividers? What would it be like? A nightmare, no doubt. Everyone in his or her street clothes, looking dirty and smelling accordingly. As we continue our rounds, I feel a mixture of pity, sadness and anger. The patients' obvious lack of education and often innocent ignorance tug at my heartstrings.

A few people are introduced to me as my patients. A girl with a severe burn scar and a damaged knee is disabled and confined to her bed. An old man who is in the hospital for the treatment of his eye infection, complains of a painful, stiff shoulder. A boy in a coma with malarial encephalitis has been paralysed for several days. An old diabetic woman who has recently undergone a below-the-knee amputation for a gangrenous leg needs to get out of bed.

I try to smile at everyone, although my rebelling gut has sucked out my confidence. How will I ever treat these patients in our little two-room department with the fancy title 'Physiotherapy'? I look at the faces and see only tragedy. I reach out to greet a patient and meet the eyes of accepted suffering. The poverty, the dirt and the diseases overwhelm me. My heart cries, and my boldness plummets. If I can help any of these patients even a little bit, it will be a small miracle.

SIX

LHAMO

A t first, I see only a small, wrinkled face with a lovely smile peeking around the corner. My desk in the physiotherapy room is set back beside the door frame, and so the next thing I can see from this vantage point is a pair of thin, bony legs floating a few inches above the ground. Then the figure of a tiny lady, and lastly Lhamo who is being carried piggy-back into the treatment room.

Baffled, I stare at the surprising appearance of mother and daughter. Though Lhamo is as thin as a beanstalk, she dwarfs her mother who stands at no more than four and a bit feet tall. At thirteen, Lhamo's shoulders are several inches wider than the ones carrying her. It seems impossible that the petite lady does not buckle underneath her heavy load. Yet there she stands, steadily balancing Lhamo on her back. She even manages to untangle one of her arms to point at the bed beside me.

I snap out of my stupor and quickly pilot them inside the room. We manoeuvre Lhamo onto the bed, and there she stays lying in a fetal position, nervously staring at me. I try to make her feel comfortable by talking to her in English as soothingly as I can. My efforts are rewarded with a shy, uncomprehending smile.

A few moments later, Pema enters and tells me that she has called Lhamo for treatment. Confused, I ask if they do not have a wheelchair. Pema explains that Lhamo's mother is used to carrying her daughter, and it really is no problem. 'Of course this is a problem,' I think, but for now I keep my thoughts to myself and take out an assessment sheet.

Pema pulls up a stool beside me. The main goal of my stay in Mongar is to teach Pema as many of my physiotherapy skills as possible. Through her training as an assistant, she already has some basic knowledge of anatomy as well as physiology, but her treatments are solely based on a cookbook approach of using a diagnosis made by the doctors as her prescription. During my year in Mongar, I will try to help her become more independent in assessing and treating patients. For the first week, we have agreed that she will act as a translator and watch what I do.

My pen and paper poised, I am ready to take Lhamo's history. Lhamo's mother, however, is not. In an uninterrupted torrent of words, she talks to Pema in Sharchhopkha. When she finally finishes, I ask Pema the meaning of her outburst.

'She wants to know will Lhamo walk again.'

A little exasperated, I ask what else she said.

'Nothing,' Pema replies and turns back to Lhamo.

Over the better part of an hour, we patch together Lhamo's history. Lhamo's family comes from the district of Trashi Yangtse, from a small village two days' walk from the main road. Like most villagers, her family has lived on the same farm for generations and produces a small crop on a bit of land. Lhamo herself has never attended school.

According to her mother, five or six years ago Lhamo fell over a pot of boiling water and burned the back of her left leg. It healed, but since then, she has had a severe scar from the buttock right down to below her knee. One year ago, a knife injury damaged her right knee, and now it is stuck in its present position and hurts.

The details and dates of this story vary from what the nurses had told me, and on further repeated questioning of Lhamo's mother, the injuries now range anywhere from eight years ago for the left leg, and three years to a few months back for the right. It seems pointless to harp on a detail that obviously does not hold priority in their lives, and we move on, marking the category 'Time of onset of injury' with a big question mark.

What does become apparent, though, is that this second injury has caused much hardship for Lhamo and her family. Since the trauma, Lhamo has not stood or walked. Confined to her bed all day, Lhamo is carried outside by her mother only to urinate or defecate, or at the odd time, to have a wash.

They have tried several 'treatments'. The village lama has come to hold many a religious ceremony called a puja. Her family has prayed and made offerings for a quick recovery. No result. They brought her to the hospital, and the surgeon at the time tried to lengthen her burn scar to allow the leg to extend completely, thereby making weightbearing possible. No help. Different doctors subsequently tried the same operation. Unfortunately, the resulting fibrosis and immobility in bed only made her stiffer and, in the end, the leg seemed the same. A team of Australian plastic surgeons came for a visit, but they too shook their heads in regret. There was nothing to be done.

Between every bit of revealed information, Lhamo's mother asks me if I can fix her daughter. Gently, I tell her that I will try my best. Mom is not satisfied. In her eyes I am a foreign doctor, therefore ordained with a lot of knowledge and ability. I have to cure her daughter.

I ask Pema to coax some answers out of Lhamo, but the girl only stares at us. Her look is frightened and distrustful. Without touching her, I again start speaking to her in English, and Pema translates. I explain that I only want to have a look, that I will not hurt her, that her Mom will stay right beside her the entire time, and that she can tell me where she has pain. Ever so slowly, Lhamo relaxes. Still suspicious, she watches my every move, but at least her distrustful attitude slackens.

A few spectators have gathered in the hallway and this time, determined to get some privacy, I shut the windows and door tightly. Then I ask Lhamo to remove her skirt, a simple flowered petticoat, which she wears instead of her kira. Lhamo refuses. I try to explain that I have to look at her whole leg – but she is immoveable. Tentatively, I lift the flimsy garment a few inches, and

Lhamo starts wincing like a baby. I realise the problem immediately. Lhamo has no underwear.

Somehow we manage to tuck her skirt between her legs to cover her embarrassment and still allow me a better look. The back of her right leg is horribly deformed. A long, deep and tight burn scar covers the rear of the knee and stretches in ropelike bands all the way up to her buttock. Though not painful, it resists all movement trying to straighten it beyond a 75-degree bend. The right foot hangs on the ankle like a useless appendage. All muscles have been wasted from years of disuse, and her sole is turned in, resembling what is medically termed a clubfoot. Although she is tense and tries to resist my moving her leg, Lhamo is far too weak to put up a real fight. Instead, she continues whining and whimpering, yet whenever I ask if there is pain, she shakes her head.

Her other knee is obviously very tender. The moment I touch it, Lhamo starts screaming. After several attempts, I have to give up. I assume, from what I observe, that there is maybe a 5-degree freedom of movement, if any. We ask Lhamo's mother if the knee has always been this stiff, and she confirms. Has it always been this painful? She nods.

Neither her mother nor Lhamo have told me about any other injuries, but in her chart I see a note about dressing a bed sore, so I continue my examination. I find not one but two deep, puss-filled sores, one over her tailbone, and one over her left seat bone which explains why Lhamo does not want to sit. Thin cotton bandages have been taped over the wounds, but with moving about, they have slipped, and now the tape is partly stuck to the bleeding flesh. The wounds are oozing, and Lhamo's skirt is damp. Appalled, I ask her mother when these wounds were last cleaned.

'Yesterday.'

'Why not today?' I ask, wondering who is responsible for this needless neglect.

'Always, they are only done every two days,' Pema answers.

I am shocked. 'Do they always look like this?'

The answer is yes. From Pema's translation, I learn that it is difficult for Lhamo to use the toilet, and that the bandages always get wet from washing her buttock after passing stool. Still Lhamo's mother thinks that they are slowly getting better.

Lhamo is quietly whining to herself, and when I turn to ask her to sit up, she throws a temper tantrum and screeches in a high pitched voice. Her mother chides her sternly, but Lhamo continues her lamenting. Pain and an overwhelming terror are clearly written on the girl's face. I understand that for today it is enough and ask her mother to take Lhamo back to the ward. Relieved, the tiny mother picks up her daughter and carefully carries her out of the physiotherapy room.

I feel guilty. Did I push Lhamo too hard? Desperate to focus on something positive, Pema and I discuss the availability of wheelchairs. There are three new ones in the hospital, one of which belongs to physiotherapy and two to the wards. Unfortunately, the physiotherapy chair always disappears. I ask Pema to go and look for it, and she dutifully sets off on her mission. Minutes later she returns with a foldable, soft plastic-seated wheelchair, and I sigh in relief. At least one thing we can offer to Lhamo immediately.

A quick check of the chair reveals that the brakes are useless, overstretched and barely able to touch the wheels. For the umpteenth time since my arrival in Bhutan, I pull out my Swiss Army knife and start repairing. Luckily, the problem is easy to fix, and I take the chair for a test ride.

Although I generally find the faces of the people here very hard to read, as I wheel myself past the windows of the operating theatre's prep room the nurses' astonishment is obvious.

'Sister Britta! Where are you going?' Sister Rupali, a plump, jovial nurse sticks her head out the window and calls after me. In the hospital, I have been demoted from doctor to sister.

'Just testing out the chair!' I reply and grin.

'Sister, will you come for tea? Please come and join us for tea. Sister Pema is always coming for tea!'

I have wondered when and if we get a lunch break, and the offer is tempting.

'Thank you. I would like that.'

The window of the OT prep room closes again, and I steer back to my treatment room.

Over a hot cup of sweet tea, perfectly spiced with ground cardamom and cloves, and a couple of sugary cookies, I voice my worry about Lhamo's wound dressing.

'Do you think it could be done more regularly?'

'Lhamo is nice girl, isn't it,' Sister Chandra replies. 'It is good that you can help her now.'

Sister Rupali agrees but also dodges the issue of wound dressing.

'You have to talk to Matron about that, sister. Here in the OT, we only prepare the dressing sets. You see,' Sister Rupali points to the steaming autoclave, 'it is so difficult. No electricity and it is always broken, isn't it, sister?' This time she turns to the other OT nurses for confirmation. Everyone at the table nods seriously. 'Every day we make dressing kits, we are always busy. But this machine is never working.' Rupali condemns the whistling autoclave with another stare. Then abruptly she changes the topic to yesterday's operation.

Most of the nurses at Mongar Hospital seem to come from Southern Bhutan, and among themselves, they generally speak Nepali. Initially, I guess that the discussion centres on an emergency caesarian section, but then I get lost in the foreign language and cannot follow another word. Surrounded by eagerly chatting nurses, I am left sipping on my tea, wondering how long it will take me to understand at least enough of my colleagues' language to participate in their daily gossip.

After my interlude in the OT's prep room, Pema and I take the prized wheelchair to the ward. It is time to teach Lhamo that from now on, at least while she is in the hospital, there will be an alternative mode of transportation to her mother's back.

We find both Lhamo and her mother on the bed sharing lunch. Excited talking erupts at our arrival, and the half-empty plate of food is left on the blanket. While I push the wheelchair over to the bed, I take a look at the hospital ration. Rice, some sort of potato curry and a cup of dal compose the lunchtime feast. Earlier I saw how the cook dished it out from a couple of huge buckets in the courtyard, but now I am somehow surprised to see it here, heaped on a plate. It looks better than I had anticipated.

Lhamo eyes the wheelchair with a worried face. All new commodities cannot be trusted, and the unknown technology seems to intimidate my young patient. The little chattery mother, however, is quick to realise the advantages of mechanical wheels. With a beaming smile, she proudly assesses the chair.

Still looking more than sceptical, Lhamo eventually lets herself be convinced to give it a try. To avoid further complications, I decide to neglect the proper rules of a transfer for the moment and lift Lhamo off the bed. Mistake! Within fractions of a second, her long skinny fingers dig into my neck, and she lets out a terrified squeal. Like a monkey, she hangs on for dear life, refusing to let go of my neck. I can hear Pema talking and even the neighbouring patients giving good advice, but only the warning voice of her mother makes Lhamo relax her grip. Slowly we lower her onto the chair, and she sits awkwardly and stares at me. Determined, her mother takes the steering and starts wheeling Lhamo around the ward.

When she finally comprehends the great potential of her newfound freedom, Lhamo's face brightens into a lovely smile. Carefully she leans over the sides, testing the arm rests with a tentative pressure and playing with the foot supports.

'*Yalama!*' she calls out in excitement, and an old woman in the bed beside her starts cheering.

Now eagerly jabbering with her mother, Lhamo propels the wheels forward a few feet, then she claps her hands and turns around to look at us. Her face is radiant with joy. In her eyes shimmer hope and excitement, and childish pleasure in the little perks that must come along so rarely. As if waiting for this moment for many months, Lhamo's laughter breaks through her wall of suffering. No longer confined to her bed, on the plastic seat of an overstretched wheelchair, Lhamo has found a new independence. And for the first time since my arrival in Mongar, I know that I made the right choice in coming here.

SEVEN

BACK-BREAKING WORK

The end of my first week in Mongar is drawing near, and this dark and rainy morning promised to be slow. Feeling slightly more at ease with my new routine, I left the hospital for a few minutes to get some of my textbooks from the house. Heavily loaded, I now walk back past the OT. There is a line-up in front of our physio windows. When I left, the hallway was deserted, but now it looks as if someone has opened the floodgates. I observe the queue but cannot recognise any of the faces. Moreover, this crowd is not like the usual onlookers; they seem to be patiently waiting for me, absorbed in their own thoughts.

As I approach, the line divides respectfully to let me through. Perhaps my white lab coat is an unmistakable sign of authority. I smile at the patients and notice that most of them are dressed in Indian clothes, the women in saris and the men in simple shirts and trousers. I wonder if they are workers on the hospital construction site, or else road workers whom I have seen in little camps all along the road from Thimphu to Mongar.

Pema is already busy taking a history. Since I cannot hear any '*ngamla*' (pain) or '*oga?*' (where?), the words must not be Sharchhopkha, and I assume that Pema is talking in Nepali or Hindi. Not comprehending a word, I sit down to watch. The woman beside Pema speaks in a low, almost inaudible voice, her hands neatly clasped and folded on her lap. Her concern seems urgent and somewhat confidential. She never looks at me, but after a while, Pema translates.

The patient's name is Dhan Maya, and she is indeed a road worker at a site about an hour's walk from here. Her job consists of carrying stones to a spot where others can break them. For the last few weeks, she has been suffering from back pain, and now she can no longer sleep at night.

I look at her referral. It says 'Chronic lumbar derangement. For physiotherapy. Kindly assess and treat.' The signature is a big, bold *B* with a few scribbles behind it. I ask Dhan Maya about her doctor. She says it is Dr. Bikul, the young Indian doctor working in Outpatients.

Pema and I complete the assessment together. Sadly I realise that there is precious little I can do for this lady. Made of only skin and bones, Dhan Maya's stature is far too fragile for her heavy labour, and other than somehow altering the gruelling tasks of her day, nothing will alleviate her agony. I discuss her options with Pema.

A new job is out of the question. She is here with her family from Bengal, and she and her husband work in order to make some money to send home to his siblings. They are grateful for the work; they have been here for almost seven years.

I ask about decreasing her hours, but I only get a small shake of the head as an answer. I ask if she can take a few more breaks during the day, but again the answer is a no. I ask if it is possible for her to switch her duties with another woman, but she says that they are all doing similar things, and anyway, she is one of the youngest and strongest.

Can she come here for treatments?

No, it takes too much time out of her work. She only has this morning off.

Physiotherapy is not a profession that counts on quick fixes and easy cures, and I am used to running into problems. However, here in Bhutan, I face new challenges. At home, I would call her employer and discuss light duties or a change of duties. She could get worker's compensation or, at the very least, she could get some time off. There would be some way to lessen the constantly aggravating circumstances – but here? What should I tell her? I feel dreadful. I am facing a dead end and I know it.

I am stuck for advice, or a treatment, but somehow it becomes clear that my shy, polite patient is not really expecting any. She is already halfway out the door, and apologetically explains that she has to leave. She needs to get back to work now.

'We see many workers here,' Pema sighs, her eyes full of sympathy. 'You have seen where they live?'

I nod.

'You will be able to treat them?'

'I hope so,' I reply without admitting to my doubts.

The next few patients all have similar complaints. Low back pain, shoulder pain, elbow pain. Every time it becomes disturbingly obvious that the symptoms are caused by the brutal physical nature of their work. They are all labourers. They all need their jobs. None of them can afford to take time off, and none of them wants to. They walk in with clothes soggy from the rain, tired, dragging their feet, and they leave much the same way – disillusioned, resigned, accepting.

I feel miserable and useless. I wish that we could at least offer them a rest under the heat lamp, something to comfort them for a short time, but there is no electricity today, and our desired machines are hiding in the damp semi-darkness of the room.

At last, I am confronted with an acute, treatable condition. Pasang, a young Bhutanese man of 27 hurt his back while lifting a log. I ask him to rest for the day and teach him some exercises. My confidence is boosted, and my spirits rise. Though he is one out of many, at least he can benefit from my being here.

Pema asks why he differs from the other patients we have assessed so far, and we take the time to discuss his condition in more detail. I want this to be a learning experience for Pema. Finally, I send Pasang back to the doctor to ask for a prescription for some anti-inflammatories. Within a few minutes, he returns. The doctor wants to speak to me immediately.

I am not even surprised. All of the outpatient referrals today have come from Dr. Bikul, and this is the first one I have actually been able to treat. Now Dr. Bikul is questioning my methods.

Already this morning during rounds, I had a run in with him over the diagnosis of one of his patients. He thought it was a case of L3 (lumbar vertebrae 3) paraplegia. To me it looked more like an incomplete L4, and I voiced my opinion. We argued for a while over whether it could be caused by a tumour, an autoimmune disorder or a compression fracture. Then he tested me on the nerve supply of the entire lower extremity, all the while waiting for me to foul up. I did not falter. I stood my ground and demonstrated my knowledge. He seemed astonished. Finally, he admitted that he knew next to nothing about physiotherapy and abruptly turned back to his patient.

Now he probably wants to grill me again. Well, he can wait. There is another patient outside who has been expecting to see a physio for almost an hour. I will finish here first and then go. After all, if it is so urgent, why can the good doctor not come here himself? With a sweet smile, I ask Pasang to go back and let Dr. Bikul know that I will come soon.

Half an hour later, Pema and I enter Chamber No. 4 behind a thick, blue curtain. Dr. Bikul looks up from his papers. 'Please sit,' he says and directs us to two chairs facing his desk. His attitude is distant, and his arrogant expression gets under my skin. Defensively, I square my shoulders and then look at Pema for reassurance. As always, she is smiling.

'You wanted to talk to me?' A little bout of panic wells up in me, but I try not to let it show.

'Yes.'

The foreboding silence that follows evaporates my earlier courage. I cannot read his expression. Maybe I did do something wrong. Again I look at Pema, but she does not seem perturbed. In my mind, I quickly run through the cases which I have seen this morning. What does he want from me?

His question pulls me out of my thoughts. 'How do you like Mongar?' For the first time, a tiny shadow of a smile whisks across his face.

'Well, I am not sure yet,' I stutter. Then I quickly add, 'It seems like a nice place.' Quietly I scold myself for not displaying more enthusiasm.

'I am sorry that I sent you so many patients this morning. I did not know if physiotherapy could do something for them, but I thought you would try.' He seems almost sincerely apologetic. More relaxed now, I wait for what is to come.

'Could you explain to me why you gave Pasang those exercises?'

Here is my trap. Again I feel my body stiffening, but then I remember that he is the one who knows nothing about physiotherapy.

'From my examination I found that Pasang has a mechanical low back problem.' I launch into a long explanation of mechanical back pain, its causes and applicable physiotherapy treatments.

Dr. Bikul listens attentively. At one point, I feel like I am convincing myself, and not him. How do I explain the other mechanical back pain patients to whom we did not teach any exercises? Will he take offence if I talk about the back-breaking working conditions of the labourers? This is only my first week here; better not to stir up any trouble.

Dr. Bikul is still occupied with Pasang and calls him back into the room.

'Pasang, do you understand the madam's exercises?'

'Yes, sir.'

'Could you show them to me?' Dr. Bikul points to his examination bed.

'Yes, sir. Of course, sir.'

Carefully, Pasang climbs onto the bed and demonstrates his homework. Not totally correct, but acceptable, and I say nothing.

Dr. Bikul seems satisfied. 'Hmm. Good. You do the exercises like the madam has told you. Come back if you still have pain in ten days.' He turns to me.

'Are you finished with Pasang?'

'Yes,' I answer.

Dr. Bikul nods at Pasang. 'OK, Pasang. You can go home.'

My nerves are settling, and with a new confidence, I eye Dr. Bikul. He is definitely handsome. Young, maybe my age, he has an athletic posture and wide, strong shoulders. His hair is thick and black, and his dark and smooth features are beautifully underlined by his white lab coat. His eyes are big and expressive, and now they sparkle with a shy smile.

'I would like to talk to you more about physiotherapy. It is very interesting.'

'That would be fine,' I reply. 'Any time.'

Our discussion seems to be finished. Pema and I rise to leave. Throughout the entire visit Pema has been quiet, but now she teases him. 'Doctor, you still have many girls out here waiting for an examination.' Suddenly, I feel embarrassed and rush to leave the room. Outside, Pema smiles from ear to ear. 'You really told him about physiotherapy. Isn't it?' We both laugh. I have to agree with Pema. We earned our first small victory.

Back in our physio room, I do not feel quite as victorious looking at a neat pile of referrals, which are stacked on my desk.

'Where did these come from?' I ask.

'Inpatients, sister. They are referrals from the wards.'

With a sigh, I look at the diagnoses; an old woman with chronic low back pain; a leprosy patient with an ulcerated foot; more back pain patients.

A young woman, perhaps thirty, enters the physiotherapy room. She comes from a village two days' walk from Mongar where she heard that a new foreign doctor has arrived. She insists that I have to treat her. At first, I am confused by her lack of a referral, and when I ask her if she has already seen another doctor, she nods. She saw the gynaecologist before, but now she wants to see me. After more prodding, her concern finally becomes obvious. She has come because she wants me to check her IUD, or intra uterine device that is part of her family planning. I am not sure if I should laugh or cry.

Helplessly, Pema explains to her that although I am a 'doctor', I am not *that kind* of doctor. Obviously disappointed, the woman asks repeatedly if I might not look at her. Guiltily I think about her long journey through the rain to the hospital. How quick the news of my arrival has spread to the villages, and how happy she was at first, thinking that finally a woman would look after her private concerns. Although this misunderstanding came about through no fault of my own, I cannot help but feel overwhelmed and wonder if I will be able to meet the high expectations of a foreign 'doctor'.

At the end of the day, we finally arrive at the bottom of the pile of referrals. Tshering Dema, 68-year-old female from Mongar district. Stomach ulcer. Scoliosis. Low back pain.

Pema tells me that I can call any older woman Abi, instead of addressing her by her given name. We agree that I will try to do as much of the talking as possible to practise my Sharchhopkha.

The old abi from Ward B is a delight. The intense sun of high altitudes has wrinkled her face like a prune. A single stained tooth sticks at an odd angle in her mouth and accentuates her glowing smile. While Pema takes a history, Abi mumbles a continuous flow of words, not once ceasing to grin.

My turn arrives to start the physical assessment. Immediately, Abi peels herself out of her kira and before I have a chance to protest, she is lying on the bed, stretching a pair of incredibly large (and even more notable, incredibly dirty) feet towards me. Awkwardly I clarify to her that she needs to be upright. Abi gives me a toothless smile, points at her back – and continues to lie on the bed. When I finally convince her to stand, she busies herself putting her kira back on. With much difficulty I get her to stay undressed long enough for me to throw a glance at her back.

Her trunk is deeply rutted just above the hips, perhaps from continuously wearing a kira belt much too tightly. That, combined with extremely heavy fieldwork and years of carrying the children and later grandchildren on her back, is enough to cause pain in even the strongest of spines. Abi's vertebrae are oddly twisted and turned, making the diagnosis of scoliosis almost an understatement. I ask her to do a few movements. Abi just smiles.

While I am contemplating my helplessness in resolving her pain, the lights come on, indicating a functioning electricity supply. Like a flash, Abi is back on the bed, looking at me with great expectations. I switch on the infrared lamp, which has become an object of great desire, and Abi mumbles happily. Within a minute or two, she is fast asleep. Unfortunately (but not surprisingly) only ten minutes later the lights go off again. I tell Abi 'No lights, no machine!', so again she smiles, dons her kira and, in leaving, insists on squeezing a bunch of walnuts into my hand.

'*Kadinche la*,' she thanks me. Slowly, bent over, diminished to maybe three-quarters of her real size, she limps out of the room and waves goodbye. I noticed on her referral that she was discharged from the hospital today, and I am sure that I will not see her again. She is probably already on the way home to her village, back to the fields and a myriad of chores.

EIGHT

OM MANI PADME HUM

'Don't move.' Pema rushes towards me and quickly pinches the front of my lab coat between her fingers. 'I got him!' She inspects her catch, focusing on her fingertips. 'They really like you.'

Throwing my hands in the air, I have to grin. Yes, the fleas seem to thrive on me. Since my arrival two weeks ago, every day in the hospital is flea-collection-day, and I am the designated collector. No one else seems to have a problem with those awful, tiny blood-sucking beasts. I have asked several doctors what I can do, but they just give me a puzzled look and tell me to change my clothes after I get home. 'Of course I change my clothes!' I think, but what good does it do when I simply refresh my flea supply the next day as soon as I touch a patient. Sometimes I can see them jumping over, other times I just feel that annoying itch somewhere inside my shirt. And they always head for my underwear! Like a rash caused by cheap laundry detergent, I have semi-permanent red dots all along the elastic of my panties and the outline of my bra. Hats off to mosquitoes and blackflies, but they are nothing compared to fleas. I have spent a few sleepless nights already, trying not to scratch, trying to ignore the unbelievable itch. No chance. By now, my skin is overly sensitive and bleeding in some areas.

Pema is full of sympathy. 'They are terrible. Nima gets many bites all the time. I don't know, they never bother me or Chimmi. Maybe it's because we have darker skin.' Her concern for me is genuine, but she has no solutions either.

We return to our previous discussion. Pema is studying the anatomy of the shoulder, and possible causes of pain in that joint. Mongar is turning out to be typical of any physiotherapy referral pattern: syndromes come and go in spurts. You might not see a single shoulder patient for months, and then within a day, there are four patients with similar symptoms. Yesterday, we were flooded with chronic shoulder pains.

Pema wrinkles her forehead in concentration. 'What are rotator cuffs?'

'They are the supporting muscles of the shoulder, the little ones inside. These ones,' I point to the picture in the book.

'How we can treat them?' Pema is eager to get to the interesting stuff.

I try to be as unspecific as possible, to encourage her to think on her own.

'Well, how do you treat other inflammations of tendons?' I ask instead of replying.

A *'Jang oma exercise pincha mo?'* interrupts our studies. 'Should I do my exercises now?' An old, leathery face twinkles its remaining teeth at us. I laugh. This meme (a Sharchhop title for old men) is another one of my favourite characters.

'Nan odo, Meme!' I reply. 'Come in, come in.'

Meme shuffles through the door, pulls his gho off his shoulders, and heads straight for the stool beside the heat lamp.

'Mangi, Meme,' No, not now! I try to explain that there is no electricity, and therefore no heat lamp. Pema doubles over in laughter at my attempt at speaking and signing Sharchhopkha, and then translates in a few short words. Meme looks disappointed that his idea of exercising is not available today. I point towards the pulley system in the doorframe.

'Nan exercise pi. Nado?' You exercise now, OK?

A reluctant *'Dikpe, dikpe,'* is the answer. OK, OK.

I watch Meme as he gets ready. His legs are bowed from years of hard work in the mountains. His trunk is thin and fallen in, every rib is showing, and his collarbones stick out like two thin shelves. He wears a farmer's tan on his lower arms, and the rest of his body, except for his feet, is rather pale. His hair is grey but still thick. A wispy moustache and an equally thin goatee underline his marked cheek bones, and permanent laughter lines are etched deeply into his face.

Meme scrunches up his already squinting eyes. Skeptically he inspects the pulley and draws the string tentatively. It moves. Surprised, he pulls some more. Look at that, it works. Meme turns to me triumphantly. His face smiles with a thousand wrinkles, a thousand proofs of a long and happy life. He starts joking with us and clowns around with the rope. His efforts cannot exactly be described as exercise, but they serve their purpose. At that moment, the light bulb springs to life again. In an instant, Meme drops his preoccupation with the rope and sprints towards the heat lamp. Lights mean electricity, electricity means taking a rest under the comforting heat of the infrared rays. Meme's life is indeed blessed.

Soon, another old man pulls up a stool beside the heat lamp. He brings with him his tattered physiotherapy referral, a prayer wheel and his rosary. While he patiently waits his turn for treatment, the two pearl-sized globules hanging from the handheld prayer wheel make round after round, swishing and pulling the cylindrical drum on the top, as he slowly rotates his wrist in a clockwise direction. The other hand is busy with the rosary, his thumb steadily counting and moving the beads. He mumbles something under his breath, but I cannot understand the words, so I ask Pema.

'He is saying "*Om mani padme hum*",' she explains.

Om mani padme hum? Is that a prayer, or is he hypnotising his pain away by repeating the same words over and over? I ask what it means.

In response, the old man murmurs his words loud enough for me to hear. '*O manee peme hu, O manee*

92

peme hu, O manee peme hu, O manee peme hu...' the
same syllables are repeated over and over, slightly
slurred, and each time a rosary is moved and the
prayer wheel completes a few turns. I ask for the
meaning, and find myself pleasantly surprised that
this praying meme has an answer for me. Generally
I have noticed that the Bhutanese are extremely
religious and follow their rituals diligently; however,
few are able or willing to explain the deeper meaning.
This meme is obviously well learned and well spoken
because he seems to have many things to say. With
much difficulty and many long pieces of explanation,
Pema translates for me.

From what I understand, '*Om mani padme hum*' is a
mantra, a prayer which, through its devout repetition,
brings one closer to a desired outcome. There are many
mantras in existence, but in Bhutan '*Om mani padme
hum*' is the most common one. Literally translated it
means 'Hail oh jewel in a lotus'. *Mani* means jewel,
padma means lotus, *om* is the sound of the beginning of
all things, and *hum* is the end; om together with hum
represents the universe.

It is believed that with each turn of the wheel, merit
is accumulated. Each time the mantra is murmured, it is
added to the many prayers out there, thereby increasing
the likelihood of the enlightenment of all beings. The
act of reciting the mantra gains merit for a spiritual path
that will lead closer to enlightenment.

Having exhausted Pema's translation vocabulary, the
old man turns, closes his eyes and presumably continues
murmuring for the enlightenment of all beings.

The news of the heat lamp has caught on, and soon we have a queue of eager patients waiting for a blissful holiday at physiotherapy. Unfortunately, the power surge is short-lived, and a little later, we again sit in the semi-darkness of the room. Our patients disappear.

When at noon the power still has not returned, Pema rushes home to bring Nima back to the hospital. The little boy's cough has worsened, and Dr. Pradhan, the medical specialist, has promised to have a look at him. Pema seems relieved but nervous when she returns to the physio room with Nima on her arm.

'He thinks it's only a cough. I get cough medicine for Nima.'

I have noticed that Pema puts great trust in Dr. Pradhan.

'What does Dr. Pradhan think of Nima not crawling?' I ask carefully.

Pema twirls one of Nima's fine black curls around her finger and the little boy begins to giggle. She then gently picks him up and supports him in a standing position on the floor. Nima wobbles and sways, but keeps his shining eyes fixed on his mother.

'Perhaps he got injury to the head. Or maybe it happened during birth.' Nima continues to giggle until a bout of coughing rattles his little body and Pema hugs him tightly. 'But I think he was fine in the beginning.'

Determined, Nima frees one of his hands from Pema's embrace and raises his fingers to his lips. His expression becomes distant, almost thoughtful, while in slow, steady circles, his index finger caresses his lips.

'Don't!' Pema gently scolds her son, then turns to me. 'I am not sure that he can hear me, you know. Sometimes he smiles when we talk to him, but we just don't know if he hears us. I want to take him to Vellore. Dr. Pradhan also thinks that only in Vellore they can give good diagnosis.' For the first time since we met, I can see a tear rolling down Pema's cheek. It leaves a little dark mark on the front of Nima's sleeve.

I nod and turn to the papers on my desk to give Pema some privacy. From Dr. Pradhan I have learned that Vellore in Tamil Nadu is one of India's foremost diagnostic and research hospitals. Due to lack of equipment and resources, many conditions simply cannot be diagnosed properly in Bhutan, and for complicated diagnoses or treatments, patients are sent to India. However, the costs for the Bhutanese government for each referred patient are huge, and the waiting list for outside referrals is long. And yet for Pema, Vellore signifies her only real hope. So far, no one in Bhutan has been able to make a diagnosis for her baby. Myself, I am confused by the little boy's signs and symptoms which, if nothing else, point towards cerebral palsy.

'We only live for him now,' Pema says with a sigh. In a sudden impulse, I reach out and put my hand lightly on her shoulder. The young mother looks at me and tries to smile, but her dark, sad eyes betray her. I stroke the soft curls on Nima's small head, and the boy rewards me with a little gurgle. Unnoticed by Pema, he has managed to again free his hand which is promptly on the way to his lips.

Then he turns his head and I think I see happy recognition on his face. I follow his glance to the door.

'Good afternoon, ladies.' Pema's husband enters with a box of sweets from the bakery. He offers me a tired smile, then reaches down to cuddle his son who squeaks in delight. 'I thought you might be hungry.' Turning to Pema he asks: 'What did Dr. Pradhan say?' For a while the two parents discuss quietly.

'You're not working today?' I ask Karma.

'I took the afternoon holiday so I can take Nima home.' His answer is slow and drawn out with the slur of fatigue. 'Nima didn't sleep well last night,' he apologises, and I can guess that none of them did.

'Why don't you go home, too?' I say to Pema and point at the powerless bulbs. 'I am sure we won't get many more patients.' For a moment I wonder if I am overstepping the boundaries of my authority, but then reassure myself that no one will notice anyway.

'You will be OK by yourself?' Pema asks, then gets up quickly, perhaps afraid I might change my mind.

'Of course,' I lie with fake confidence, searching for one more rationalisation for Pema's early departure. 'We always advise our patients to take some rest, don't we? And I think that is what Nima and you need most right now, too.'

And it is true, after all. Perhaps there is not much we can offer here in our little physiotherapy department, but at least I can put a small part of my western training to use.

NINE

CHODEN

I noticed Choden a few days ago during rounds when Dr. Shetri explained that she was a case of transverse myelitis, admitted to the hospital for a urinary tract infection caused by her catheter. A little unclear about this diagnosis, I had asked further, and the doctor explained that transverse myelitis is a viral disease, attacking the spinal cord and leading to neurological deficits. The disease left Choden partially paralysed from the waist down, and for about four years she has not walked or stood. When I watched Choden that day, I noticed that the muscles of both of her legs seemed to violently contract in frequent spasms, leaving her curled up on the bed, helplessly writhing in pain. When I enquired as to whether she was receiving any treatment for her legs, the answer was no. She was only here to fix the urinary tract infection.

No one seemed to think that Choden was a candidate for physiotherapy treatments – except for me. I wanted to give it a try. I asked permission to work with Choden, and reluctantly the doctors wrote out a physiotherapy referral.

The apparent hesitancy with which I am granted a trial period of treatment irks me a little. I am puzzled by the doctors' attitude towards my role at the hospital. Although I am seemingly welcomed as part of the staff, there is an unspoken underlying resentment whenever I suggest something different from what has already been prescribed. At times, I wonder if it is all in my imagination; perhaps I am a little paranoid and hear criticism where none is meant. Yet I cannot shake the miserable impression that I am treading on somebody's toes.

In any case, today Choden is coming to physiotherapy, accompanied by her mother and her little five-year-old daughter, Yeshey. Choden is a very pretty young woman of twenty-six, with large brown eyes and a full head of short-cut black hair. She smiles readily, and her expression is one of intelligence and understanding. Self-confident and remarkably agile, Choden has learned to manipulate her legs in such a way that she can get around by supporting her bodyweight on her extremely muscular arms and pivoting her hips to the side. This method allows her to at least move from the bed to a chair or, if needed, to the ground.

Transverse myelitis struck her a few years ago. Again, the number of years varies between different versions of the story, but it seems clear that the onset occurred after her daughter's birth. Since then, she has gone from being completely paralysed below the waist to her present status of painful lower extremity spasms. She says that her catheter is the main problem. She only has one and, in her village, it is difficult to keep it clean. Over the past few years, she has been in the hospital several times for urinary tract infections.

Curious, Yeshey, the little daughter, looks at me. She appears intrigued by my blond hair and pale skin, but remains quietly standing beside Choden's wheelchair. Like a tiny guardian, she assesses my trustworthiness.

'Do you want to sit on the bed with your mom?' I ask. Yeshey nods seriously. She does not intend to leave her mother for even one minute.

I ask Pema to translate our assessment plan to the three women. Choden's mother asks a few questions, but Choden remains quiet. Smiling, she pulls her daughter closer, and although Yeshey must not understand all that is being said, she visibly relaxes.

Pema turns to me with a frown. 'It would be better to be in Thimphu.'

'Why is that?' I ask.

'Thimphu has more equipment and better room. It is much easier to work there.'

'I don't think it'll make much difference for the assessment,' I counter.

'Still, it is better to work in Thimphu.'

'Well, let's see what we can do here. We should be OK.'

Pema's sudden appraisal of our primitive conditions in Mongar astonishes me. Could it be that Choden reminds Pema of her son, and now Pema is wondering if Nima could get a better treatment in the capital? I resolve to encourage my faithful assistant to bring Nima to our physio room. Maybe if we see some success with Choden, Pema will feel more confident in my treatments and let me try with Nima.

I look from Pema to Choden and am struck by the same quiet determination which both of these two young women share. But for once I am grateful that my patient does not speak English.

'Please don't discourage Choden before we have even started,' I plead with Pema.

My usually diligent assistant shrugs her shoulders but affirms once more, 'Thimphu has better facility.' Then she starts the physical assessment.

After several attempts at moving Choden's legs to evaluate her range of motion, Pema has to abort her efforts. The more she tries to push, the more Choden's legs go into spasm. Once triggered, the strong involuntary muscle contractions grip Choden's legs like a vice, pushing them into a pointed-toe, straight-leg position, or pulling them into a tight crouch. The harder Choden concentrates herself, the more her muscles play havoc. Nothing can be done but to wait for them to relax in their own time. Eventually when the tension slackens, Choden is able to put her legs into a reasonable position through stiff, jerky kicks.

Still, Choden is eager to keep trying, and after a short rest, we again attempt a meaningful movement, this time more slowly. Initially, it looks as if we could succeed. Then, completely unexpectedly, I feel Choden's legs tighten, and before I can react she has kicked me against the wall. My hip bangs against the iron bar of the suspension frame, and loud rattling echoes through the room. Embarrassed, Choden apologises, and I can see that she is now ready to give up. Through Pema I try to reassure her, try to tell her that it does not matter at all. How can I make her understand that I am the one who feels silly? I should have been prepared. I promise myself to watch out the next time.

In full concentration, we continue for another twenty minutes. Finally, we find a solution. Bending Choden's knees to 90 degrees and pushing the soles of her feet with an even pressure onto the bed seems to interrupt the constant waves of spasm. Choden smiles through her exhaustion. Perspiration has plastered her hair against her forehead, and little rivulets of sweat are running down her cheeks.

Choden's mother disappears to fetch a glass of water. Yeshey climbs onto the bed and lays her head on Choden's stomach. Tenderly, the two whisper to each other. Then Choden laughs and brushes a curl off Yeshey's forehead. I am touched as I watch the closeness and confidence between mother and daughter, and ponder the stormy weather that must have strengthened this trusting bond.

Just like Lhamo, Choden and her family live in a small village far away from Mongar. A trip to the hospital is like a voyage to a different continent. At home, her parents and her husband run the farm and Choden is left to herself for most of the day. She gets around the house by sliding along the floor, pulling herself with the help of her arms. Still, her happy spirits do not seem to suffer. Now she is joking with Yeshey, and together they tackle her transfer to the wheelchair.

Encouraged by our modest success, I plan my treatment strategy. I want to help Choden to walk. Her body is strong, and she is a determined woman. Somehow we will make it; we will find a way. I ask Choden to come back tomorrow morning, first thing before rounds, so that we can divide the treatment into two shorter sessions. Upon my arrival in Mongar, the DMO had enquired if I needed anything else, and now I know what is missing: a set of parallel bars! We need a solid grip for each hand to help Choden stand up, and a narrow walkway to prevent a fall. There is enough space along the far wall of the exercise room to accommodate a bar of ten-step length. Just long enough. And we need a mirror. Choden has to see herself stand; she has to see that it is possible.

I explain my ideas to Pema. 'Do you think we could find a really tall mirror?'

'Why not!' Pema answers enthusiastically. All signs of her previous wariness have vanished.

'You should speak to ADM.'

Shortly thereafter, I discuss my plan with the hospital's administration, and the ADM sends Arup, man of all trades, to assess the situation. We agree that for the parallel bars we will use a couple of old pipes and make a base out of wooden boards. Immediately, Arup asks me for an exact drawing of what I have in mind. Perhaps my enthusiasm is contagious.

Two more 'general mechanics', Dendrup the electrician and Tenzin the assistant, join our little group, and like a team of engineers we survey the building site.

'If the base is too long, it will not fit around the corner here,' Pema cautions, pointing at the hallway that leads to the TB ward.

We study everyone's palm size and estimate the required circumference of the pipes needed. Then we discuss stability problems. I show them how ideally we would need the bars to be able to move up and down to accommodate different sized patients. Arup answers my every suggestion with a return confirmation, 'You would like it like this… isn't it?' followed by an encouraging little sideways shake of the head, 'yes, yes, I think that is possible, OK, OK!'

Arup is eager and seems quite knowledgeable. Pema is ready with critical comments, and Dendrup and Tenzin nod obligingly. I have every reason to put full trust in our mission.

In the afternoon, I am standing with Arup and Dendrup in the laundry-drying hut, a simple covered wood structure held up by a few posts. There is a fireplace at one end, and wire clothes lines run parallel throughout the length of the shed. The hut seems to double as a storage room, and below the drying sheets and pillowcases, there are piles of wood scraps, old doors, dented, rusty night tables and broken windows consigned for… I don't know what.

Though all sides of the hut are open for a breeze to circulate, the air smells stale and musty. An old woman, probably a relative of one of the patients, is cooking something over the fire and smoke creeps through the mist to settle on the freshly washed sheets. Arup and I are discussing the engineering principles of building parallel bars, and I watch as Dendrup hammers the four corner supports into place.

I am flabbergasted by the speed of the whole operation. In my experience, the hurried, fretful West and most of nonchalant, unruffled southern Asia run on a different perception of 'on time'. Bhutan is no exception. Usually things promised for tomorrow arrive the day after, if you are lucky. So far, I have learned that patience is probably the one survival technique, which I will have to perfect. Yet here I am watching the makings of my parallel bars, less than a day after the idea was conceived. It is a miracle.

Another miracle blesses that wondrous afternoon. The rain stops! As if someone in the heavens was grabbing chunks of the white fluffy stuff and flinging it into space, the clouds break up. Torn to this side, then to that, the fog loses its grip on the ground, and evaporates in one slow huff. Warm yellow sunrays flood through the patches of blue sky and burn away the remaining shadows. Steam starts to rise from the earth, as water droplets on trees, bushes, and grass turn into vapour.

Around me, an entire spectrum of green explodes in the sunset. Out of the mist, the mountains rise to meet the sky. They are beautiful, gentle mountains, softly curved and cushioned by jungles of dense green foliage. Valleys carve themselves through the ranges, zigzagging between the slopes only to lose themselves behind the next corner.

In front of the hospital, in a little courtyard half enclosed by the infectious disease wing and the operating room, a small crowd of attendants and patients gathers to enjoy the glorious evening. Women chat quietly, their fingers all the while busily finishing off a piece of weaving, spinning some wool, or picking lice out of someone's hair. A group of men sits off to one side, absorbed in a game of cards. In a large depression in the ground where the new hospital construction is planned but has not yet begun, children play on a pile of sand. Some are engaged in a game of hide and seek; others are strapped with a saggy piece of elastic which is the instrument of a lively jumping contest. A few boys noisily play football.

Choden's wheelchair has been pushed up the ramp to allow her to watch some of the activities, and Lhamo's mother wheels her daughter over to the grass. Timidly, Yeshey and another little girl in a tattered kira begin a game of catch with Lhamo. For the first time, I hear laughter that is loud and free. Unconstrained and relaxed, the afternoon is marked with happy songs and games. Only when the sun sinks behind the mountains and the cook announces the arrival of dinner does the little community slowly move back inside the walls of the hospital.

TEN

COMPASSION FOR LITTLE THINGS

In the third week of June, blessed with a full day of beautiful sunshine amidst the dark days of the summer monsoon, I move my bed and buckets into my newly assigned two-room quarters below the hospital. My spirits soar. Within no time, my cheerless classroom abode is forgotten. Although the neighbourhood of construction sites has tripled from there to here since I arrived in Mongar, if I can ignore the noise, the view is superb. Before my doorstep, a steep valley drops out of sight, climbing up the opposite side on the southern slopes of Chali mountain.

My set of rooms is one of four identical apartments in a cement building that skirts the lower hospital campus, and if it were not for the construction noise around me, I could make believe that this is indeed my palace at the end of the world. My neighbours are friendly even if not overly eager to become acquainted. Only the OT nurse Sister Chandra to my left is happy to exchange a smile and chat. The inhabitants of the two units above me prefer to share only our vista.

In front of my entrance door, there is a little overhang of the stairs leading to the upper units. I quickly designate it as my own laundry-drying room. On the first Sunday morning after my arrival, my small could-be porch is promptly christened by a chicken, which very unceremoniously blesses my doorstep with a couple of squishy droppings. Apparently satisfied, it then proceeds to stick its head through my door, inspecting my all-purpose living/bedroom. I never find out whether my decorations meet approval because a rooster comes speeding around the corner, and the two take off in a feather-flying cackle.

Then the telephone rings. A real phone, my own telephone, in my own apartment! It is not any old telephone either. For the last five years, Mongar has been connected to the outside world via satellite, a luxury beyond measure. I am reminded again that when new technology arrives in Bhutan, it is often accepted only in its most useful and sophisticated form. In eager anticipation, I pick up the receiver, and find that the line is clear and static free. But I cannot recognize the voice at the other end.

'This is Dr. Bikul,' the voice repeats.

Yes, of course, the sceptical doctor. Why is he calling me on a Sunday morning?

'Do you want to play badminton with us? All the doctors are going to play a game at about ten o'clock.'

Me, play badminton? Help! I have not held a racquet since high school. I am not convinced that this is the time to start delving into a game against all of the respected high society of Mongar Hospital.

'Well, I don't have a racquet,' I answer.

'That's OK, you can borrow one from somebody else,' the doctor insists enthusiastically.

I try to think of another excuse, but my mind is blank. My reply sounds hollow and lame even in my own ears. 'Thank you, but maybe not today. I might come up later and watch.'

Dr. Bikul does not seem satisfied with my answer, and hangs up after a disgruntled 'OK. Bye.' I feel guilty for turning down his first social invitation. Nonetheless, I am off the hook for today.

By noon, a little stab of loneliness shames me into watching at least one game. Fully expecting the inevitable stares and hushed snickering at my appearance, I climb the path to the main campus and head towards the hospital. To my relief, I meet no one.

On a small cement island amidst the staff quarters, a men's double is under way. ADM and DMO are facing Dr. Bikul and Karma, Pema's husband. The game is fast and cutthroat. No laughter breaks the tension. Though I assume that they are enjoying themselves, the players look as if they are fighting a war. Clenched teeth, eyes pinched into a narrow squint, they attack the bird. A fumble of the shuttlecock is greeted with a loud groan by the teammate and a triumphant cry by the opposition.

I linger for a few minutes, and then continue along the road leading through the hospital campus. The Class A quarters surround a grassy patch with a few trees and an old volleyball court. Dr. Shetri, Dr. Kalita, Dr. Bikul and Dr. Robert each have separate houses with little gardens, and a spectacular view over the valley. The DMO, ADM and matron have flat bungalow versions of Class A, located in the heart of the campus. Around and to the sides lie Class B and C quarters for nurses, lab technicians and other support staff.

I know that there is an acute housing shortage. All of the present construction is for new staff quarters. However, the space is limited and old quarters had to be demolished in order to build new ones, leaving many employees without a home. They had to move into the town itself; however, there too, everything is occupied. A place like Mongar does not see a lot of change, and an influx of new bodies simply cannot be accommodated.

On completing one loop of the hospital road, I end up back at the badminton court. The game is over, and the ADM and Karma are dismantling the net. Dr. Bikul saunters over to join me. Immediately, my nagging guilt returns, and I smile.

He seems to have something on his mind, but not the words to say it. Shifting nervously from one leg to the next, he looks at me, then at his racquet, again at me. 'Do you want to have dinner at the guesthouse tonight?' he finally asks.

Dinner? I can hardly believe my ears. Yes! Of course! A dinner that has been cooked by someone else. A real dinner, not like my brew last night. I think of my rice, which turned into a pot of porridge-like gunk, and the green beans that were tasteless too, not forgiving the lack of spices or sauces. For far too many days, I have been living off potatoes and bread. Honey and peanut butter are already coming out of my ears.

Does he know that I am a lousy cook, or is this a social invitation? Well, one way or the other, dinner means a full stomach to sleep on. Trying not to sound too eager, I quietly accept the offer.

The Sunday turns into a hot, muggy day, the kind that leaves you gasping for air, dreaming of fresh lemonade and ice cream. We start our climb from the hospital at five o'clock. The evening is warm and cloudy. Finally, the day's heavy humidity has ceased to throttle our energy, and the agonising heat has cooled to a pleasant mild summer's night.

Dr. Bikul marches slightly ahead with short, purposeful steps, and I do my best to keep up. By some unspoken law, we walk in silence until we reach the bazaar. Then, amongst the hubbub of Indian labourers, villagers and young men drinking and noisily playing carom, a game similar to pool, we slide into a serious conversation. Dr. Bikul is now eager to talk.

'I like Canada. It is a good country. Canadians do a lot for the environment. They are an international leader in environmental protection.'

'Hmm.' I answer with a vague confirmation.

Dr. Bikul continues, 'I like especially the Hudson's Bay Company. I have heard that they do a lot to protect the forests in Canada.'

This time I have to interrupt. I am not sure that he really means the same Hudson's Bay Company that I am thinking of. 'Did you also know that the Company was originally based on fur trade? That is not an entirely environmentally friendly business,' I say.

Dr. Bikul seems surprised but not in the least put off. He continues to inform me about the advantages of Canadian attitudes, about our environmental consciousness, and then moves on to issues on a global scale. I do not get another say. Somehow, the topic shifts to a future world war, although the doctor firmly insists that such a possibility is out of the question. When he finally dives into a lecture about Germans and Hitler, I have had enough.

'Did you know that I am originally from Germany? I really do not appreciate you generalising about a country you have never been to. That is dangerous! That is how prejudices are formed!'

I am steaming. Who does he think he is? A bookworm, full of arrogance and theoretical knowledge. I feel like turning around, but instead we continue further and further up the road, leaving Mongar and the guesthouse behind us. As our feet strike the irregular pavement, we gradually steer the conversation back to safer ground, but the friction continues.

Maybe twenty minutes out of town, we reach a bend in the road. I look back. Below us lies Mongar. All around, the mountains stretch in a curvy silhouette, greying in the light of dusk. Dr. Bikul points to the individual peaks and tells me their names, sometimes the local name, sometimes the one he has given to them.

'Over there, across from Mongar, is Chali. I like the people there. They are really funny. No one can drink as much as a Chalipa!'

Dr. Bikul acts out a drunken little dance and I have to grin.

Then he points to the next mountain. 'The high peak beside Chali is Takchhu. To the right, the pass at the end of this valley is Kori La.'

I follow his finger to a ridge of mountains where the thin serpentine road disappears into the trees. It is a beautiful view. Farms dot the hillsides of terraced paddies and cornfields. The houses and tiny figures of people blend with their surroundings naturally and effortlessly. Again I marvel how the traditional Bhutanese buildings, often fantastic in their sizes and architecture, harmonise with the awesome splendour of the highlands.

Quietly, Dr. Bikul continues. 'I call Kori La *Krishna Pahar*, in memory of my father. *Krishna Pahar* is where the sun rises every morning, and where the new day begins.' Then he turns further south. 'And these two peaks I have named *Hurja* and *Anonda*. If you stand here before sunrise when everything is still dark, the mountains are only a thin outline. And then, all of a sudden, you can distinguish *Hurja* and *Anonda*. Their shapes become clear, more defined. They glow in the first rays of the sun, just before it peaks over Kori La.'

Looking at his mountains, Dr. Bikul's attitude softens. The stern arrogance of his face gives way to something dreamy.

'I love my nature,' he says quietly. Then he smiles. It is a heart-warming smile that innocently erases the carefully guarded demeanour from his face. His dark eyes glow with passion, and for a second, I am charmed by his smile. Then abruptly Dr. Bikul sobers, and as if to protect his vulnerable confession, marches ahead a few steps.

A dog comes limping down the road, and my fleeting moment of utter content crashes in one sad look. The poor creature is nearly furless, and the red raw patches of skin are covered with pussy sores. Every rib lifts his skin a few centimetres from his hollow skeleton of a body, and several wounds on his legs are quietly bleeding. His eyes are swollen and weepy, and he salivates in long, slimy beads onto his paws and chest. He sniffs the road as if there was hope of any food coming his way, and then drags himself on, resigned to hunger.

He is not the first dog I have seen in Bhutan in pathetic condition, but of all of them he is certainly the one closest to death. In Mongar as well as in Thimphu, the streets are filled with stray dogs; most of them mangled and disfigured by scabies. No one seems to care. I see no one reaching out to these poor creatures; instead they are kicked and yelled at, and children learn from a small age that they are only useful as living targets for flying stones.

I stand there and helplessly watch as the sad little beast forces itself to make a big loop in order to avoid us. Dr. Bikul turns to me, and I tell him my grief. Not that I expect him to understand, but I cannot keep my frustration inside. To my surprise, he is quite attentive. 'You are very kind-hearted,' he replies, instead of laughing at me. 'I never really thought that much about these dogs. They are just here, and that's it.'

'But you are a doctor,' I reproach. 'At least you should care about these poor creatures.'

'But I am a human doctor! I have no ideas about animals.'

'But you see them suffer! I just mean, to me, it is beyond comprehension how all these Buddhists in Bhutan watch the dogs suffer.'

'Perhaps you are right.' Dr. Bikul nods. Then he produces a small red package out of his pocket. Holding it out to me, he asks, 'Do you want to feed the dog?'

'What is that?' I ask.

'KitKat. I usually keep some with me for the children.' His face has softened and lost all pretenses. I feel a wave of gratitude. With a new closeness, the doctor and I are bonded by our joint compassion.

I break some of the KitKat into little pieces and place them carefully on the ground. The dog does not look over and shuffles on. Hastily I pass him and start a little trail of chocolate, one piece after the other, towards the rest of the bar. For a moment, it looks as if the poor thing will walk on. He does not seem interested; or else, his sense of vision and smell has been deadened beyond recognition. But then he carefully licks one tiny crumb off the road. His difficulty in swallowing is obvious, and I quickly break up the rest of the bar.

He eats another piece, and another, slowly, cautiously, not looking up, saving his energy for the tiring task at hand. Tears begin to burn in my eyes, and leaving him to finish his meal in peace, Dr. Bikul and I walk back towards the guesthouse.

At the primary school, a steep road veers off to the left, and we follow it to the Royal Guesthouse. We enter through a heavy red gate and find ourselves in a fine English garden. Big trees palisade the path and the air is sweet with the smell of blossoms. The lawn is thick and well kept, and a tall stone wall surrounds the garden. Beyond that enclosure lies the dzong and, below that, the houses of Mongar. Kesang, a young, friendly man, asks us to sit in the little sheltered porch in front of the main building.

Self-assured Dr. Bikul orders a beer for me and raises his eyebrows in surprise when I tell him that I do not drink. I order a Coke instead.

The menu must have been prearranged because within minutes we are served a plate of fried peanuts, followed by several dishes, most of them containing some form of meat. It is the first time since my arrival in Mongar that I lay my eyes on any kind of meat, and I am wondering about its safety for my stomach. Still, I do not want to refuse the meal. Instead I eat only modest bites and try to explain that I am not a big meat eater. Again, Dr. Bikul seems surprised. He orders another Coke for me, and then offers a cigarette. I refuse politely. I do not smoke. I can see that he is struggling hard with his prejudiced image of Westerners. Don't we all drink and smoke and eat meat? He asks if I mind if he smokes, but then stubs out his cigarette after a few puffs. Awkwardly, we finish our meal.

It is only after the last bowl has been cleared from the table that we somehow reconnect.

'Dr. Bikul, about your religion, I mean about Hinduism and Buddhism – I am still very confused.'

'In what way?' Dr. Bikul asks.

'For example, I thought that Buddha is a god. But the other day, I learned that Buddha did not believe in God.'

'Well, sort of,' Dr. Bikul replies. 'Buddha neither denied nor recognised the existence of God. Buddha emphasised the importance of a noble life, a non-violent way of life. Buddha did not ask us to believe, but to realise and experience our own spiritual life.'

This does not make total sense to me. Every house, every temple I have been to, has one or several statues of what I thought were gods. 'But the Bhutanese worship Buddha as a god, don't they? I mean, our patients, those villagers, they believe in Buddha.'

'They do.' Dr. Bikul nods. 'Believing is easier and more romantic than realising, you know what I mean. We like to believe, because we are human.'

Dr. Bikul gives me a conspiratory smile and leans back in his seat. He is obviously comfortable with this topic. It must be familiar ground to him, and he opens up with his deep philosophical ideas. I learn about Buddha and Guru Rinpoche, about the religious behaviour of my patients, and about the Bhutanese attitude towards suffering. He tells me about the monks living in the mountains in isolation, meditating undisturbed, and about how Buddhism and Hinduism are related.

The hours pass. At almost midnight, under a pale moon and a multitude of twinkling stars, we stumble through the darkness back to the hospital.

ELEVEN

CHILLI CON CARNE

I wake up early with a feeling of pure joy. A warm radiant light floods my room. Indulging in the luxury, I lazily get up and make a strong cup of coffee. I throw my windows and doors wide open and let life wash over me.

A green and gorgeous giant greets me from across the valley, a distinguished character amongst the neighbourly peaks. Marked through the years by monsoons and dry winters, the face of the mountain is furrowed with shallow wrinkles. Rivers separate him from his mates, cutting deeper into the ground each season, lengthening his rounded back.

Perched on his steep slope over the Kuruchu river, the farms and terraces of Chali bask in the morning sun.

Trees and shrubs surround parcels of land covered with paddies in all different hues of green. Billows of clouds reflect the low rays of the sun, painting the mountain's features with brilliant colours.

Below me, I can hear the roaring of the Gangola as it thunders towards Lingmithang. The sound echoes through the valley and bounces along stones and rocks following the river's path. Joining its tune, the melody of a myriad of birds celebrates the break of day.

My morning routine begins. After my daily adjustment to the weather's follies, I cram as much as possible into the hours before hospital duty calls at 9 a.m. Cleaning myself and my home in addition to preparing food takes up most of the time. If, as today, I finish early enough, I try to get the laundry done.

I fill the big blue plastic tub with water to the rim. Unbelievable how much dirty washing keeps piling up. Every day after duty I have to abandon my flea-infested outfit to the tub. If I go for a walk after that, the humidity and the heat combine into such a powerful steam bath that I come home drenched in my own sweat, and I have to change again. Finally, if at night more fleas find their way into my pyjamas, there is no other solution but to wash those too.

Drying the stuff afterwards is a completely different challenge. On cloudy or rainy days, there is practically no chance of success in that matter; my clothes hang on the line for several days before I can even think of taking them inside. Still partially damp, they then start rotting in the cupboard and are usually completely dried only by my body heat upon wearing them. That leaves them with a few minutes of dryness, before sweat and dust sully them again. Heaving the heavy bucket of wet clothes out the door, I resolve to become less fussy about smell and stains. I will simply blend in more; I will adapt to the laws of the monsoon.

This morning, I am almost finished decorating my clothes line when a small, furry dog bounces up to the porch. I try to call her over, but she only looks at me with big, brown eyes. I crouch and drum my fingers on the floor. She wags her tail very tentatively but keeps her distance. About the size of a terrier with a long reddish coat, she looks healthy, not at all mangled like most of the other dogs. I doubt that she is someone's pet; I cannot recall anyone in Mongar admitting to the ownership of a pet.

The little red mutt inches closer to me. She sniffs my hands, my feet, my dress, and then, apparently satisfied, turns into a leaping, barking bundle of energy. Laughing, I head for the kitchen to get some leftover rice. All I can find are potatoes, though, and suddenly remembering the name of one of my friends' teddy bear, I call my new friend Spud.

In the late afternoon, when my hospital duties are over, I decide I will walk up to the bazaar to find some underwear for Lhamo. The hospital campus is deserted, and only one door to the outpatient chambers is still open. I poke my head through the curtain. Dr. Bikul is deeply absorbed in his books.

'Hi!' I call into the resounding silence of the cement walls, 'you are still working?'

He looks up puzzled, then slowly recognises the intruder. 'Oh, hi!' With a quick motion, he stuffs his pack of cigarettes into the desk drawer. I cannot let him get away with that, so I smile.

'No need to hide the cigarettes.'

Dr. Bikul looks as guilty as a little boy caught with his hand in the cookie jar.

First a little annoyed, then relieved, he grins. 'How did you see them so quickly?'

'Well, I have sharp eyes for such things,' I reply. 'So what are you working on?' I ask, and walk closer to his desk to get a better look at his books. They are medical textbooks, volume upon volume filled with tiny print.

'I came to Bhutan to get some quiet time to prepare for my PG entrance exams.'

'PG entrance?' I repeat.

'Postgraduate school,' Dr. Bikul explains with a little self-importance. 'I have my medical degree, but I need to join postgraduate school in oncology.'

I nod. Oncology is the study and treatment of cancers. A very specialised field, and I can picture this serious doctor well in that role.

'When are you going to apply?'

'Next year. The competition in India is very tough. Imagine, there are more than ten thousand doctors every year applying for oncology, and only two seats.'

'Ten thousand doctors will compete for two seats?' I repeat sceptically. Perhaps another exaggeration to underline his importance?

Dr. Bikul is quick to qualify his statement. 'Well, two seats in Chandigarh Postgraduate Institute. There are other medical institutes. But everyone competes to be in Chandigarh. That is the best place to do research against cancer.'

'I didn't realise that a doctor working in this remote hospital could have such big plans,' I admit.

Bikul nods. 'Initially, I came to Bhutan only for three months. Bhutan was looking for doctors and I thought, what better place than this to get away from the noisy hospitals in India. It is quiet here, plenty of time to study. But then, I liked it so much here. The untouched nature, the ancient civilisation. I decided to stay longer. Actually,' Bikul grins, 'this is my third year.'

'So that's why you are always sitting in this room?'

'Yes, in the evenings, this is my study. No one disturbs me here.'

'Don't you ever eat?' I enquire, looking at my watch. 'I never see you leave this room until night-time.'

Now he hems and haws a little. 'I will eat at the hotel.' Then, obviously sensing my need for a further explanation, he adds, 'You know Norbu, the pharmacy assistant who got transferred this week; he used to cook for me.' He pauses for a moment. 'I cannot cook.'

'So you always eat at the hotel?' I ask in amazement. Even I, the self-proclaimed terrible chef, cannot believe that.

'Well, I only eat one big meal. In the morning I have some tea and coconut.' He seems embarrassed now.

'Oh.'

I am not sure how to respond. I always assumed that all single men who have endured years of bachelorhood know how to feed themselves. Actually, I thought that I was a pathetic exception to all over-twenty-year-olds, with my minute knowledge of fine cuisine. Obviously, I was mistaken.

Feeling awkward, I decide to leave the hungry doctor to his studies. Halfway out the door, something makes me stop, though. Before I can grasp the full meaning of my own words, I hear myself extending an invitation. 'Please come for dinner tonight. You can eat with me, I have to cook anyway.'

Why did I say that, and worse, why did he accept? All the way up to the bazaar, I scold myself. What am I going to cook? What will he eat? What will we both eat? What kind of food should I buy? I have no idea how to cook for myself, let alone prepare Indian dishes. I do not even know the name of this yellow spice that seems to be the characteristic ingredient of curries. What if he eats only extremely spicy food with lots of chillies, like the Bhutanese? I wish that I could take the invitation back, but it is too late. Somehow, I have to dream up SOMETHING!

I decide first to get the underwear issue out of the way, and then tackle the question of food. One of the sisters recommended that I look in Yeshey Pelden's shop, and I find it halfway up the road, the shop set slightly underground, in a sort of mezzanine. The right wall is packed with drinks of all sorts: beer, rum, orange squash, lemon squash, tins of pineapple and orange juice, and some fruit concoctions in lunch-sized drink cartons. In front of the drinks is a long glass case with all kinds of cookies, sweets, stale-looking chocolate and crackers. At the far wall, I detect a shelf with garments. I ask for underwear.

'What size?'

'Small,' I reply. 'Really small.' The girl behind the counter snickers, and I feel obliged to add, 'It's not for me. It is for one of my patients, and she is only thirteen.' The girl pulls out a couple of packages of plastic-wrapped underwear with little butterflies on them. Not too bad for the middle of nowhere. I pick the smallest pair and quickly leave the shop. That mission accomplished, I devote my full attention to the question of food.

In Rinzin Tshockey's shop I look around for a while. There is a big basket with tomatoes which must have come up from Samdrup Jongkhar with the bus. Tomatoes – what could I cook with tomatoes? A brilliant idea strikes. Chilli con carne! Except for the carne. There is no meat available for regular mortals in Mongar. I remember that somewhere I have a recipe for a very tasty chilli without meat. I turn to Rinzin Tshockey.

'Can I buy some chillies?'

He looks at me with a question mark across his forehead. 'You are going to cook with *chilllies*, madam?'

'Yes, I am going to try. Can I have, um, maybe five?'

'Five chillies, madam?'

'Yes, only five.'

Rinzin Tshockey grins from ear to ear. 'Please,' he says handing me five green chillies. 'For you. No need to pay.'

I toil over the gas cooker, sweat over the chillies and cry from the onions. I pray and talk to the pot in the sweetest of voices. I run back and forth between the kitchen and the living room in nervous anticipation. Did I set the table nicely? Are the potatoes done yet? Will the lights stay on long enough for us to finish dinner? I had better get some candles, just in case. Then again, candles? A little bit too romantic for a simple shared dinner. Nevertheless, this is Mongar; everyone eats by candlelight. No, better use the kerosene lamp; better not give him any wrong ideas. He is simply going to have dinner with me because I have to cook anyway.

To my surprise, the chilli turns out quite tasty. However, if I heat it any longer, it will surely transform into another ugly mess of overcooked everything. I fret and worry and experiment with the low settings of the gas cooker. I turn it off and, a few minutes later, back on in a panic that the food might be cold. I watch the clock as if it was going to jump out at me. Spud comes by and I share some potatoes with her.

At nine o'clock I sit at the empty table and try to eat a bit of my, by now cold, chilli con carne without carne and without company. The disappointment tastes bitter.

The lights flicker and dim a shade. Without much thought, I strike a match to light my candle before the room gets lost in complete darkness. A spider sprints across the floor and hides under my shoes, another one drops from the wall onto my bed. Get off! The thought of finding myself locked under my mosquito net with this creepy-crawly sends me clambering across the room, shooing the unbidden guest off my property. In the kitchen, a metallic sound makes me wonder about rats. I remember the odd hairs on my cutting board yesterday. Did I close my meat safe properly? How can I stop the fruit flies, and how can I slow the mould? Did I boil my water for filtering? No, I forgot. Will it be enough for tomorrow morning?

Almost asleep, my mind starts spinning around the same annoying question: Why did Dr. Bikul stand me up?

TWELVE

FRICTION

It is barely day yet and already I have spent a full hour, and then some, hunting my most dreaded enemy – the flea! First I wanted to snuggle back in bed after half-starved devouring the better part of my dinner and a bar of chocolate (all at 4.30 a.m. when the first rooster in the neighbourhood woke up). Then I felt something on my leg, and when I shone the light on it, it jumped.

Now, after a fortnight of agony, scratching myself every day and night until I bleed, there is no way, simply no way, I can go back to reading when I know that my blood enemy is still somewhere out there. So, reluctantly, I get up, take my sheets and blanket outside, shake them hard, and hang them on my under-the-roof line for the day. Then I am off to the bathroom where I diligently check myself and my nightgown – but to no avail. The little bugger has escaped.

OK, I think, I will get dressed. I pick up one sock and immediately recognise this suspicious black dot. I set off to crush it successfully. Then, however, I notice another black dot on my leg (at this point, I am standing stark naked in the bathroom). With much skill, I catch it. Knowing how quick those critters are, I immediately squash it in some toilet paper, but... when I carefully open the paper, nothing is there. Was the cushioning effect so strong that the paper ate the insect? But no – boing! It jumps out towards me and is gone.

There is a certain paranoia which goes along with losing one of those bloodthirsty tiny creatures, and it prompts me to go on a search for the bug's whereabouts. With no result. So in the end I got one and lost two, rather an average outcome for most of my hunts; especially considering that there are probably still half a dozen or so sitting in my room, my clothes, my everything, waiting for me to walk by so that they can hurl themselves at my innocent flesh. I spread the mothball powder everywhere. That means they jump from there to somewhere else – big success.

Have I become too violent? I know the Buddhist philosophy demands respect for all sentient beings – and I do feel guilty. Normally, I would not hurt a fly, but lack of sleep makes me cranky. Praying for forgiveness, I submerge my entire heap of worn clothes in my oversized bathing bucket.

The hospital is filled to the brim. Twenty-one new admissions overnight! Patients are lying on mattresses on the floor everywhere, absolutely everywhere. I.V. poles are set up in the middle of the hallways and attendants are crowding the already scarce free space. Dr. Bikul is busy giving instructions and briefing the incoming day shift of nurses. There is no apparent order to the chaos, but somehow everyone understands to stay quiet. There is no complaining or nagging; no one demands immediate attention. Patients and attendants alike passively wait their turns.

At 8.30 a.m. I unlock the doors to our physiotherapy rooms. The blue double doors squeak open and I flick on the lights. A clean sleepy room welcomes me. On the bed, some donated stuffed animals for the children greet me with their never-failing grins: a furry Gremlin-like ball of fluff; a green frog that makes a noise when you shake it; a little dog; a handmade cotton bug whose red eyes are about to pop out of his head. The doctors raised their eyebrows when they first saw them, but I like our little squad. They are the guardians of Pema's and my castle.

The lights wink at me, flash brightly, and then turn off for the day. I throw open the windows towards the courtyard and survey the scenery from within the safety of our refuge. I feel at home in the physiotherapy department. Here in these two rooms, Pema and I are allowed to make decisions, to assess, treat and discharge as we see fit. As soon as we leave these walls, we abide by the unspoken laws of Mongar Hospital; we bow to rules of rank and respect that do not always have an obvious connection with wisdom or the best interest for the patient. Out there we have to play the politics, but in here we talk freely and openly. There are no secrets in physiotherapy.

Proudly I examine the new parallel bars in our exercise room. The yellow paint gleams from the long iron bars, and the whole construction has an air of prized solidity. At the end of the bars, a half-length mirror has been fixed on the wall and, for a minute, I look at my somewhat distorted reflection. Sister Britta, here you are. Only three weeks in Mongar, and already I feel almost at home. With a smile, I give the bars one last shake to reassure myself of their sturdiness, and then walk over to Ward B to tell Choden that I am ready.

The atmosphere in the wards is lively. Some patients and attendants are still having breakfast, others make a bed, line up for the toilet, or try desperately to continue a bit of slumber. They have half an hour left before the doctors start their rounds, half an hour of unhurried morning business.

Choden is not quite ready for me, and the hustle of the ward occupies my senses. Across the aisle from where I am standing, a naked toddler starts peeing on a pillow, and within seconds her mother swoops her up and holds her over the side of the bed. Urine splashes on dangling feet and the neighbour's' plastic slippers. A small puddle forms on the floor. No one takes notice. Satisfied with her save, the quick-witted mother settles on the bed, unbuckles her kira and starts breast-feeding the now contentedly suckling little girl. All continues as before.

Then a bit of commotion attracts my attention to Ward A. Two nurses are arguing loudly with a small group of people standing around the bed of an old, wrinkled abi who is slowly getting dressed with the help of a young man. I know from yesterday's rounds that this abi is suffering from a severe ulcerated stomach, and is scheduled for surgery today. However, by the looks of it, she is leaving. I ask one of the nurses what is going on.

It turns out that Abi's family wants to take her home to perform a puja, a religious ceremony to ask for a quick recovery. They do not want an operation today. It is not a good day for surgery, they say. After the puja, they will come back, but now they have to go. The nurses continue trying to convince Abi to stay, but it's no use. Her family does not want to hear what the doctors say, they have heard enough. Their lama told them to come home, and so they must leave. Before anyone can stop them, Abi's son carries the little lady out of the hospital.

I return to Ward B. Choden is ready now, and together we head to the physio room. For three days we have tried the same routine, and I feel that we are making progress. I can now move her legs throughout their full ranges without too much difficulty. Choden has learned to relax, and I have learned to go slowly. Today I want to try something different. The new parallel bars are waiting in all their glory in the exercise room, and I have planned for Choden to try standing for the first time.

As soon as Pema arrives, we tackle the challenge. First, we secure a transfer belt around her waist. Then we manoeuvre the wheelchair to the open end of the parallel bars. From there, Choden transfers onto a wooden stool, which has been placed at the entrance of the bars, facing the full length mirror at the opposite end. We explain to Choden what to do. I will kneel in front of her and steady her feet to prevent them from slipping. She will hold onto the parallel bars with both hands. Then on one, two, three, go! I will pull her towards me while she pushes herself out of her wheelchair and straightens her legs. If all goes according to plan, she will stand securely between the parallel bars, supporting herself as needed with her arms.

Choden is obviously nervous. I kneel down and motion to her to put her feet between the bars. Tentatively, Choden tries to extend her toes to the floor, but her thigh muscles contract and she forcefully kicks the air. Again she tries – unsuccessfully. Finally I guide her foot to the floor, and then push it down with all my might. Her muscles relax. We try the other foot. This foot, however, does not budge off the footrest. Again we have to trick her muscles, and it seems like hours until finally we have both feet firmly planted on the floor. Choden is sweating. Her palms are damp, and I can feel her grip tightening on the bars. Her strong forearm muscles are contracted into tight bundles; her whole body is shaking in anticipation.

'*Dikpe?*' Ready?

A quick sideways shake of the head and a nervous smile say yes. Ready. With an encouraging 'Up!' I pull Choden towards me. She lurches forward – and her knees buckle. All of a sudden, I am holding her entire body weight in my arms. I groan and my back starts screaming, then Choden recovers and suspends herself between her powerful arms. Pema comes to our rescue. Gently she pushes Choden's knees into a locked position, and holds them there firmly.

Choden is still shaking, but I think this time it is out of fear. She mumbles something which I think is a plea to stop, but I tell her to wait. In my best Sharchhopkha, I ask Choden to look up. No response. Choden is leaning forward onto me, watching her disobedient legs as her muscles try to pull her feet out from underneath her. Again I ask Choden to look up, and at last she lifts her head and stares at the mirror behind me. First surprise, then disbelief and finally joy washes over her face. Gradually, her tension eases, and she starts talking in excited tones to her little daughter Yeshey. I cannot understand what she says, but I know that it is good news. Her words are filled with smiles, and her voice speaks of giddiness and pride. Choden can see herself standing up properly for the first time in years.

A few more seconds of well deserved triumph pass, and then we help Choden back into her chair. She is exhausted but wants to try again. I look at her legs. The continuous ebb and flow of muscle contractions is flinging her legs off the footrests, and her toes splay and curl without any apparent rhythm. Choden might be ready for another try, but her body needs some rest.

A small, frightened face peeps around the corner. Lhamo must have watched our difficult exercise and feels scared now that she will have to face the same trial. I smile. She too has made a lot of progress already, and I am proud of her. With a shake of my head, I wave her in. Not too agile yet with her wheelchair skills, Lhamo crashes against the doorframe a couple of times before she comes to a halt in the middle of the room. I leave it to Pema to direct our stubborn patient to the bed.

The daily whining begins. I never know if it is fear or pain, or both, that turn Lhamo into a heap of quivering anxiety as soon as she lies on the treatment bed. I can tell from the level of her vocal cords at which point she really starts to hurt, but the background sobs do not seem to have a specific cause; all the same, I cannot take all of the pain out of our treatment.

Upon seeing her X-rays and discussing her left knee with the surgeon, I know that any work on that leg would be an excruciating waste of time. Nothing other than an operation will ever move that knee again. So far, every surgeon has refused to touch her knee. Dr. Kalita says he would try, but in Mongar, we simply do not have the surgical equipment required. I am told to forget about the left knee.

The right knee, however, has minute potential. Though Lhamo's burn scars are massive, and several surgery efforts were of no benefit, she is young enough that she should be able to stretch them by several degrees. Even if we can never restore her leg to normal, maybe one day I can get it strong enough to support her with the help of crutches. Anything is better than her present condition.

Pema has designed a strengthening routine for Lhamo's wasted muscles, and every day after her stretches, we supervise our little patient's exercises. Through her repetitions, I learn to count in Sharchhopkha: *thur, nigzing, sam, pshi, nga, khung*, and so on.

Sitting over the side of the bed, dangling her legs, Lhamo reclaims the happy nature of a teenage girl. Her head is always filled with nonsense. Flashing a bright, mischievous smile, she tries to cheat a little, forget a few repetitions. A little scolding or a warning look from us seems to enhance the value of skipping a few counts.

To my utter surprise, though, she always completes her exercises. She is far too lazy to strain herself, or overly fatigue her muscles, but she ploughs through her routine in her own time. Some days it takes hours, and I get the definite feeling that she is prolonging her routine in order to stay with us and have some company.

I can understand her longing for some excitement. The ward does not hold much appeal for a young girl. The times when I have visited Lhamo there, she has always been sitting on her bed, playing with her mother. Mostly, her games are simple. One amusement consists of someone tying some rope into a knot, and the other person trying to undo it. Another favourite is using a little bowl and some small stones to play catch.

Now, however, nothing compares to physiotherapy. Here, she can explore an unknown creature. Sitting beside me, she questioningly touches my blond hair, wrapping it around her finger or watching it against the light. She observes my blue eyes, comparing them to Pema's, and voicing her opinions loudly. Gently she feels the pale skin on my arms and stares at my freckles in wonder. She wants to see how I write, how I assess other patients, what exercises others have to do.

She welcomes my attempts at speaking Sharchhopkha with a delighted giggle, and soon becomes my impatient teacher. Together, we memorise the body parts one by one. I point at something and she tells me the name of what I am indicating. Then I repeat it. She laughs but will not say it again. I have to try different pronunciations, different ways of twisting my tongue into bizarre positions. I say the same thing repeatedly, until finally I am rewarded by a satisfied smile from her, and we move on to the next word.

When other patients come, Lhamo retreats onto the vacant bed and watches. Sometimes she continues her exercises but mostly she sits there, with a perplexed look on her face, studying the world of our physiotherapy room. These four walls have become her second home in the hospital, and whenever she is not in the room, I expect to see her face peeping through the windows. Her wheelchair has given her a new freedom, and physiotherapy a new travel destination.

THIRTEEN

ARE YOU FEELING BORING?

I have just returned from the hospital when the telephone rings. It is Dr. Bikul.

'Do you want to play badminton?'

I am torn between saying yes just to be brave and the overwhelming lump in my throat when I think about the all-male every-man-for-himself attitude during the games. Embarrassed I excuse myself, admitting that I am not a very experienced player.

'Please come, you will like it,' Dr. Bikul insists.

Nervously, I play with the cord of the telephone. I am glad that he cannot see me now. Mustering my utmost courage, I ask if he would like to go for a hike instead.

There is a little pause before Dr. Bikul answers. 'Well, I'm on emergency duty today, but maybe after five o'clock?'

I am relieved and agree quickly. Thankfully, he does not mention badminton again.

We meet in front of his quarters and slowly climb the muddy road around the helicopter pad to the bazaar. Once we leave the hospital campus, the air seems lighter, fresher.

My steps carry me eagerly up the hill. The clouds have moved back in, and a soft, warm drizzle dampens my hair. The road is deserted; reaching the first few houses, I marvel in the calm around me. Only an old man sits in front of one of the shops, faithfully turning a large prayer wheel filled with mantras. A little wooden peg on top of the wheel strikes a bell on each turn, reminding me to include an act of compassion or devotion in the day. The man looks past us somewhere into the distance while his thumb moves bead after bead on the rosary. Never interrupting his prayer, he slides deeper into the corner of the bench, and continues turning the large cylinder with a steady rhythm. Cling... cling... cling, the bell echoes through the market place, each pause filled with the complete silence of the mountains. Dr. Bikul and I adjust our stride in unison, the mesmerising sound begs us to listen more closely. Slowly, step by step, I can feel my body relaxing.

The bazaar behind us, we again climb towards Kori La. Lost in our own thoughts, we walk silently into the clouds. The rain-soaked branches wave at us, and the clouds seem to drift along with our steps, enveloping us in a peaceful cocoon. As if we were the only two people on earth, walking a path which has never been trudged before.

Halfway up to Kori La, we turn back. The rain has become heavier, and Dr. Bikul in his T-shirt and jeans is soaked through. Still, he seems to enjoy the rain, as if it too were his friend. I glance at him from the side. The stern doctor, who generally looks aloof and ready to fight, has been left at the hospital. Instead I see a young, joyful man, with a merry step who embraces life all around him. The dark eyes that can blaze with such conceit are now deep and vulnerable, so much more like the ones of a boy, refusing to grow up.

'Dr. Bikul,' I start, but he interrupts me with a frown on his face.

'Please do not call me doctor. I am just Bikul. OK?' He smiles pleadingly at me.

'Oh, OK,' I stutter with a mixture of pride and excitement. 'Bikul,' I try out the sound and find that the name rolls softly off my tongue. Then I push myself, for better or for worse, to broach the question that has been nagging at me all day.

'Why didn't you come for dinner last night?' I hope that my voice sounds matter of fact, and that my disappointment will not show through.

His steps hesitate. 'You mean, you really invited me?' Do I imagine dismay in his voice? I nod.

'You cooked for me?' he asks.

'Well, I cooked enough for both of us, and I thought that you would come. Did you have dinner somewhere else?'

Now Bikul looks truly upset. 'Actually, I didn't eat anything at all. I had to go back to the hospital for a case that arrived from Lhuntse, and then I stayed in my OPD room and studied.'

Confused and somehow relieved, I am at a loss for words.

Meanwhile, Bikul studies his feet intently and then confesses, 'I thought that you were joking.' He looks at me apologetically. 'I am so sorry. You waited for me long?'

'Not that long,' I lie. Actually, I had wanted to tell him how rudely he had behaved. Last night I had envisioned a stern confrontation, or else decided I should just ignore him today. Obviously I had already failed my first intentions, but now I find myself relieved, too ready to forgive and forget, just to see him smile at me. Has he really gotten under my skin so deeply already? I want to dismiss this as ridiculous, and yet, when I look at him, his beautiful dark eyes, I have this urge to reach out, to touch. I wonder what it would feel like if we walked hand in hand... I jolt myself back to the reality of Mongar. If someone was watching us, the gossip mill would run endlessly.

So instead of continuing to admire the two lovely dimples in Bikul's cheeks, I turn my eyes to the sight of Mongar's bazaar, and by the time we pass the first houses in earshot, I manage to resume my official attitude.

At Rinzin Tshockey's shop, we part ways. I still want to buy a few things for dinner, and Bikul has to return to the hospital to check on some of his patients.

'Bye,' I whisper a little hoarsely and then repeat it louder to reassure myself and everyone else. 'Bye, see you later.'

Bikul turns around and waves, and a tiny bubble of joy starts bouncing around in my stomach.

'How are you today, doctor? Where you and the doctor went?' Rinzin Tshockey looks at me quizzically. Despite my nervousness, I have to laugh. Of course, I should have known that my every move is an open book to the nosy stares in the bazaar.

'We just went for a walk,' I answer honestly, and then quickly comment on today's new arrangement of the furniture. Rinzin Tshockey surfaces from behind the laden counter and grins. 'Nothing to do all day, so I look after shop.'

That much seems obvious. He has somehow relocated all the goods and food into the left side of the store, and built a little bar with a table and a few chairs on the right. Already a couple of older, skinny-legged villagers occupy half of the seating arrangement. Satisfied, they chew betelnuts, each cradling a nearly empty bottle of beer.

'Not much to do in Mongar, isn't it doctor?' complains Dema, Rinzin Tshockey's wife. 'So boring here.'

Then, as if she understands how miserably unexciting my life *must* be, she says, 'Come, we go to see my friend Choden Karma.'

On the way to her friend's house, we pass Mongar's petrol station – a prehistoric hand pump, which (on good days) will dispense some petrol to the desperate driver. A big blue Tata truck pulls up beside the pump, and a group of boys immediately surrounds the gloriously decorated vehicle, viewing the worn tyres and dented bumper in awe. Dema and I skirt several puddles filled with rainbow coloured gasoline rings. The entire vicinity of the station reeks of diesel and kerosene.

Inside Choden Karma's house, the smells of the petrol station are replaced by heavy incense that threatens to make me dizzy. Gratefully I sink onto a small bench. As if our arrival was expected, our host, a short lady wearing a resolute posture, immediately offers a bowl of zao and two cups of tea. She is full of news and gossip and wants to know all about my reasons for being in Mongar.

Between lengthy explanations, I contemplate the dilemma of how to eat the offered rice. Choden Karma instructs me to scoop it into my cup. Thoroughly embarrassed, I show her my dirty hands and refuse politely. Choden Karma gives me a quizzical look and inspects my pale skin, which must appear perfectly clean. Then, with a cheerful 'Just wait a moment!' she disappears, only to return moments later with a bowl, a can of water and a bar of soap. While she pours the water generously over the bowl, I awkwardly wash my hands in the middle of her sitting room. Water droplets and soap splash everywhere but that seems of little consequence. My host smiles, well satisfied, and continues to urge me to have more tea.

Dema and Choden Karma launch into an animated conversation in Sharchhopkha, and I take the chance to quietly study the room. Across from our bench, there is a little house altar with offering bowls and a few flowers. A shelf to its left bears a TV and a VCR. Television programs are not allowed in Bhutan, a ban which is strictly regulated and reinforced. However, Hindi films and western movies found their way into the kingdom a few years ago, and have obviously spread to a few select houses as far as Mongar.

Choden Karma follows my eyes and then proudly nods at her TV. 'Watching movie is the only thing you can do in Mongar. It is so boring here.'

She tells me that her husband has been transferred here from Paro, a larger town on the other end of the kingdom, and that she dislikes the move a lot. 'You must be very boring here, doctor. Mongar feels not good, isn't it?'

I look at her red lipstick that seems so out of place in this modest town and shake my head. I try to explain that I like the silence and the serenity of the mountains, but I get the distinct impression that we are on different wavelengths. Both women only stare at me in obvious confusion. Then they repeatedly tell me how boring Mongar is and that there is *NOTHING* to do here. They inform me about the advantages of living in Thimphu or Phuntsholing, two large towns in Bhutan. Although we chat amiably, our conversations run in different directions, and we fail to meet at any crossroad. Trying not to seem too much an outsider, I keep my opinions about city life to myself. When I finally take my leave, I have to promise to return soon. The ladies are still worried that I will be too boring by myself.

There is no electricity that evening and by the flickering light of a candle, I pour my heart out to my diary. A knock interrupts my thoughts. Startled, I check my watch and only tentatively open the door. I am greeted by a big cardboard box from the bakery and an apologetic Bikul peeping over its edge. He thrusts the box into my hands. 'I brought these for you.'

I open the lid and find myself ogling several lovely pastries. A peace offering for last night's misunderstanding? Or perhaps…? To answer my unspoken query, Bikul apologises for the missed dinner. Then he looks sheepishly at his feet.

'Do you want to come in?' Self-conscious and acutely aware of the impropriety of the situation, I hesitantly open the door all the way. Spud jumps up from beside the bed and with a loud, annoyed bark, disappears into the darkness. My guest settles onto a chair beside the door.

'Have you had dinner?' I ask.

'Not really,' Bikul mumbles.

I suggest eating some of the cakes now, but Bikul refuses immediately, insisting that he has brought them only for me. Despite his protest, I fetch a knife from the kitchen and divide each pastry into half. Having successfully manoeuvred around the Bhutanese social formalities of turning down offered food at least twice before accepting, we devour most of the cakes in a few scrumptious bites.

Then Bikul reaches for my little photo album, and together we study the pictures. I imagine a new closeness between us. Bikul seems to be delighted with my photography. He admires each scene at length and then comments on it. To my dismay, however, he quickly reverts to his know-it-all attitude. I try not to let it get to me and remember the look on his face earlier when he arrived with his box of apologies.

We talk about this and that and the evening rushes by. At times I wonder if he is stalling his departure, if he is looking for a reason to stay, but at a little past ten o'clock, Bikul lets himself out through my front door.

My 'Goodnight!' is partly relieved, partly disappointed. Spud sets off into another barking concert, and embarrassed, I look around to see if anyone noticed my late evening guest. In the quarters around me, all the doors are closed and the curtains drawn – but still, I get the uneasy feeling that the walls have ears.

FOURTEEN

MINAKPA AMA

The first sound that penetrates my comfortable cocoon of peaceful slumber is the proud, piercing morning call of the neighbour's rooster. The second is a loud knock on the door. Drowsily shaking off the insistent memory of my unfinished dream, I stagger to the door. Dorji, a cheerful wardboy dressed in blue hospital uniform and grinning from ear to ear, heaves a bucket into the room. 'Your water, madam.'

Perplexed, I stare at him. He continues grinning.

'Why are you bringing me water?' I enquire. Still fighting off sleep, I try to understand the meaning of this hallucination, doubtfully gaping at the pouring rain outside my doorstep.

'Pipe broken, madam. No water,' he explains, and then adds, 'Doctor said to bring you.'

Too bewildered to ask which doctor, I stutter an embarrassed thank you and carry the bucket to my kitchen. Unbelieving, I confirm the state of affairs and, indeed, the faucet spews out only a few gurgles, then croaks and hisses accusingly until I turn it off again. Interesting. The outside world is drowning in downpours, and we have dried up. I am discovering another one of the monsoon's little idiosyncrasies.

An hour later, I trudge up to Bikul's house to ascertain if he was my morning benefactor. A middle-aged Bhutanese woman opens the door. Undoubtedly, she is a villager. Her red-and-blue-checkered kira is wrapped carelessly, and her bare feet are stuck into mere reminders of plastic slippers. She smiles at me, and I smile at her. Though she seems in no way surprised by my appearance, I cannot remember having met her before. She eagerly tells me something of obvious importance in Sharchhopkha, heedless of the fact that I cannot understand a word of her rushed speech. She nods and smiles, and all I can hear is a repeated 'doctor' and *'jonsho'*. Then she retreats inside the house. Feeling at a loss, I remain standing on the doorstep.

'Ama,' I call after the woman awkwardly. At least I am grateful for the Bhutanese way of addressing a person by his or her title without having to know an actual name (any woman who has obviously outgrown her teenage years can be called Ama).

'Dr. Bikul…?' I want to ask if he is there, but of course, I cannot think of the necessary Sharchhop words.

Ama replies something but again the meaning eludes me. Should I leave or enter? Embarrassment gets the better of me, and I turn on the grassy walkway back towards the road. Halfway down the lane, however, I decide to give it one more try, and gathering all my courage, I walk around to the back door at the kitchen. There, I do not find Bikul but the same smiling Ama, expertly chopping onions with a huge, sword-like knife.

The usually deserted kitchen is filled with evidence of an upcoming feast. A plastic bag of rice is opened and half spilt onto the counter. Mud-caked potatoes fill the sink. A heap of beans lies on the floor and, beside it, looking almost as innocent, a stack of small, green chillies. Ama is busy handling the steel, all-purpose war instrument. With precision, the heavy blade thunders down just millimetres beside her fingertips, its curved tip barely clearing the lined up pots and pans. The pressure cooker whistles. It smells of dal and fried spices. Experimentally, I venture into a little Sharchhopkha.

'Dr. Bikul *gila?*'

'*Cha,*' she answers and wiggles her head from side to side. Yes, he is there.

The only other thing that comes to my mind is '*Nan hang pile?*' What will you do?

Ama cannot interpret my feeble attempt at bridging the language barrier and abandons her cooking to come closer. Again she smiles, showing off her big brownish teeth and creasing her face into many suntanned wrinkles. Rapidly she utters something.

I try again: 'Dr. Bikul?'

'*Cha, cha,*' she nods and points to Bikul's bedroom. Then in a sudden flash of genius, she walks to the kitchen door and calls him.

I can hear Bikul's answer out of the back of the house. His tone is joking, and it is obvious that he is completely at ease with Ama. He looks around the corner, inspects the contents of the pot, then at last notices me perched on his steps.

He laughs. 'So you have met my Norbu Ama. She is Pema's mother.' As if that explains everything, he turns to Ama and the two start to discuss something in animated voices, interrupted only by her bouts of giggling laughter. My ears are burning, and I get the uncomfortable feeling that yours truly is the topic of discussion. Impatiently I ask Bikul to translate.

With a mischievous grin, he explains that Norbu Ama is suggesting that I cook for him. To confirm, he addresses the smiling woman who nods enthusiastically, looking at me and then pointing at the kitchen. Exasperated I tell Ama that I cannot cook at all. Bikul translates. Norbu Ama does not agree. She says that she lives too far from here, she cannot cook for Bikul. He needs someone to look after him. She thinks that since I am single, why cannot I cook for both Bikul and me. Norbu Ama flashes me a winning smile, showing off a sparkling silvery cap on one tooth. The topic seems settled for her, and quickly she resumes dedicating her time to the rice and the curry on the stove.

I can feel my face flushing wildly. To make matters worse, Norbu Ama then insists that I come into the living room and eat with them. 'With them' turns out to be only Bikul, since Norbu Ama disappears in the kitchen, where she noisily cleans up.

My stomach revolts at the thought of rice and curry for breakfast. Bikul organises a fork for me and then proceeds to scoop up the dish quickly and expertly by hand, almost finishing his plate before I have had my first taste. Self-conscious, I try my first forkful while Bikul watches me expectantly. Immediately, my throat starts burning and tears sting my eyes.

Bikul dives into the kitchen and emerges with two glasses of water. 'Too much chilli!' he exclaims before downing the contents of his glass in one urgent gulp. Unhappily, I pick at my food. Norbu Ama is still busy in the kitchen, and finally Bikul takes pity on me. Before anyone can notice, he promptly clears my plate.

When Norbu Ama returns, it takes more than three polite refusals to turn down further heapings of the spicy meal. Norbu Ama shakes her head and tries again, but this time, even Bikul is firm. The only thing that appeases her is the promise that we will visit her home soon. With one last generous smile, Norbu Ama shoulders her heavy bamboo basket and walks off into the rain.

'Where does she live?' I ask Bikul, curious about this bubbly lady who does not look like Pema at all. Until now, Pema's childhood home was a picture in my imagination, and she did not talk about it much. And with her recent declaration that she wants to go to Thimphu, I had almost forgotten that her family lives close by.

'Their farm is in Bargompa, at the top of that mountain.' Bikul points somewhere above Mongar into the clouds. I am getting used to the idea of villagers living somewhere 'up there' where the sky meets the earth, and so I do not question this answer further.

'But why didn't I meet her before?'

'She cannot come down to Mongar that often in the summer. There is a lot of work to do on the farm. I think she visits Pema every Sunday after the market.'

'And how come you know her so well?'

'Ah, that's because her husband, Norbu, is the pharmacy assistant who used to cook for me. He used to live in one of the Class C staff quarters before he was transferred. Norbu Ama used to come down to visit him. They always invited me for the festivals to Bargompa. Ama's family are real *minakpa*s!' Bikul smiles.

'Minakpas?'

'That is what the villagers call each other. If you talk to a villager and say, *'Eh, minakpa, o dele?'*, they will immediately feel more comfortable with you. Minakpa is a respected term among villagers, like Abi or Meme.'

'So Pema's whole family comes from the village?'

'Yes, they were all farmers. Just like most Bhutanese villagers. It is the custom here in Eastern Bhutan for the daughters to inherit the house and land – so it is Norbu Ama who owns the farm and runs it. Actually, soon it would be Pema's turn to take over, but I am not sure what they will do. Pema obviously won't return to the farm, and her little sister is studying in Thimphu. Her brother is a monk.'

'And Norbu is working in the hospital to make some money?' I ask.

'Yes, that's true. Villagers don't need much. They grow mostly maize, and some vegetables. Only on special occasions they eat meat. At the Sunday market, they sell some of their produce, but most things are grown for their own needs. Norbu's salary at the hospital was supposed to be additional income and help to cover the medical costs for Pema's son.' Bikul's expression turns serious as he starts talking about Norbu. 'He is a good man, of course, but you know, he has a bad problem with alcohol.'

Bikul sighs. Drinking, and in many ways excessive drinking, is very much part of the Eastern Bhutanese custom, but it is usually limited to alcohol home-brewed out of maize or other grains. Norbu, however, being paid in cash by the hospital, is totally incapable of budgeting for the family and spends his entire salary on buying alcohol. Pema has never seen a penny of her father's earnings, and with her younger sister away at school in Thimphu, the family is short of a cash income.

Frustrated, Bikul recounts how he has tried to help Norbu to stop drinking, and how after a few months, his attempts have proven useless. Somehow, Norbu does not fit into this split life, stuck between the old world of the mountains and the new world of the hospital. Two different sets of expectations, two different rhythms of time. For Norbu, who is a soft man yielding to the pressures of the world around him, the temptations of alcohol prove too much to resist. So Ama continues to carry her vegetables over the tiring footpath down the mountain to the market, hoping to make at least enough to support her little daughter in Thimphu.

'Minakpa life is not easy,' Bikul says, then adds, 'But they never cry. For them, life is good. No matter what happens, you laugh.'

I think about Ama's face, creased with many wrinkles, deep furrows caused by her work outside in the high mountains, but patterned by the fine lines of laughter that look like crows' feet at the corners of her eyes. What about Pema? Will she look like her mother one day? Somehow I doubt it. Like her father Norbu, Pema has chosen a life away from the stability of her family and the village. Unlike Ama, Pema is learning how to cry.

FIFTEEN

BUTTERTEA IS WARM AND SALTY

An Autumn Evening

The looming peaks of the rising mountains
Sink into the lingering shadows of the sunset
A crescent moon hangs over an ancient sky
The villagers gather near the campfire,
And centuries-old legends and myths
Transpire an illusive symphony of magic.

Nostalgia of age-old seasons
Reverberates in their confused minds
As they move the rosary beads

And listen to the radio noise.
Through the burning edges of their hearts
Tradition moves, refreshes and creates a sense:
A sense of living together,
A sense of being cornered.

Remote, forbidden yet excessively romantic
Here in this land of the tranquil dragon
My heart has been shaken by fear;
The fear of losing this perfect harmony.

I wish that I could enjoy the next autumn
I wish that I can enjoy this land in peace.

Annitt Kumar, 1996

One day when the rain lets up and the mountains steam in the afternoon heat, we plan to climb the slippery path to Bargompa. Pema tells me that she and the children will spend the weekend with her family, and she urges me to visit them. 'Bring Dr. Bikul too!' Her wink is undeniably mischievous. 'He has been there often. He knows the way – and I think he would like to go with you.'

The trail winds through the bottom of a little river valley and then steeply ascends the eastern slope of the ridge. We cross a creek, waltz through a meadow, and balance on the big boulders penetrating the ground like stony birthmarks. At one point, an umbrella of big oak branches shelters the trail. The path continues to scale the hill with little relief for my screaming lungs. Bikul seems to have no trouble with the altitude and jumps ahead in his old, worn out running shoes. Every few hundred metres we stop for me to catch my breath.

The views are mesmerising. On the slope across from us, farms of the village Phosrang are spread between densely wooded jungle. The houses with their adjacent cornfields and rickety barns form a mosaic with patches of burgeoning bushes and fields full of flowers. The colours of blossoms and crops in bloom underline the deep green of the forest, which thickens as you go higher, spreading up the grade with a dense cover of leaves. Interspersed with the human dwellings are little white chortens, gleaming in the first afternoon sun.

We pass an old building whose red painted horizontal band around the upper walls indicates that it is a temple. From afar, it looks nothing more than a big old farmhouse, but on closer inspection, the structure reveals its religious design. A continuous ribbon of small, hand-powered prayer wheels wraps around the entire circumference, interrupted only by weathered patches where the odd broken wheel has collapsed over time. The gable and the eave are richly decorated with woodcarvings of different animal designs and shapes. There is no sign of people and the sacred building looks abandoned and somewhat forlorn. The red entrance door, painted in faded colours with a big auspicious parasol, is secured with a rusty padlock.

Further on, we meet a few minakpas and are greeted with a friendly 'O dele?', which literally translates into 'Where are you going?' Our answer is always accepted with an even brighter smile and an encouraging cheer, '*Lasso la*, doctor!', which means something like 'That's great!'

We must be a good hour's walk away from Mongar, and the apparently purposeful comings and goings of the villagers amaze me. In big, efficient strides, they effortlessly climb the hills or run down the steep slopes. Along the way, they yodel or sing, or shout to each other, their voices echoing off the mountains. There is a relaxed merriment in their motions, a cheerful accomplishment of whatever needs to be done. Their ease is contagious.

The path divides at a little chorten and becomes even steeper in our direction, forcing me to pay attention to my every step. I struggle with the mud and my fatiguing legs. Even Bikul slows and like a gentleman offers to carry my backpack. I look at him with renewed surprise. Again, the strict doctor has metamorphosed into a relaxed young man with a boyish grin and sparkling eyes. As if we were approaching his own home, he pushes on eagerly, explaining every tree and every familiar sign.

When the roof of a farmhouse appears over the tops of the cornfield, a loud, rather unfriendly barking greets us. Respectfully, we stop in our tracks. 'We get many dog bite cases in the hospital,' Bikul warns. Then he calls a drawn out 'Oieehhhh' through the fields, and it echoes off the strutting ridge.

Minutes later, Norbu Ama comes running down the trail. '*Kuzuzang po la! Jonsho! Jonsho!*' Excited, she waves us towards her. Her welcome is heartfelt and her laughter immediately includes me in her conversation, of which I understand not a word. The dog is locked safely into the barn, and we are led through a gate to a set of steep wooden steps, the only entrance to Ama's big farmhouse.

Off a little platform halfway up the stairs, a single door opens into a large, black-stained kitchen. A tiny cobwebbed window throws a few rays of light on an earthen fireplace; from its holes, flames lick eagerly at three big sooty pots. Almost unnoticed, an old woman sits close to the fire, methodically stirring her spoon in a thin wooden tube.

I am eager to explore the secrets of this intriguing place of cooking, but polite guest behaviour requires us to follow Norbu Ama upstairs to the main family room, where two blankets are quickly converted into the best seats in the house. Ama motions us to sit down. '*Jonsho* doctor!' The room is big and airy. The window shutters are slid wide open, and our view is guided over the valley to the minuscule nest of Mongar town roosting on a slope in the distance. Immediately below the house, a field of tall maize stalks waves to us through the breeze.

Norbu Ama disappears, leaving Bikul and me alone. I look around for a sign of Pema or her children.

'Have you seen Pema?' I finally ask.

Bikul shrugs his shoulders. 'Maybe she is with her grandfather. He lives not far from here in a tiny meditation hut.'

Feeling a little awkward in the huge empty room with Bikul at my side, I twist my hair around my fingers and wish for Pema and the children to return really soon. Eventually, though, I am distracted by the family altar, an impressive structure right across from our seats. The central offering place is large and well built, with glass cases on either side. There are five podiums, each encircled by an arched frame in the style of Bhutanese windows. Inside each receptacle sits a colourful statue, wrapped into a silken frock. The two large statues dominating the middle of the altar are bronzed; the others are smaller, and one has blue skin.

As an offering, three butterlamps (candles made out of hardened butter or vegetable oil in a solid dish) burn quietly beside a couple of incense sticks and seven bowls filled with water.

'The seven bowls symbolise the seven offerings made to Buddha,' Bikul explains. 'They represent what we want to share – things like food, drink, or water for washing.'

I look at the little vessels with renewed interest. Water, a plain and simple offering. The people in the Himalaya are not rich, but everyone can afford water. It is a universal offering, something causing no hardships, no greed, and can be given with pure faith.

An extension on either side of the altar houses the family's holy books, each volume bound in shiny silk cloth. Two photographs of yellow- and orange-clad lamas round off the colourful altar, and each picture is respectfully draped with a white ceremonial scarf.

The intriguing sights of the altar spark my curiosity, and we leave our drafty corner to take a closer peek. The first thing I notice underneath the bookshelves is a sort of cupboard – a pantry. Its door is covered with a simple fly mesh, and behind it I can see chunks of cheese and banana- leaf-wrapped parcels, which look like the butter packages in the subjee bazaar. Obviously, the food storage lives in harmony with the precious inhabitants of the altar.

I again study the seven bowls. They are delicate silver vessels with intricate designs, symbols that remind me of an old Chinese chest that my father brought back from one of his travels years ago. The water twinkles at me from the polished basins. Standing guard in the middle of all these treasures is a vase for holy water with one large peacock feather, a symbol of the wisdom of Buddha's love.

Bikul picks up a rosary from between the other decorations and hands it to me.

'You see here, these bands.' He points at a few short leather straps with ten metal rings. 'Each rosary has a hundred and eight beads, and after each completion of one count of the beads, you move this first ring to the other end of the leather strap. Then you continue. When you have completed ten rounds, you move to the second band and start over.'

'Why is it necessary to count your prayers?' I ask.

'I guess it keeps you on the right track.' Bikul shrugs his shoulders.

The answer is not wholly satisfactory to me, and I return to examine the altar. A tiny white object catches my attention. It looks like a tooth. 'What is that?'

Instead of an answer, Norbu Ama enters with a huge pot full of tea. We guiltily stop our nosy examination of the family treasures and return to our prepared seats. Norbu Ama is in high spirits. Under constant chatter, she pours our cups. The liquid is slightly cloudy, and I imagine bubbles of grease floating on the surface. Carefully I sip the brew. It is greasy! And salty, very salty! What kind of tea is this? Norbu Ama looks at me expectantly and I fake a smile. Secretly I imagine how my tongue and the inside of my mouth contract, and my stomach bars its doors in revolt of the strange infusion.

'Seudja,' Bikul explains. 'Buttertea. Have you had it before?'

I shake my head.

'It is great, isn't it?' he says and I agree half-heartedly. More like soup, I think to myself, and brave another sip.

'Here, add this,' Bikul suggests and heaps a generous handful of zao into my cup. Skeptically, I eye the ensuing potion. It looks no more appetising than the initial serving, with the exception that the grease is now hidden by the floating rice kernels fighting for space. Politely, I take another swallow. To my surprise, the flavour has become rather pleasing. I crunch on the zao and the salty nature of the tea slowly warms my insides. I drink again and find that the more I have, the better it tastes.

Eventually I lose count of how many refills Norbu Ama generously pours into my cup. Just when I am sure that we must have successfully finished the entire pot, Pema appears with Nima and Chimmi, carrying another flask.

'Auntie!' Chimmi shouts and bounces excitedly up and down. Then she pulls Nima to sit beside her, facing us, and both children watch us with interest. Or at least Chimmi does. Nima's eyes are for once focused on us, but still I am not sure that we are the objects of his contemplation. As always, he is busy rolling his lower lip between his fingers.

'Auntie!' This time, Chimmi makes sure that I give her my sole attention by driving a little home-made car, which consists of two short sticks for the axle and wheels and a flat piece of bark for the body, back and forth over the floor in front of my folded legs.

Pema places a wooden bowl between her eager daughter's 'tyre tracks' on the hardwood. 'Welcome to my family's home!' She offers a warm smile which I now realise is just like Norbu Ama's. 'It is a long way, isn't it? Please, have some *arra*.'

'Arra?' I smell the drink gingerly and nausea rises in my throat. The pungent scent stings my nose and makes my eyes water. So this is arra, the famous alcoholic home brew.

'I think I better not,' I apologise, and Bikul quickly gives a more flowery version of my excuse to Norbu Ama, who has come to join us. Pema's mother looks unhappy and again nods at me. '*Zhe, zhe!*' Afraid to offend her hospitality, I point at my stomach and make a grimace. '*Pholang ngamla!*' I remember the phrase for stomach pain from the hospital. Norbu Ama and Pema laugh heartily. My apology is accepted, and although I am urged a few more times to try the drink, I get away with my tentative sniff.

Pholang ngamla, I repeat the magic words to myself and notice in astonishment that they seem self-fulfilling. My stomach is indeed feeling quite bloated, and the buttertea has clumped like a stone somewhere above the belt line. There it sits and sits, and I dare not move for fear of my whole gut dropping out the bottom. With horror, I look at my refilled cup.

When dusk reminds us to bid farewell, Norbu Ama, Pema, and the old woman (who turns out to be Pema's grandmother) try to load us with at least two bags filled with *thengma*, dried and beaten corn, and another one with *kharang*, a coarsely ground version of dried corn. Kharang is the main dish for villagers. The corn kernels are dried and shredded, and stored for later cooking much like rice. When we politely insist on accepting only one bag of each, Norbu Ama supplements our gifts with four fresh eggs, carefully hidden amongst the corn for safe transportation. All three women seem reluctant to say goodbye, and Pema tells me that they were hoping we would spend the night in their house.

'This is a wonderful home!' I say while Pema clasps my hands. 'Wouldn't you like to live up here all the time?'

Without hesitation, Pema shakes her head. 'Oh, no!'

'I mean if Karma would stay with you, of course.'

Again Pema shakes her head. 'It is too boring up here. I don't want to live on the farm. I would like best to live in Thimphu.'

Yes, I think, I know that. Still I cannot quite understand why.

'What will happen to your farm when Ama and Norbu get old? Your sister Rinzin Tshering is studying in Thimphu too, isn't she? And your brother is a monk. Who will look after your parents?'

'Ama is thinking about adopting a little girl,' Pema answers with obvious relief in her voice. 'Rinzin wants to be a teacher. And when Chimmi grows up, I hope she will be a doctor. But it is not good to live here.'

I think about Pema's cramped quarters at the hospital
– then I imagine Ama and Abi taking care of Nima in
this spacious house, giving Pema a chance to relax and
look after herself. But of course, Karma would need to
live in town, or he would have to walk the hour and a
half each way to the dzong. Pema does not seem to have
the same regrets as I, for she continues: 'After I went
to school and learned English, I knew that I would live
somewhere else. I wanted to get a job, to earn money. It
is not good to live in the village always.'

I look from Abi and Ama to Pema and Chimmi. Four
generations of women, with the same lovely smile, the
same dark eyes. And yet, two different sets of hopes
and aspirations.

We are about to put our shoes back on when Norbu
Ama walks over to the altar and triumphantly picks up
her prized possession, the little white something that I
had inspected earlier. She sticks her fingers in her mouth
and begins squawking, all the while pointing to her
cheek, making us understand that it is indeed her tooth.

Pema laughs. 'Ama can put the tooth in and out, but
she only wears it if she goes to town. She thinks she
looks better if the tooth is in.'

Bikul and I look at each other and smile. Even our
village Ama knows a little about vanity.

Abi too seems to have something on her mind and in
her bent, shuffling gait rushes over and waves us towards
her room. We follow her past the shrine through a set of
heavy wooden doors. The chamber is small, dark, and
smells of dust and mothballs. It is stuffed with heaps of
clothing. On a bed in the corner, several cats are curled

up on an assortment of kiras and ghos. Abi shifts a pile of orange-checkered material to the side and uncovers a large wooden box from which she pulls a *bangchung*. The little woven bamboo container is obviously as aged as Abi, but it still hints at a glorious youth with colourful designs. With an endearing smile, Abi presents me with her bangchung. Thoroughly embarrassed, I thank Abi, still confused about the appropriate response to this family's generosity.

Bikul, as always, is curious and none too shy. 'This is wonderful!' he exclaims and eagerly dives into the box. Suddenly he resurfaces holding a carefully wrapped silver necklace with many inset pearls. Abi starts chiding the nosy doctor, but to my surprise everyone else is laughing.

'What's this all about?' I ask, walking back into the room.

Bikul happily holds the jewellery to Abi's flushed neckline.

'This is how Abi attracted Meme monk to marry her.' Norbu Ama and Pema are still giggling, and Abi sends them a reprimanding glance while Bikul amiably lays his arm around the old woman's frail shoulders. I can see that he is about to launch into one of his favourite stories.

'When Meme was a young man, he vowed not to marry. Then one day, he announced that he would stay in the dzong and become a monk. That day, Abi was really sad. Her family used to live very close by, and every day they took their cows to the same grass field. She had been in love with our Meme for many years. Every day she put on her prettiest dresses, but Meme never noticed her.

'Abi did not want to give up, and one day, she went to see the local priest who could play tricks to attract a man to marry a woman. For one month, Abi applied all the tricks, but nothing seemed to work. Abi was so sad that she grew thinner and thinner. Then, one day, her parents got very worried and made a plan to help Abi. They invited Meme for dinner. Abi's mother gave her daughter this beautiful necklace along with her most precious kira.'

By now, both of the younger women have stopped giggling, and even Abi has resigned herself to listen carefully to Bikul's story, narrated so lovingly in a language she cannot understand. Still, the power of the gleaming necklace keeps everyone captivated.

'Even before the meal started, Meme noticed Abi's necklace. He was so fascinated by the beautiful appearance of the girl across from him that he forgot to carefully check his drink. Abi's parents had been counting on that. You see,' Bikul interrupts himself to secretively walk closer to me, 'people in Eastern Bhutan believe that a girl's family can use black magic to attract a boy. They will put a secret herb into the boy's drink and make him fall in love with the girl.' Bikul now turns to the other women and translates his words to them. Immediately, Norbu Ama starts nodding wildly, while Abi loudly protests. She claims not to know about any black magic at all. Bikul shakes his head, also laughing.

'You know, Britta, Norbu Ama even told me to always spill a little of my drink three times when I go to other villagers' houses. That is the only way to protect yourself against the magic of the herbs. Norbu Ama did not want any girl to hook me like that.'

166

'Do you actually believe in it?' I ask incredulously.

'You never know,' Bikul replies. 'Anyway, Abi's parents were quick to distract Meme all evening, and Abi's mother even invited Meme to come a little closer and have a better look at the pearls. All of a sudden, Meme felt shy. He wanted to seek permission from Abi, but she only smiled at him. Finally, for the first time, Meme looked into her beautiful dark eyes. He had never before seen the charm and warmth of a young woman. Now he realised how much he wanted to hold her close. For a long time, the two looked at each other, and that night, Meme stayed in Abi's house. Next day, they were married. So, you see, the magic did work.'

Bikul is obviously pleased with his story and gently puts the necklace back where he found it. Abi, Norbu Ama and Pema all start talking to me at once, and I nod in pretended understanding. I do not know what exactly Pema's mother and grandmother are saying, but somehow I grasp that each is telling a slightly different version of Meme and Abi's romance. I cannot help but smile. Perhaps each of these three women does know a little magic.

SIXTEEN

MEME MONK

'Where did you get this from?' I ask in a faltering Sharchhopkha, pointing at a small, yellowed picture of Jesus Christ that is sharing the altar with the colourful statues of Buddha and several honoured tantric deities. Pema's grandfather thinks for a minute and then answers, 'The foreigner's Buddha.' From Meme's words and gestures I gather that a doctor from the mission gave it to him. He lovingly blows away an imaginary speck of dust and lights a butterlamp. From the shrine, he seems to focus on something beyond this world. With devout respect, his gaze shifts into the distance where nirvana is waiting for humanity.

Jesus is the Westerners' Buddha. It is that easy. To him, what need is there to distinguish between Christianity and Buddhism? He believes in a higher being, no matter what He looks like. If only everyone could find such a peaceful compromise.

Meme Monk has embraced his deep belief and faith, renouncing his wishes for materialism and is content to spend the eve of his life in peaceful meditation. He is happy with where he is and what he does, and it shows in the smooth features of his 84-year-old face.

The hut is no more than a one-room shelter but built in the solid Bhutanese style of stone and wood. Meme retreated to this tiny refuge years ago to find repose for meditation, leaving his family in their big farmhouse a few hundred metres farther down the hill. He knows that Norbu Ama is quite capable of running the farm by herself, and his old bones could no longer do the heavy work anyway. Although he loves his wife and family deeply, he now needs the quiet to think and contemplate life and religion alone.

Meme Monk is a *gomchen*, a spiritual villager who has received a certain amount of religious training and is allowed to practise rituals for the common people. Gomchens have a special ranking in Bhutanese society. They have been appointed with distinctive powers through their spiritual devotion, but at the same time they are allowed to marry. Only a return to the dzong and an achievement of higher states of religious teachings is not possible for them once they have entered family life. Now, at an age when the younger generation runs the farm and can take care of his wife, Meme Monk has decided to again dedicate his life to religion.

In his tiny hut, Meme is surrounded by all that he needs. A mat on the floor with a goatskin on it makes his bed and an old gho his blanket. He wears a burgundy gho resembling the dress of a monk; his thin white jacket is stained and worn from years of honest use. Other than a couple of aluminium pots for cooking kharang and chillies, a flask to prepare buttertea, and an assortment of stained plastic containers, all the articles neatly placed on shelves and on the floor are of religious significance. Many of them are unfamiliar to me, I only know the handheld prayer wheel, the rosary, and I recognise a few religious texts, wrapped in colourful pieces of material.

His family altar again proves Meme's tolerance for the interconnection of all things. Behind the offering bowls, a bright yellow plastic bag bears the label Dalda, the locally available, hardened vegetable oil, which is used to fill the butterlamps. Two empty Coca-Cola bottles hold some fresh green branches to decorate either side of the altar. Next to the offerings of water are two lunch-pack cartons of 'Frooti' mango juice.

Since I have come up here by myself today, the peaceful quiet of the hut allows my mind to focus more sharply on all the new sights to explore. I assume that the set-back shrine above the family altar was born on the day on which the walls of this house were erected. The simple wooden case is framed by paintings of orange and blue flowers. On a shelf, protected against the frenzies of dust and drafts by two glass windows, statues of Lord Buddha and Guru Rinpoche serenely smile onto Meme Monk. They are surrounded by smaller versions of other manifestations of the two Buddhas, most of whom I do not recognise.

Although I have spent many hours reading my books about Bhutan's religion, the colourful pantheon of tantric deities is still a mystery to me. In temples and on paintings, I can merely recognise the three most common figures. First there is the historical Lord Buddha sitting cross-legged on a throne of lotus flowers, with a crown of light instead of fancy headgear, wearing simple, mostly unadorned clothing. The second, Guru Rinpoche, usually has a little curled moustache and goatee; he is pictured with his trident, and in one hand he holds a *dorje*, a religious instrument which looks like a small dumbbell. Finally, there is Shabdrung Ngawang Ngamgyel who, with his long grey beard and wearing a red pointy hat, is the most ordinary-looking of all the images.

Before I came to Bhutan, I had only heard of Buddha Shakyamuni, the historical Buddha whom the Bhutanese call Sangay. Lord Buddha founded what we know as Buddhism today. His original name was Siddhartha Gautami, and he was born in the fifth century BC to a king and queen in northern India. His father, who had been foretold that Siddhartha would either become a great ruler or a universal teacher, tried to cajole his son into staying within the confines of the palace. Siddhartha enjoyed a charmed childhood protected against the harsh realities of life, until as a young prince, he managed to venture beyond the gates of the palace. To his dismay, there he encountered age, illness and death for the first time. Upon the revelation that all human life is suffering, Siddhartha renounced luxury and materialism and became a wandering ascetic. Then, after six years of meditation and austerity, he found that starvation did not lead to discovery and formulated the 'middle path' of moderation. Under a fig tree in Bodh Gaya, Gautama attained enlightenment. He became the Buddha – the

Awakened – and began to spread his teachings, or the 'dharma', thereby initiating what is known today as the Buddhist faith.

In Bhutan, Guru Rinpoche (the precious master), also known as Padmasambhava (the lotus born), is considered the second Buddha. He was a tantric missionary from the Svat valley in today's Pakistan. In the eighth century AD, Padmasambhava introduced tantric Buddhism to Bhutan by subduing demons and the enemies of Buddhism and turning them into protective deities. One of Guru Rinpoche's main weapons against demons was his dorje – a thunderbolt of diamond indestructibility and the purity of the Buddhist teachings.

Shabdrung Ngawang Ngamgyel (literally, 'at whose feet one submits') was a Tibetan Buddhist scholar who appointed himself as the religious ruler of Bhutan in the seventeenth century AD. Under the Shabdrung, Bhutan resisted numerous Tibetan attacks, and Bhutan's many valleys and districts were turned into a unified country. For defence as well as monastic intent, the Shabdrung built the country's first dzongs where he established a dual system of administration and law. He himself was the spiritual leader, while the state monastic body was headed by a supreme abbot, the Je Khenpo. The country's administration and politics were handled by the temporal ruler, the Desi. In 1656, shortly after the Shabdrung's death, Bhutan united into its present shape and the dual system of government persisted, albeit with many feuds and conflicts, until a hereditary monarchy was established in 1907.

In Meme's house, the statues of the revered Buddhist scholars share their wall-temple with a collage of present day holy men. There is a picture of the Dalai Lama, the Je Khenpo (who still holds the position of Bhutan's chief abbot), and the third king, Jigme Dorji Wangchuk. Beside them are pictures of the temple of Bodh Gaya in India where Buddha attained enlightenment and the great Bodnath Stupa in Nepal. The bottom of the collage is filled with faded snapshots of Meme Monk as a young lama, and another picture of his wife and daughter.

Though living in seclusion from common family life, Meme Monk's day is filled with his own sort of activities, and placidly he continues sorting dried chillies into thin blue plastic bags, the new throwaway items that can usually be found discarded in trees and shrubs closer to town. Until only a few years ago, plastic bags did not exist in Eastern Bhutan, but especially now among town folks, they almost exclusively replace the traditional woven bags.

Meme's hospitality does not lag behind my other Bhutanese acquaintances. Having cleaned up the odds and ends of his chilli storage, he deftly starts preparations for serving buttertea. Over his cooking fire, he heats a pot of water to which large black tea leaves are added. Then, out of somewhere unseen, he produces a big wad of butter, and the mixture is churned in a long, wooden, brass-ringed tube. The salt is heaped into the drink in generous pinches, and a rather strange aroma fills the little hut. Meme watches me polish off thengma and buttertea appreciatively. The noise of the jungle accompanies our two-person gathering, and the conversation is limited to a few jovial smiles.

The end of tea and snacks usually signals the time for departure to visitors in Bhutanese households, and with great theatrics, Meme now pulls a hand-carved flute out of the folds of his gho. His big, callused fingers barely fit on the delicate instrument, blotting out the diminutive holes. Then, from deep within his being, a few grumbles surface like approaching thunder. He noisily clears his throat, and a load of spit sails through the air and lands in a pot on the floor beside the bed.

I bid Meme farewell and he looks at me with a twinkle. Apparently satisfied, he lifts the flute to his lips, and out of his dainty instrument, a few notes float through the air. The music is light and joyous, a simple folk tune with a bewitching rhythm. In my mind, I can still hear it from miles away, and I start skipping on the long descent back to the hospital.

SEVENTEEN

DIFFERENT EXPECTATIONS

One morning in August, Pema enters our chamber waving a note in her hand.

'I got a referral to Vellore! We will take Nima for assessment.' In Pema's voice I can hear a mixture of relief and worry.

'That's great, Pema! When will you go?' At first, I feel excited for Pema. Finally, after months of waiting and worrying, she will get a diagnosis for Nima's strange behaviour. Delighted with the good news, I give Pema a hug. A moment later, though, the full meaning of her absence hits home. The thought of our physio room without Pema's friendship, her unfailing encouragement, her beaming smile, not to mention her invaluable translations, makes my heart drop.

'How long will you be gone?'

'I don't know,' Pema replies and turns her hands over in a helpless gesture. 'It is far to the hospital. Vellore is right at the southern tip of India. The travel alone might take two weeks. Karma will come with us. Maybe we come back in six weeks?'

I picture myself alone in our physio room, surrounded by patients I cannot understand. My first reaction is panic. I will never make it! Over the past two months, Pema has become my pillar and my strength when all around me seemed to fall to pieces. Together we have survived many a hot, dark, powerless day at Mongar Hospital. But without her?

'Don't worry, OK?' Pema reassures me. 'We will telephone you – and you will have Dr. Bikul.' Her wistful remark does make me smile. My frequent visits to Bikul's chamber have not escaped her attention; neither, of course, has the official town rumour that Bikul and I are married, since he now seems to take every meal with me AND we are seen walking together.

Pema opens the treatment record and studies the names of our patients that are scheduled for today. Despite her good news, she looks tired. As always, her thick black hair is neatly combed, her kira spotless and perfectly ironed, and her face composed, with the trace of a smile playing in the corners of her lips. Yet something has come undone. The summer has been all but easy for her.

'Maybe if we get a diagnosis, we can stay there for treatment also.' Pema's thoughtful remark makes me wince.

'Yes, maybe.' I want to agree with her, but I have my doubts. If it is cerebral palsy, there will be no cure. The chance that perhaps Nima is suffering from something else, something that is indeed curable, is slim. But I do not want to shake Pema's hope unnecessarily.

'May I leave for some time? I have to book train tickets.'

'Yes, of course.' I nod and watch Pema quickly gather her things. Her comportment is brisk, her steps confident, but her hands are shaking.

For a while, I forget about Pema's looming departure. With the modern day athletes of Mongar's volleyball and soccer teams filling the physiotherapy room to capacity, my workday remains busy, and yet what gives me the most satisfaction are my two daily visitors, Choden and Lhamo.

Choden's progress is phenomenal. Thanks to her incredible strength and extraordinary will-power, after only a couple of weeks of practice, she manages to walk more or less independently two full lengths of the parallel bars. During her rest periods, she stands proud and erect. The daily onslaught of spectators, young and old, attendants and visitors, curiously watch her progress. In many ways, they become her cheering fan club. Little children, not able to understand Choden's disease but aware that they are watching something important, stand and gawk in admiration at her efforts. Her walking becomes a shared goal, every step a miracle to all.

Only occasionally when a ballistic muscle kicks her leg out from underneath her, Choden still needs a firm hand to help control her knees. Standing between the parallel bars, watching herself in the mirror, she works hard, the perspiration dripping off her forehead in the overpowering heat of the summer monsoon. She never complains or winces; her jaw is set in unshakeable determination. When her palms become sweaty and slip off the metal pipes, she stops only long enough to dry them on her shirt. In addition, just when I think that she is tired, that her legs will not walk another step, she asks me to go one more length. Her inner strength carries her through the pain and fatigue of the battle with her misguided nervous system.

I admire her boldness. Day by day, she progresses faster than I ever thought possible. The regular weight-bearing exercise has another beneficial carry-over. Choden tells me that since she started walking her legs are relaxing better, and now she can sleep through most of the night without being awoken by painful spasms. I imagine Yeshey, Choden and her mother, how they spend the long nights in the ward, three women sharing a narrow hospital bed.

Our daily sessions, the hard work and her rewarding improvements all help to connect me through a special bond with this determined young woman. I feel excited for Choden, and I am proud of her success. Soon she will be independently mobile. A few more weeks and she should be able to go home with the help of a walker or crutches. After years of handicap, she will be able to live an almost normal life in her village.

Nevertheless, the tremendous effort that Choden has to make is exhausting and, a few times a week, she misses her treatment because she is feeling feverish or too tired. On one such occasion, I ask Pema to come to the ward and help me with translations. We find Choden sitting on her bed, playing with her daughter, looking happy and relaxed. Confused, I ask why she is not coming to physio. With a shy smile, Choden replies that her urinary infection is under control, and she will be going home. I cannot believe my ears. Surely, Pema misunderstood. Choden cannot possibly be giving up. No, she cannot quit; not now, not after making such remarkable progress, not with our goal in graspable reach!

I look around me but the curious stares from the other beds offer no suggestions. Bewildered I ask Pema to confirm. Again, I get the same answer. They will be leaving here tomorrow. Pema points at the neatly packed bag with Choden's belongings. Her husband is already on his way to pick them up. Incredulous, I realise that somehow the news of Choden's upcoming departure bypassed me. On enquiring with the doctors, my worst fears materialise. Choden has already been discharged.

Nervously rocking on the chair behind the desk of my treatment room, I debate what could be done to change the course of events. Choden is not ready to go, not yet. Finally, I speak to the DMO and plead to keep Choden for a couple more weeks, at least until she has practised walking outside of the parallel bars. The DMO agrees. With a sigh of relief, I hurry along the yellow corridors to share the good news with Choden, but my joyous message is greeted by a long face. Choden's mother insists that they have to leave anyway.

I do not understand. Again, I ask Pema to find out what the hurry is. Certainly, after all this work and effort, Choden will not throw everything out the window just because she no longer wants to stay here. Impatiently I wait for the answer. My confidence reappears as I listen to the quiet discussion in Sharchhopkha. It was all a misunderstanding, and in a minute, I can plan the next week of treatment for my determined young patient. However, after what seems like hours of talk, I find out that there is a different reason. It is harvest time, and Choden's mother cannot afford to look after her daughter at the hospital any longer. She needs to go home and bring in the crops. Choden has to go with her.

Unbelieving, I weigh the facts. I cannot argue with a family's livelihood, and it is true; in Mongar, a patient like Choden cannot stay in the hospital without an attendant. Many personal tasks, such as using the bathroom, Choden could never do alone. She needs someone to stay beside her at all times, especially during the night. The nurses do not perform such support roles here. Someone from outside has to look after the patient.

I feel trapped in the system but refuse to relinquish our goal. So close to success, so close to independence, it seems ridiculous to throw in the towel now. I discuss with Pema the possibility of finding a woman in town who would like to earn some extra money and be Choden's attendant for a few weeks. The idea seems promising, and I take my new proposal to the hospital's administration. They agree in principle but interject that there is no budget for such a service. Another obstacle, but this one will not stump me. How much can it cost? The average monthly wage for the wardboys is 700 Ng, less than thirty Canadian dollars. Without much hesitation, I offer to pay whatever is necessary, but although my proposal is accepted, I meet a few raised eyebrows.

Ignoring the sideways glances of whoever deems it their business to frown at this foreigner throwing around her salary, I lay out my plan to Choden. I am exhilarated at the possibility, and eagerly expect an equally excited Choden. Not so. After another lengthy discussion with her mother, Choden informs me that she will go home. Why exactly I will never know. Whether she feels uncomfortable at the thought of a stranger helping her with her personal affairs, or whether she is convinced that we will not find anyone, I refuse to believe that her walking matters so little that she is unwilling to overcome a few minor obstacles.

Still, in the end, I look at her gentle but set smile, and I know that I have lost her. She promises to come back in one month, after the harvest, but now, she needs to go home. I think about her long journey, about how miserable the ward must look to her after weeks of boredom in an overcrowded room abounding with disease. Still I try my best to convince her. I beseech her and beg her to stay, but at the end of the day, I have to accept her decision.

With a heavy heart, I wish her a safe journey and wave goodbye the next morning. The empty parallel bars stare at me from the exercise room. Now there is no one to breathe life into them, they no longer give hope or support. Through the whims of farming law, they have been cast off and labelled useless. Deep down I know that Choden will not come back in one month, and probably not thereafter. All I can do is pray that she will continue to improve at home.

Without Choden's daily treatments, I now focus my attention with renewed energy on my other problem child, Lhamo. Her right leg is making slow yet steady progress, but I am still racking my brains over the immovable left knee.

'These villagers are tough, don't worry about it,' was the advice from the surgeon after he discovered that he himself would not be able to reap any praise for an ingenious operation. 'There is nothing that can be done,' was the final most unhelpful diagnosis from the other doctors. I am frustrated by such passive comments. Lhamo is only thirteen; there MUST be something that can be done.

At the hospital in Thimphu, North American orthopaedic surgeons volunteer for one-month rotations. I decide to send Lhamo's X-rays for a consultation. Finally a glimmer of hope.

'We can try,' the surgeon says on the other end of the telephone, 'but we would have to fuse the knee completely. She will not be able to move it again.'

I weigh the consequences. Lhamo can always sit with a straight leg, but she cannot stand with it bent.

'The operation will be difficult. We would have to cut into the knee, and I am worried about the arteries and nerves. They might be damaged in the process. You would have to think about it carefully.'

I do think about it, and the enormous responsibility of my position weighs heavily. But I believe that even if the worst came to the worst, and they would have to amputate, Lhamo would be better off with an artificial limb than with the crooked knee she has now. I am all for trying – but Lhamo refuses.

She is scared. Scared to the point that she comes wailing into the physio room one day, repeatedly yelling that no one will cut off her leg. I sit beside her and put my arm around her shoulder. I try to explain that the doctors are not just going to 'cut off her leg', but Lhamo will not listen. Even her mother shakes her head in silent refusal. No operation for Lhamo.

Afresh every day, I remark on the issue, and every time I run into the same brick wall. Lhamo's participation in physio dwindles, and more often than not, I have to summon her to come and complete her exercises. Then, one morning on rounds, I make the connection.

In the bed beside Lhamo lays a shrivelled old Abi with diabetes. Due to a gangrenous leg that could not be saved, this Abi had to have a below-the-knee amputation. It was the only thing to do, and Abi is lucky to have survived the operation. She comes to me for exercising the stiff knee, and I try to teach her family how to wrap the stump. Lhamo, of course, sees her all day long, and must assume that any leg operation means cutting the leg off, a thought which would terrify anyone.

Having discovered the culprit of her fear, I assume that now I will be able to clarify the misunderstanding. I spend hours explaining the operation of a fusion to Lhamo and her mother. The answer is still a vehement NO.

In a desperate attempt to motivate Lhamo, I introduce her to the parallel bars. At first, my mission ends in disaster, with a crying and sulking Lhamo who complains about everything from foot cramps to sore palms. She seems dead set on sabotaging my efforts.

One morning, when all the doctors are on rounds and I am sitting at my desk discussing a few cases with Pema, Lhamo rolls her wheelchair to the open window. Her cheeky smirk greets me before she sticks her head through the opening. Reassuring herself that the air is clear of unwanted listeners, she waves her mother over. Like a conspirator, Lhamo's mother starts whispering with Pema. '*If* they did the surgery, when would they do it?'

I explain that we would have to wait until September when the next American surgeon arrives in Thimphu.

'How long would Lhamo have to stay there?'

'Maybe a month, maybe two, depending on her recovery.'

Lhamo's mother decides to come inside the room for further privacy and, without looking at us, mumbles something to Pema. Somehow I can feel that whatever is being said has the utmost influence on Lhamo's future. Finally Pema turns to me and translates.

'They cannot go Thimphu. There is no money to pay accommodation and food.'

I sigh in relief. A surmountable hurdle. Pema and I agree that there is no problem. I will find enough money to feed them until they return to Mongar.

With that promise, the way is cleared. Lhamo's mother does not doubt my sincerity for a second, and does not bother to ask how much I will give them. I must have proven trustworthy and now they will put their fate into my hands. They will go to Thimphu.

As if touched by a magic wand, Lhamo's attitude changes dramatically. She pushes herself without needing a reminder. Pema makes a list of all her exercises, and every day adds a few repetitions. Lhamo keeps up. Defying death and disaster, she throws herself between the parallel bars until honest exhaustion forces her to stop. Her strength increases in leaps and bounds, and every day she looks healthier and happier. After a few weeks, we prepare the next vehicle to take her to Thimphu.

Too soon, shortly after Lhamo's departure, the day arrives for Pema to say goodbye – and I feel as if my own departure date has been set. My teaching job, which is supposed to be the basis of my work, is essentially cut off. Both Lhamo and Choden are gone. What will be my role over the next few months?

Above all, I will miss Pema. Her unruffled, calm presence has become my lifeline to communication with the hospital staff. Her smile has cheered us through the rain and fleas of the monsoon, and her resourcefulness has bridged many a day without electricity. No doubt, my real challenge in Mongar is about to begin.

'Good luck!' I whisper to my friend who is standing with Nima and Karma in front of the post office, waiting for the bus to Samdruk Jongkhar.

'Don't worry!' Pema repeats and shifts Nima on her hips. The boy is in the best of spirits, happily drooling on Pema's kira and spreading his dribble with his mechanical wiping motions around his mouth and evenly over Pema's toego.

'Bye Nima!' I wave. Nima gurgles and looks past me towards the mountains. Suddenly his little hand extends in my direction but then pulls back to once again spread saliva over himself and his mother.

'It's good that you are going,' I can hear myself say aloud. Pema nods. Her smile brightens and affectionately she wipes Nima's fingers on her handkerchief.

'Take care of Dr. Bikul,' she grins.

I make a face at her, but silently promise to do just that.

'Bye bye! My thoughts will be with you!' With a heavy lump in my throat, I wave as the overloaded bus finally pulls out of Mongar bazaar.

EIGHTEEN

CHORTENS AND PRAYER FLAGS

A hot day is drawing to an end. The warm air feels sluggish, but a touch of coolness is just beginning to set heavy dew on the ground. In front of me, a group of banana trees in lush green grass watch over a gnarly old pine tree with a long beard of lichens and mosses. A butterfly with orange wings, dotted black and tipped in blue and white, flutters gracefully between a few patches of pink flowers and then surfs the breeze to disappear in the hazy sky. Through a faint hole in the clouds, I get a vision of the mountains beyond. Washed and faded by the humidity, they look steady and solemn, yet fleetingly illusive.

From the garden, the soft haunting tune of Bikul's guitar stirs the quiet. After a while, the melody hesitates, and only the wind rustles in the leaves of a rhododendron. Unhurriedly my feet follow the familiar path to Bikul's house.

Sometimes I wonder why of all the people here, Bikul is the one who makes me feel at home. I have started to count on our daily walks, the philosophical discussions, the shared meals and the comfortable camaraderie. I wonder if we would have gotten so close had life not thrown us together like this. Two strangers in a strange place – so you become friends. Some days I question the sanity of this bond, but perhaps we have more in common than I am allowing for. One thing is for sure, though; whatever may happen, we need to be friends above all else. Mongar is too small to start a squabble with someone. There is no room for lost romances. Can I trust him and myself? There is so much that I want to share – but will we get hurt?

I find Bikul in his garden gazing at the clouds. His handsome features are soft and dreamy. He does not hear me approach and turns, a little startled, when I call out to him. I ask him what he is doing, and he answers, 'I am looking at my sky.'

My sky. He says it so sincerely; he seems so much in harmony with his surroundings that I feel that this world is truly his. He belongs here. Something about the sight of his lonely figure amidst the mountains and the clouds makes me tremble. Deep inside I feel the earnest wish to be part of this moment, whatever it holds.

'Bikul,' I try timidly, 'will you share your sky with me?'

Bikul looks at me with surprise. I can see that at first he is bewildered by my question, but then he seems pleased.

With a tilt of his head, he wipes away all differences of culture and thought. Tenderly, as if cradling the idea in the crease of his palm, he says, 'Of course!'

Together, we wander towards Kori La, through a world full of mystical shadows and fantastic beauty. I wonder what makes Bhutan so special. Is it the mountains that tower all around, or the untamed beauty of the jungle? Perhaps I am enchanted by the radiant smiles of villagers passing by, or maybe my heart feels at home with the peaceful murmur of a prayer.

Our trail dips into a narrow valley and emerges from the trees on the opposite hilltop. Bikul runs ahead, recklessly jumping over small creeks that have grown to sizeable streams by the plentiful feeding of the monsoon rains. Pausing for a moment to contemplate my safest crossing, I listen to the splashing of the water.

A little white structure on the opposite bank reminds me that in Bhutan, chortens instead of signposts mark the trail. Ancient Buddhism is the heartbeat of this kingdom. Looking at the old monument and its few neighbouring prayer flags, I ponder the boundless presence of the dharma, the teachings of Buddha. They are the basis of daily life in the Himalaya.

Everywhere there is evidence of the overwhelming devotion of the Bhutanese to their religion. The rushing water of many a stream or creek turns a large conical prayer wheel, sending mantras to heaven and blessing the fields that are fed by its waters. Chortens are erected on waysides or passes, turning away evil spirits and remembering great lamas. Sometimes white, sometimes colourful, prayer flags flutter on mountaintops and overlook rivers, spreading their prayers through the wind and the water. Village temples and farmhouses are decorated with artistic paintings of lotus flowers and the eight auspicious symbols. Even kiras and ghos have religious patterns artfully woven into their designs. Bhutan without Buddhism seems impossible.

I watch Bikul as he walks around the chorten three times; careful to turn clockwise, to keep the sacred site to his right. His belief is honest and pure, and his knowledge about Buddhism and Hinduism is vast and detailed. He has introduced me to a world of meditation and rituals, of Hinayana and tantric Buddhism, of philosophies that are still only vague concepts in my mind. What I have managed to grasp is so little, so modest compared to the sacred teachings that are out there, combined with a myriad of local village beliefs. Some of these practices stem from the animistic and shamanistic views of the ancient religion of Bonism, others from histories about demons and deities.

My eyes wander back to the chorten – a simple white structure. Often chortens are not much taller than I, and yet to me their sight is always precious. Their presence in the hills, amongst the trees and fields, is humble and unpretentious, though somehow reassuring. Even if you have lost your path and are straying through the jungle, you know that someone was here before you. Someone prayed on this very patch of earth, and built a monument in sincere devotion. Its shape symbolises Buddha's mind, a place for offering, a sacred spot.

I walk up to the little pious construction and feel the soft mosses, which cover the rough whitewashed stones. The chorten harmonises with its surroundings in a structural and philosophical way. The angular base that supports the tiny tower looks somewhat like a pedestal, and symbolises the earth. The dome above it stands for water. The conical spire signifies fire, and a crescent moon cradling the sun represents the air. There are thirteen steps in the spire, which stand for the thirteen steps to Buddhahood or enlightenment. On top of the pinnacle is a spike or flame; ether, the sacred light of Buddha.

Slowly I stroll around the chorten, thinking about the hands that once laid these stones in such a symbolic fashion. In my mind, I imagine what might be contained within it. I know that hidden inside all of these consecrated structures is a 'tree of life', a wooden pole inscribed with prayers. In addition, sacred religious relics are placed within the receptacle, sometimes books, sometimes statues or weapons, sometimes even the bodies of great lamas.

Chortens are built for different reasons, and I wonder what may have been the cause for the initiation of this one. Sometimes they commemorate the visit of a saint; sometimes they are supposed to ward off or subjugate demons and evil spirits from dangerous locations such as cross roads, mountain passes or bridges. Whatever the reason, to me they symbolise the precious devotion of the Bhutanese, a reminder of spirituality amidst the mountains and valleys.

Bikul is eager to push on, to reach a certain spot before sunset. After a while, the trail drops into a valley surrounded by long, gentle mountain slopes. The wind nurtures lush green rice paddies, and hundreds of dragonflies dance in the breeze. The setting sun floods through the clouds and reflects off their tiny transparent wings as they sway and drift here and there. Like sparks of fire, in glittering gold they illuminate the air, creating a dazzling festival of lights.

After we climb through a thick wood, we emerge onto a tree-lined field. Here, an old mani wall, a stone wall with inlaid carved or painted prayer stones, links two chortens. Time has made this sanctuary one with the mountains. Tall grasses and mosses have covered the flat roof in patches of green, and the once whitewashed stones have returned to their original yellow and brown. In some places, chunks of rock have broken out of the wall, and the paint is faded on many of the stone slates. Still the edgings of a mantra remain clearly visible. As I pass the wall to my right, I listen for the sound of a murmur. Then, tentatively, my lips form the sounds of six precious syllables: *Om mani padme hum.*

Beyond the mani wall, where the jungle again encroaches on the path, we meet an old villager with bowed legs and bare feet. He smiles at us and interrupts his prayer for a greeting, never ceasing to turn the little wheel in his hand. Bikul and the old man exchange a few cheery remarks and the villager nods in approval. He has watched us walk around the chorten, and he is happy that we respect his religion. With a regretful shrug of his shoulders, he remarks that the young people today try to forget the old ways. He points to his prayer wheel.

'There is a lot of wisdom in a mantra.'

Bikul asks if I may turn it a few times. With a delighted grin, the old man hands me the wheel and I hold it in astonishment. It is heavier than I thought, yet it spins effortlessly, each rotation creating a sweet humming sound. The old man encourages me with another smile.

'*Om mani padme hum,*' he murmurs for me.

I try to recall the meaning of what he is saying, hoping that if I understand the message, I will feel less self-conscious about pronouncing it myself. Quietly I ask Bikul to explain again.

'Padme is the lotus, and mani the jewel,' he says. 'Mani can refer to the intention to become enlightened. Or it can mean Guru Rinpoche or Buddha, referred to as the precious jewel, resting in the lotus heart of the devout.' As with so many religious meanings in Bhutan, there seem to be several explanations.

'Don't worry about it,' Bikul then adds. 'Just feel it.'

I try. Still self-conscious about Bikul and the old man beside me, I listen to the wheel spinning around, and then the need for an explanation vanishes. The more I turn, the more even the wheel's motion becomes. The old man continues murmuring his mantra for me.

After a while I gratefully return the prayer wheel to its owner, who bows with another lovely smile.

'*Lasso la,*' he acknowledges my thanks and waves in farewell. Still enrapt by the calmness of the moment, I too raise my hand in farewell. Then I turn to Bikul who watches me with a tender smile. While the old man retraces our steps back to the chorten, Bikul holds out his hand, and with a little jump of my heart, I put my hand in his.

Soon, the heavy air makes our walk just a little more difficult, giving our breath a dense, cloaked tinge. Gently we are reminded to slow down, there is no hurry.

Moments later, the sun disappears. Twilight guards the mountain's secrets in a pale blanket of mist and just a few rays of light pierce the approaching nightfall. Only the serenade of a lovesick frog and a cricket choir accompany the peaceful quiet. Around us, the clouds hang so low that a short walk up the mountain we find ourselves within them, embraced and cushioned. Later yet, we feel the air part, feel a welcome breeze, a coolness, and we look on a sea of cottony white fluff.

Wordlessly, we watch the mist in the valley as it shifts, lifts and settles in an endless game of weight and flight, of floating and drifting. I turn my gaze upwards, and in the muted harmony of the evening, I feel close to heaven. The boundaries between here and there seem no longer visible. In my mind, reality becomes a dream and illusion the presence.

Is this where we feel God? Is it His presence I feel? I do not know – but if God is peace and goodness, soothing and comforting, then surely the silence can be nothing else but God's words to us. Time slows down and no longer matters. I feel that words are not needed, neither are thoughts nor firm ideas, all that counts is this feeling of complete silence.

Gradually the darkness melts all shadows and forms, and the distant mountains sink into the horizon. With the last glimmer of fading light, the birds hush their songs, and the activities of the day move inside. Side by side, Bikul and I continue our path, wandering a road into the vast expanse of the imagination.

NINETEEN

A TRULKU STAR

Amidst a twinkling night firmament, a single bright star shone on the western sky. Its light was clear and splendid, cutting through the night like the beam of a lantern. Sparkling and glittering, it reached down, bridging the gap between earth and heaven.

A little boy in red robes looked up into the night. In awe, he stared at the brilliant celestial body, his mouth opening in silent words of admiration. Unconsciously he raised his hands, and with his palms joined in prayer, he bowed deeply.

A few villagers gathered, and together they gazed at the dazzling appearance. In hushed voices, they whispered, and the solemn weight of an auspicious night settled on the land. The mountains rose and fell in deep sleep, and the wind stirred the dozy leaves of a cypress. All was quiet, yet in a village in the high mountainous country, the hearts of a people were awake with wonder.

For three nights, the star appeared and shone down from heaven. For three nights, its light radiated to every part of the

Himalaya. The little monk watched every evening, and joined his hands in prayer. On the third night, with bright eyes and a quivering voice, he turned to his friends. 'It is a Trulku star!' he whispered. 'Somewhere, a great lama has been reborn.'

On a chair by the window sits a young man clad in red robes. He flips through the pages of a book, seemingly uninterested, his mind perhaps preoccupied. When I enter, he looks up with a sweet, innocent smile. He studies me quietly with a mixture of curiosity and welcome.

'Hello,' I stammer freezing in my tracks. 'I just came to, um, to ask Bikul if he has some sugar.' The sight of the unfamiliar figure throws me completely off balance.

'Bikul is there,' says the young man, pointing at the kitchen. His voice is soft and a little husky, as if I had woken him from deep sleep.

I feel the heat rising in my cheeks. Blushing for no reason, I remain standing fixed to my spot on the floor. Bikul enters to my rescue.

'Phuntshok, *chai piyange*? He addresses the monk as if it was the most natural thing in the world.

'Phuntshok is my friend,' he explains while walking over to where the young monk is sitting. 'He is a great *Trulku*, a reincarnation of an important Tibetan lama.'

Phuntshok (pronounced as Phuntsho) offers me another shy smile. He says something to Bikul in Hindi, and gathering the various ends of his robe, he slowly rises from the chair.

'Do you want to come for a walk with us?' Bikul translates.

At first I hesitate, but the prospect is too tempting to turn down. I look at Phuntshok who is patiently waiting beside the door. I imagine that his grin is almost as awkward as mine, and I nod sheepishly.

A young monk with a head of closely cropped black hair, a bouncy chattering Indian doctor and a blonde blue-eyed girl – we make a funny threesome, strolling along the street. The road is busy with girls and boys in school uniforms, reciting something out of their books. For a while, Bikul and Phuntshok converse fluently in Hindi. Then, to my greatest embarrassment, Bikul urges us to start a conversation.

'Phuntshok speaks a little English. Why don't you two talk about something? Talk about anything,' he advises and then retreats into silence.

My head seems empty, and I am completely tongue-tied. The great Trulku seems to have similar dilemmas and we walk on, each studying our feet, until Bikul again pipes up.

'Why don't you ask him about his life,' he says to me and nods encouragingly at both of us.

Out of the corner of my eye, I look at Phuntshok. He does seem rather like a normal young man. I gather all my courage. 'Are you a *gelong*?' As soon as it is out, I wish that I could take my words back. The question seems silly, as if I was asking the obvious.

Phuntshok smiles. 'Yes, but actually still a *getsul*.'

I ponder what to ask next, but before I have managed to formulate an intelligent question, my tongue gets the better of me.

'What is a getsul?' Embarrassed I cough and look to the ground.

'We live in dzong or monastery. We study Buddha's words.'

'Getsuls first have to be fully ordained as monks before they become gelongs,' Bikul explains. 'But around here, we call them all gelongs. It's easier that way.'

Phuntshok grins and seems to agree.

'Oh.' Another lapse of silence, then I ask Phuntshok if he is allowed to marry. He says no.

'At what age did you become a monk?' I think of the little red-robed boys in the market, tiny monklets, or 'little Buddhas' as Dr. Kalita calls them. How can they decide at such a tender age to dedicate their lives to religion?

'My mother take me to dzong in Lhuntse when I am six. I always know that I will become gelong. You know because of Trulku.'

Trulku – the word sounds like 'tikku' when he pronounces it. I ask again about the meaning of Trulku. The answer, however, is too complicated for Phuntshok's English, and Bikul has to translate from Hindi.

Buddhists believe in the reincarnation of all beings, Phuntshok explains. No one is born for the first time, but has lived through many, many lives, has died and been reborn since the beginning of time. Trulkus are reincarnations of great masters who are successively reborn in different people. The consciousness of the lama is passed on to a newborn baby, and the child and eventually the grown man embodies this later consciousness. A Trulku still has to learn or relearn many things, but he is able to do so quickly, and has an inborn propensity for the dharma, the 'right way'.

The concept seems rather confusing to me, but over my past months in Bhutan, I have come to understand that the Bhutanese believe deeply in the rebirth of all beings.

I ask if all Trulkus are monks. Phuntshok shakes his head. Trulkus do not have to take monastic vows, but most feel the need to live in the monastic community and live like the other ordained monks. There they cannot drink or smoke or marry. If, however, a Trulku does not join the monastic community, he can have a family and lead a village life. No matter what his profession, he will always remain a Trulku.

Phuntshok was born in Kurtoe, a district north of Mongar, in 1970. At that time, a group of monks from the lower Tsangpo valley in Tibet came searching for the reincarnated lama of Samye Monastery. Samye is a place shrouded in historical legends and stories. It is said that Guru Rinpoche built it in the eighth century AD, signalling the solid entry of tantric Buddhism to the Himalaya. Since that day, Samye has been an important stronghold of the oldest sect of tantric Buddhism.

The monks of this famous monastery knew only that their lama had been reborn somewhere in Kurtoe, and they searched for several weeks. Guided by time-old rituals and traditions, they visited families with newborn babies. However, none of the children showed signs of reincarnation. The monks employed many techniques to identify the precious child. Besides using landmarks of the baby's home and characteristics of the family, they checked the infant's birthmarks and showed him relics of the previous lama. However, none of the children fitted the necessary criteria, and none could differentiate between objects out of the late lama's personal use (such as his teacups, rosary or handheld drums), and relics belonging to someone else. Finally, the group of monks returned to Tibet without success.

In the distant village of Kupinesa, however, soon after the birth of her baby boy, a mother realised that her son was different. His first words were spoken in a language none of the villagers could understand, and his expression was calm and serene, gazing with dark eyes into the distance. As soon as he could walk alone, Phuntshok would go to the dzong and pray with the other lamas. He knew how to pray without being taught, yet the language he had spoken soon after birth disappeared. When he was six years old, Phuntshok's mother took him to the dzong, and he became a monk. Phuntshok was comfortable in this role. His training and education progressed rapidly, and soon he surpassed the knowledge of many of the older lamas.

A year later, the Tibetan monks returned and recognised him as the twentieth reincarnation of the great lama Kinley. His formal education began when he was sent to school in Thimphu, where, among other things, he learned Hindi and some English. During his time in Bhutan's capital, an important minister took him in. Since then, he has been studying at the monastic school of Ngatshang, 25 km by road east of Mongar.

Phuntshok seems to tell his tale in a matter of fact way, and, if Bikul's translation is correct, without a trace of conceit or boast. While he has been speaking, our steps have slowed, and now we are standing above Mongar dzong, looking down at its gleaming pinnacle.

'Do you remember your previous birth?' I ask.

'Oh no!' Phuntshok smiles.

Thinking about the monastic school in Ngatshang, I ask him how he came here today.

'Walk,' he says.

'You walked all the way?' In renewed respect, I look at his plastic sandals.

'We take shortcut over mountain,' he says, and points to a ridge beside Kori La.

The sun is about to set behind the western peaks and throws long, yellow rays onto the high pass. I imagine a red-robed figure, clambering over the rocks and running through the thick forest. I imagine the reincarnation of a great lama getting blisters on the hot pavement of the road. I look at Phuntshok as he and Bikul walk amiably side by side down to the entrance of the dzong. From behind, only the red robes distinguish the Trulku from the familiar figure of the young doctor.

For nearly a week, Phuntshok comes to see Bikul daily. Often the two young men are absorbed in discussions about the possibility of a trip to Aza, a remote monastery three days north of Ngatshang. Bikul knows that he cannot leave now. The monsoon is still heavy and brings with it a multitude of diseases and conditions related to contaminated water and dangerous insects. The hospital is still filled to the brim, and there is a shortage of doctors who can respond to emergency calls.

Phuntshok does not question the timing of their trip. He spends his days at the dzong and the late afternoons with Bikul and me on campus or walking through town.

I learn to see in him a gentle boy who is eager to please and grateful for friendship. His family is poor, and his mother lives alone in a village in Kurtoe, giving what she can to her distinguished young son. With a little regret, I compare Phuntshok to children of royalty who are born into a certain rank and status, thereby losing the option to lead a regular life. This view of mine is unfounded, though. Phuntshok seems happy with his fate, and Trulku or not, he proves to be a modest, caring young man.

After a few days, I feel completely comfortable in his company. He is like a steady pole, a soothing presence in the often-tense hospital environment. It is endearing to observe the bond between Bikul and Phuntshok, their genuine admiration for each other. Each in his own way is more experienced, the doctor in the hard lessons of life's realities, and the monk in the teachings of the dharma.

On Sunday when Bikul and I return from the subjee bazaar, Phuntshok is ready with breakfast – a huge pot of rice is served to provide the base for colourful curries (and in my case to neutralise the sharp bite of the spicy dishes). Phuntshok has prepared a feast – *alu dam* (potatoes in a curry sauce), *saag* (spinach) and onions, *ema datsi* (the Bhutanese national dish of chilli peppers cooked in the local fresh cheese) and, at the side, *chapati* (Indian fried flat bread). In Bhutanese custom, our grand cook remains in the background until we are finished. Then he takes his bowl and eats his own meal, adding generous portions of fresh chilli peppers. Afterwards, Phuntshok even refuses to let me do the dishes. Firmly insisting, he claims possession of the kitchen and starts cleaning up.

Without any fanfare, Phuntshok's presence becomes part of our daily outings, and his visit passes all too quickly. I admire his quiet understanding, his unpretentiousness and his humble respect for everyone around him. Unlike some of the hospital staff who raise their eyebrows when they see me with Bikul, Phuntshok never shows any surprise at my appearance.

One day, I am told by the hospital administration that it is not suitable for me to be seen walking in the bazaar with Bikul. 'You would have to be more discreet… You should be careful about spending time in unsuitable company… It would be better if you go walking with the single nurses…' The comments hurt me deeply and make me withdraw further from the hospital.

Luckily, Phuntshok has no such prejudices or objections. His unspoken approval gives me new strength. Gratefully I tell myself that in matters of the heart, the opinion of a monk should count much more. I only wished that Phuntshok would stay.

On a clear autumn night, we walk Phuntshok back to the dzong. He will take the bus early the next morning to return to Ngatshang. I wonder when we will see him again.

'Bye!' Phuntshok waves to us in his carefree, unruffled way.

Bikul and I return his gesture. Not exactly sure why Phuntshok came to Mongar, and even less certain of what he will do next, my eyes follow the Trulku's red robes disappearing through the gate of the dzong.

I slip my fingers into Bikul's hand.

'Do you think that I could see a Trulku star if it appeared in the sky?' Questioningly I look up at the deep firmament.

'Sure, why not?'

'Maybe I would need to be more religious, you know, maybe I don't believe enough in reincarnation and all those things. I mean, I am not a Buddhist.'

Bikul looks at me seriously. 'I am not a Buddhist either.'

'But you believe,' I counter.

'Hmm,' Bikul thinks for a while. 'I believe in many things.'

'You believe in Buddha, don't you?' I press further.

Bikul seems to weigh his words carefully. 'It depends. My traditional Bikul believes in Buddha as an incarnation of God, because I am raised in a traditional Assamese Hindu family. And my rational Bikul believes in Buddha as an idea. The very idea that human beings have this potential to experience the mystery of life, the mystery of enlightenment. I think it is a great idea. We exist because we have ideas. And we create gods to serve our ideas.'

The idea of Buddha, the idea of enlightenment – why does Bikul never speak in easily understandable sentences? His complicated answers irk me.

'Well, I am sorry, I still don't understand. Are you a Hindu or a Buddhist then?'

'Neither! I follow dharma. It is the essence of Hinduism and Buddhism put together. At the core of dharma is the essence of feeling, and experiencing. You know, Britta, in this world, what matters is what you feel. Not what you believe. I cannot feel reincarnation, but Phuntshok does. So, I respect his feeling. You know what I mean.'

OK, I think. He does not really believe in Trulku stars then. I personally like the idea. It speaks to my romantic side. And I want Bikul to feel the same. Isn't he a romantic? I am longing to have him on my side. Our philosophical discussions are all well and good, but I am frustrated that we never see things from the same angle. Is this the eternal East meets West problem? How can I win him over to my side?

'But you do believe in love?' I ask hesitantly.

'Not really. Love is not a religion to believe.'

Pang. His answer hits me in the gut and I can feel a hot gush of panic rising inside me.

'You mean,' I lower my voice a bit and dare not look straight at Bikul, 'you do not believe in love at all?'

Bikul seems unruffled. 'I do not think love needs to be believed.' With those words, he turns to look at me. I cannot read the expression in his dark eyes. Is he making fun of me now? In defence, I want to pull my hand away from his, but then, I feel Bikul holding on tighter. He smiles at me, and I imagine a faint blush appearing on his handsome face.

'You know, I do feel love, the presence of love.'

'Do you?' I want to sound sarcastic, but my voice does not cooperate. Instead I stifle a sigh of relief and squeeze his hand lightly. Now, I can feel the heat rising in my own cheeks.

Bikul winks at me and pulls me back towards the hospital. Then he adds, 'Let's look for a Trulku star tonight.'

A little later, we spread a blanket under an old rhododendron tree in Bikul's garden. Idly we lean against the twisted trunk and gaze up into the night. A deep calm surrounds us, hushing even the frogs in the damp leaves on the ground. The stillness is complete and uplifting. I could not describe it as a lack of noise, it is not a soundlessness, but rather it feels like a foundation, the beginning that all else is built on. As if the mountains were brooding on the bustling life, soothing it to sleep while the day turns into night. The peace of the air is almost palpable, reaching for us with a gentle touch, a caress with tender strokes.

In the east, a bright half moon climbs through the silhouette of branches and trees. Bikul points to a few stars.

'Do you know that constellation?'

'No,' I whisper, trying not to disturb the tranquil mood.

'Over there is Sagittarius.'

I nod quietly and lean my head against his shoulder. I wonder if he feels me right here. A little wind makes me shiver, and I nestle closer to my trusted friend. I look at the moon. He seems to smile, he seems happy with us too. Drowsily I close my eyes.

A soft hand brushes over my head. I can feel the tender touch of Bikul's fingertips sliding over my hair, careful, a little questioning. For a moment, I keep my eyes shut in delight, but then peep through half closed lids at the sky again. Perhaps we will see a Trulku star tonight. Perhaps under these wrinkled branches of the rhododendron tree, time will stand still for just a little while.

TWENTY

TO SCHOOL ON CRUTCHES

The following day shines with a clear morning after a rainfall late in the night. The air is so clear that everything has been outlined like a sharp pencil drawing, and houses, trees and even the clouds emerge on the mountains as if carefully placed there by an artist's hand.

It feels odd to wake from this magical land of romance to the sobering reality of the hospital wards. As I open the physiotherapy department at nine o'clock, I withdraw into the safety of sweet memories, stubbornly trying to hang on to the tenderness of the night. Although I know that I need to concentrate on my patients, I am simply not yet ready to let go of that new tingling in my stomach. I want to shut the department and run to

Bikul's chamber, if only to confirm that he is there, that he is real, and that he feels as enchanted as I do. My work loses importance. Time spent in the hospital seems wasted on this perfect morning – but then I meet Ugyen, a little girl with spina bifida.

In her tattered kira, supporting her weight fully on little wooden crutches, she immediately appeals to my sense of motherhood. With calloused, disfigured bare feet, she follows her father, a well-known officer with Mongar police, through the hospital. She does not say much, she hardly smiles, and no matter how hard I try, I cannot cheer her. Despite her father's urgent appeal, she refuses to come to the physiotherapy room – but when I take her to Bikul's chamber to enquire about her history, she unexpectedly relaxes. Bikul laughs.

'Ugyen and I are good friends. She comes to see me often.'

For a few minutes, Bikul and I discuss the gravity of the little girl's disability. All the while, however, Ugyen is in a hurry to leave. It is obvious that she loathes the hospital.

'What can I do for her?' Feeling helpless in light of Ugyen's impatience, I look at Bikul.

He discusses something with Ugyen's father in Sharchhopkha, and then comes to my rescue.

'They have invited us for tea to their house. Perhaps you and I could go there.' Bikul winks at me. 'Maybe Ugyen will feel more comfortable once she gets to know you.'

I look at Ugyen who seems to be waiting for an answer. I nod and just to make certain add '*Dikpe!*' OK!

And to my greatest surprise, Ugyen smiles.

Although we have walked at least part of the way dozens of times before, today, every sight of Mongar town seems new and unfamiliar. I feel as if my vision has cleared. Walking beside Bikul, I now feel confident, even a little important. After passing the bazaar, we take a road twisting up the slope towards the dzong, and then follow a gravel path to the courtyard of the police quarters. The whole area is teeming with life. A long building stretches before us, the twenty-odd doors each leading to a tiny dwelling, two small rooms per family. The sewage gutter dominates a narrow alley which connects many paltry kitchen rooms. Everywhere there are children in dirty clothes, playing, screaming, running. Older siblings are busy washing laundry or scrubbing the floors. Women look out of the doors of dungy kitchens, the smoke of kitchen fires blurring their curious stares.

We are greeted respectfully, and children clear the path as we make our way to Ugyen's home. Bikul questions a couple of people, and we are shown to a door towards the end of the alley. A middle-aged woman with short black hair sticks her head around the corner and blushes. Apologetically she wipes her hands on her kira and quickly ushers us into her home. In the larger one of two rooms, she asks us to be seated on the only bed and pulls a small wooden table closer. Carefully she opens a cupboard that doubles as the house altar and pulls out two plastic cups and a packet of cookies. Then she disappears.

Bikul and I are left alone, sitting side by side on the colourful kira that serves as a bedspread. A little awkward, we both stare in different directions. Nevertheless encouraged by the secure knowledge that no one here speaks any English, I whisper my most pressing concerns.

'Have you been here before?'

'Only once,' Bikul answers. 'I feel sad to come here. Everything is so crowded. I have a good friend though… who lives in a house over there.' He points behind us and away from the camp.

My mind skips to the thought of my little patient. 'How can Ugyen possibly keep her pressure sores clean here?' I have not noticed toilets anywhere, and the lack of privacy is screaming through the overcrowded doors.

'I think there are outhouses somewhere,' Bikul answers.

I ponder the problem. Though Ugyen can walk around on crutches and seems to have adapted well to her spinal disorder, she truly is handicapped in these surroundings. Hygiene is not a top priority for most families in Mongar, but here it must be impossible. Bikul had told me that the reason for Ugyen's frequent visits to the hospital over the last few years has always been an infection of some sort; either a urinary tract infection from a dirty catheter or a bacterial infection in the deep open pressure sores under both of her seat bones.

Ugyen's mother reappears with two cups of tea, followed by a shy, quiet Ugyen herself. I try to coax the girl into sitting down with us, but she remains standing in the door, leaning on her crutches and watching. Her expression is neither frightened nor unfriendly, but rather sullen. All attempts at making conversation are greeted with a brief yes or no. Disappointed, I realise that it will take much more than just a visit to gain Ugyen's trust.

Ugyen's mother asks us to stay for dinner, but Bikul and I both apologise and turn down the offer. Bikul needs to go back to the hospital. He has emergency on-call duty. Not wanting to offend the family or lose whatever tiny crumb of favour I might have gained in Ugyen's eyes, I am left hoping that they will assume that I am needed for emergency duty, too. Ugyen does not say anything, but her mother seems to understand and, gratefully, we escape the noisy camp.

Once the cramped police quarters are behind us, big trees and the beautiful sight of the dzong welcome silence and serenity. I try to inhale deeply the fresh mountain air, but the smell of urine and rotten vegetables still occupies my senses. I imagine feeling the stare of a set of eyes in my back and turn around. Ugyen is standing at the edge of camp, leaning on her crutches and waving – but not smiling.

I swallow hard. Urban life, no matter where, is always more congested, more difficult, but never has it been as evident to me as here in Mongar. The pristine beauty of the mountains, the peaceful chortens and temples, and the miles and miles of forest, are mocked by the ugliness of cement buildings such as the police camp. I guess we all want to believe that somewhere there is a Shangri-La – and yet the piled up garbage in town and the dirty stinking sewage pipes are reminders of how fine that line between paradise and suffering can be.

Ugyen is part of this other reality of Bhutan which I stubbornly try to ignore. As the weeks pass, I grow more and more fond of my little spina bifida patient. Ugyen has never gone to school. Her four-point walk with wooden crutches is awkward, and her incontinence sends her shambling to the toilet at unpredictable times. In the stubborn way of a teenager, Ugyen decided that she does not want a catheter. It labels her, it is troublesome, and she sees no reason why her urine should run into that see-through bag.

Initially, I cause quite a bit of turmoil in the hospital when I insist that the obviously neglected pussy pressure sores on Ugyen's buttock must be treated. With the help of Bikul and some of the nurses, we convince Ugyen to come to the hospital daily for a week. Nodding seriously, her family promises to look after the wounds, and we spend several sessions teaching her parents how to keep the ulcers clean. At the end of the week, Ugyen leaves with a big package of cotton pads and tape, and we even convince her to try a new catheter – but unfortunately the one that is inserted is too big. The hospital has run out of her size.

The following week, Ugyen returns with fever and a urinary tract infection. Like so many times over the past years, she is admitted to the ward, and again, she occupies B12, the bed immediately beside the toilet.

I start to sympathise with her reluctance to stay in the hospital. Ugyen is left alone on her wretched bed most of the time. Occasionally her father comes to visit her, her mother brings her food, and her sisters play with her in the afternoon. Overall, though, she is left unattended. Lonely and forlorn, Ugyen looks like a little heap of misery on her stained bed sheet reeking of urine.

Once a day, she shuffles along the hallway to come and see me; another time she gets her pressure sores cleaned in the minor OT. She makes no noise, and she seldom smiles. Nurses and doctors look her up and down. Some of the other patients stare relentlessly. I can almost feel her pain. I know now what it is like to be stared at, to be assessed based on appearance and a certain strangeness, and to be labelled as different.

Whenever I see her, I try in my inept Sharchhopkha to make her smile, but I rarely succeed. The lovely features of her young face are hidden well behind an impenetrable blank mask. Determined to be independent, she allows no one to help her, and no one to get close.

One particularly gloomy afternoon, I ask Ugyen to visit me in my quarters. I make tea for her, and hot chocolate. She sips both politely and then leaves them to get cold on the table. She does not look around and stares unimpressed at Spud. The only thing she takes mild interest in is my tiny photo album with pictures of my family. I tell myself to give her time, to let her relax, but the afternoon passes, and Ugyen sits politely on my sofa and does not say one word. While Spud suspiciously eyes the new visitor, Ugyen turns into a silent statue.

Exasperated and somewhat disappointed, I dive into my big hockey bag and pull out a package of crayons and a colouring book; my reserves for emergencies such as this one.

Finally, Ugyen perks up. Her eyes sparkle in surprise, and a smile lights her face. Clumsily she starts colouring the dress of a girl. Drawing seems foreign to her, and for a while, she fumbles with the crayon.

'Would you like to go to school?' I ask Ugyen.

Her answer is a little uncertain, but still a timid yes.
Yes, she would like to go. When I ask if she can write her
name, she says no. Still, if she goes to school, she wants
to go straight to class one (instead of pre school) because
her younger sister Karma Dema studies in that class.

I am relieved. Maybe we can make this work. I have
thought about it a great deal. Ugyen is a town girl, born
and raised amongst a newly developing working class
that does not live in a tight and supportive community.
In a village, Ugyen would be surrounded by friends. She
might get help, and maybe even be pampered, but in the
police camp in town, she is forsaken.

Does her hardworking family consider her quite
useless, or worse, a burden? I like Ugyen's parents. They
are simple, honest people, trying to make ends meet. But
do they understand Ugyen's disease? I wonder whether
Ugyen's stony face is born out of her quiet suffering.

The next day, I discuss the issue of education with her
mother. At home, Ugyen helps with the washing and
cleaning and, silently protesting her dependence, she insists
on cooking her own meals. She has shown some interest in
weaving, and her mother is teaching her the basics.

I ask what Ugyen's future might hold. Would she not
be more independent if she learned to read and write
and maybe one day hold an office job? Ugyen's mother
seems happy with the suggestion of putting her daughter
in school but remarks that she would have no time to
help Ugyen. Ugyen's mother is also going to school in
the afternoons. She is part of a group of women who
were unable to get an education. Now they are learning
Dzongkha, Bhutan's national language.

So, I think, of all people, she should be able to feel how important school is for Ugyen. Still I am not sure that she understands.

When Ugyen is released from the hospital, for better or for worse, I decide to take Ugyen to school myself. The primary school is located at the end of town. From the hospital, it is perhaps a fifteen-minute walk away, from the police camp about the same, unless one uses a muddy path and cuts through the bushes beside the dzong. The main timbered building of the school is four storeys high and holds most of the higher-grade classrooms. Pre school and class one have their own rooms in little cement bungalows further down the hill.

The vice principal of the school is very kind and shows me around the campus. He seems in favour of a new student, even if it is at the end of the school year. We discuss the problem with the principal. He too seems in agreement, although I am a little sceptical about his enthusiasm.

'It is children like Ugyen that should get our help, isn't it, doctor?' he exclaims. I nod. 'Actually we owe it to them to try our best.'

'Yes, you are right.' Again I agree, quietly noting that no one thought of asking Ugyen to join school before.

I suggest enrolling Ugyen as soon as possible. The principal and I agree on a probationary trial period in class one. The timing of Ugyen's entrance into school is less than ideal. The school year starts in March and runs through to December. Over the winter, the children go on a long break due to the cold weather that makes studying in the unheated rooms impossible. Now it is already October. The class teacher for IB, a thin, elegantly dressed Indian lady, assures me that she will do her best to help Ugyen, but the girl will have to make up almost two years. Will she be able to do it?

I have some doubts too, but I know that Ugyen will need the support of a sibling. Class one is better than not trying at all.

Ugyen still needs a school uniform, and having taken the initiative to enrol her, I want to make sure that my plan does not fail for the expense of buying her outfit. I ask ADM's wife for help. She explains to me where I can find the material for a kira and where to buy a toego, onju and shoes. Then, with raised eyebrows, she whispers, 'You will pay for *everything*, sister?' I try to ignore the contemptuous tone of her voice and dodge an answer.

Ugyen accompanies me to the shop and dutifully tries on the last available sizes. The shopkeeper stares at me. As a newly born foster parent, I feel shy and unqualified.

'Do they fit?'

I have no idea how to size any of the clothes and finally rely on Ugyen's preference. The jacket looks much too big, even if one adjusts for a possible (but unlikely) growth spurt. Ugyen beams an elated smile and, in the end, that settles the matter. We decide on one item each, sticking to the red rubber boots for her weak and deformed feet. Walking out, I notice that Ugyen is half drowning in her uniform, and yet her steps seem less shuffling and her head is held a little higher.

On Wednesday morning I pick Ugyen up from the police camp and, together with her little sister Karma Dema, we negotiate the curved street past the dzong and down to the primary school. Karma Dema beams with pride to walk beside her older sibling and carries both girls' schoolbooks with extra care. Neither girl says anything, but the experienced class one student is in the best of spirits. Occasionally she runs ahead to chat with her classmates, but most of the time she stays beside us, and with a bright smile, she encourages Ugyen's wobbly walking.

At the school, many curious stares and the welcoming voice of the vice principal greet us. 'Ah, so this is Ugyen. You will come to join us in school now?' I can see that the kind man tries his utmost to make Ugyen comfortable. Still, Ugyen remains shy and answers all questions with a bare minimum of words. Worried, I look at my little protégée. She seems overwhelmed by the secretive whispers and childish stares from other students but holds her head in a stubborn gesture of indifference.

The VP and I discuss the possibilities of getting Ugyen caught up with the current curriculum, and by the time we have settled on a temporary plan of action, classes have started. A proud Karma Dema heads off to class with her sister. Ugyen's teacher joins us and, confused, I enquire if she is not teaching today. The petite Indian woman reassures me with a lovely smile, 'Yes, madam. I will be teaching Ugyen, do not worry. But right now, they have Dzongkha class. Dzongkha is taught by the Dzongkha lopon. I will go back after this hour.'

We talk for a little while longer and, finally, I make my own way to the cement building that houses the first and second grade classrooms. It does not take me long to discover Ugyen. The door to the classroom of 1B is wide open, and Ugyen is perched on her seat in the front row beside Karma Dema. The little wooden table and bench are far too small for Ugyen's size, and the added cushion which I made to protect her pressure sores does not help the set-up. Still, Ugyen is sitting tall and proud. She does not notice me coming, and I am able to watch undisturbed for a few minutes.

The Dzongkha lopon, a serious-looking young man, has drawn a few pictures on the blackboard, labelled with letters that I cannot recognise but assume must be the Dzongkha alphabet. Pointing to the board, he reads out the letters and a boy in the last row recites them.

To my surprise, the lopon now asks Ugyen to repeat. Ugyen is flushed with concentration and bravely pronounces each sound. Nodding encouragingly and correcting her pronunciation, the lopon asks a few more times, and after she volunteers several timid attempts, he seems satisfied. Smiling he calls out '*Lekso!*' and on cue, the entire class starts clapping their hands in applause. Forty little pairs of hands encourage Ugyen on her first day of school. All of a sudden, I am not worried any more about how 1B will accept their new student.

TWENTY-ONE

TOWN PLANNING

After five months in Mongar, the stony, winding staircase up to the bazaar is not only familiar but also dear to me. The narrow passage leading from the football field to the shops signals freedom from the hospital and promises the world of villagers and lamas. I love balancing up the wobbly incline to emerge amongst the colourful house fronts and large prayer wheels. Today, something has changed, though. I stand beside the chorten of the village square and stare in disbelief along the road.

I always imagined change in Mongar would be slow in the making, and indeed, over the last few months, it has been. The mutations sneaked up gradually, quietly, so subtle you could barely notice them.

First, there was the undeniable shift in the town population. Where initially only a handful of villagers and shopkeepers had chatted quietly in the evening hours, now the streets are filled with dark Indian faces. The construction site at the hospital is expanding, and more and more manpower and materials are assembled in town. With no entertainment other than a few shops-cum-bars, the lonely men displaced from their country by the wish to find work collect in the streets of Mongar. They are neither noisy nor disturbing, only different, unexpected in this remote district where households have lived secluded for centuries.

After the men came the road. Town planning, as it is called. Mongar was to receive a bypass; where and how was never clear to me. In fact, *why* was not that certain either, other than the reason that Mongar had been blessed with someone's decision to develop it. What became painfully clear, however, is that town planning meant death to the trees. Every last one was felled, and after a brutal frenzy of slash and burn, Mongar is now bare and dusty, exposed to wind and weather. The green giants that used to shelter the town under their protective arms have been chopped and bundled, and are waiting to be fed to someone's wood stove.

I have watched these mutations in surprise and disappointment, wondering what will be sacrificed next to the gods of modernisation. My doubtful eye is unappreciated, I know. Mongar is embracing its advances with open arms.

Though perplexed and shocked, today I am no longer surprised by any changes – except for this one. I shut my eyes, convinced that the hallucination will fly away once I catch my breath from the arduous climb, but alas, when I peek through half-closed eyelids, the illusion remains.

On the right side of the road, where before an entire row of shops had surveyed the bazaar, now an empty hole gapes at me. The wooden shacks have up and disappeared overnight, and all that remains is scattered garbage and some orphaned plastic bags garlanding the bushes. The shops must have advanced to somewhere else.

Within a few days, the changes become more permanent. The hill on which the shops used to live is removed and the road is widened. Now instead of a one-lane dirt road, we have a two-lane dirt road. Villagers and Indians alike can be seen sprawled along the construction site, loudly hammering the mountain into gravel. The shops appear not where I had expected them higher up in town, but in the gully that leads to the hospital. There, the wooden shacks have been reerected amongst pastures of mud, and the whole market looks like a refugee camp. I am told that as soon as town planning is completed, they will move again to their permanent location. 'Where to?' I ask, but there is no answer.

In an attempt to find a piece of undisturbed road, I leave Mongar town and walk down towards Redaza. The road is filled with activities and humming with life, nowhere more so than at the Indian road worker camp, just ten minutes out of Mongar. At a bend that looks towards Lhuntse, a small shanty town has been born out of dismantled and flattened mustard oil tins, corrugated sheet iron, bamboo matting and oily pieces of cloth. The shacks line two levels of semi-flat terraces above and below the road, and are connected by a network of muddy pathways. Between the huts, strung wires are embellished with torn or worn out pieces of clothing, washed but still stained by layers of tar and grease. Children of all ages play with stones, pieces of wood and cast off plasticware. Women can be seen around their houses, sweeping, dusting and cooking, while the men have disappeared.

When I approach, a group of scrawny, runny-nosed children jump up and wave enthusiastically.

'Ta ta! ... Ta ta! Ta ta!' It sounds more like a hysterical scream than a friendly greeting.

'Ta ta!' I call back. Used to being ignored, the children giggle in obvious delight.

My unfamiliar voice draws a few suspicious stares from the surrounding huts, but on a doorstep to my left, a thin woman smiles. I squint a little into the setting sun. Her figure seems familiar. I wave. Then I recognise the slender lady. She was one of my earliest patients in the hospital. It is Dhan Maya, the Indian labourer whose back pain was my first lesson in the ways of the roadwork. We smile at each other for a while. I point at my back and mimic the universal hand gesture of a question; the woman understands. Sadly, she shakes her head. Her pain is no better.

Cautiously, she signals me to come. Her wave with an outstretched arm is polite, her palm pointing towards the ground, as if her fingers were teasing some unseen dust towards her. I look at her 'house', the pathetic shack amidst a sad pile of poverty.

All of a sudden I need her to know that she is my friend and that I am not 'too good' for her home. I would like to visit her. So I plunder through the carefully laid out rules of class and social ranking, and break all unspoken laws of Mongar town. I know that I look out of place with my clean white shirt and my flowery long dress prancing through the little shantytown. There are more curious stares but no one makes a comment. The women size me up quickly with an appraising glance and then return to their chores.

Dhan Maya beams from ear to ear. Losing no time, she asks me to enter. It is dark inside the iron hovel, but everything is tidy and clean. Immediately beside the door on the ground is a fireplace, and to its left, a kitchen corner with a couple of pots, a plastic container and a dented aluminium bowl. There are no windows, and the light falling through the door barely illuminates the bed on the far wall. I cannot see what exactly the bunk is made out of, but it is covered by a big, clean blanket, and from now on serves as my honourable seat. An older, shorter lady, another familiar face from the hospital, comes in and begins to stir the fire. Then a young boy enters with a bucket of water, and Dhan Maya fills a pot.

Our conversation is patchy at best, and must sound comical to any outside ear. Dhan Maya communicates in Bengali, and I respond in my broken Sharchhopkha. The cards are definitely stacked in her favour since she can at least understand some of what I am saying, while I am one hundred per cent ignorant of the translation of any of her words. Still we chat amiably.

Dhan Maya moves over to where I am sitting, but instead of joining me, she pulls out a key from somewhere within her sari. Quickly she unlocks a big steel box beside the bed. Her 'cupboard' makes me feel at home. I have one of those boxes myself. It stands in my bedroom, and I keep my camera and diaries locked in it – Bikul calls it my 'Vietnam box'. For Dhan Maya, though, this seems to be the genie's case. She pulls out a cup, a spoon, tea leaves, sugar and milk powder, then carefully locks the treasure chest again.

While Dhan Maya prepares tea, she crouches in front of the fire. I look at her back, and my thoughts drift to her daily work on the roads. Her spine looks like a ridge of high bony bumps underneath the thin cotton blouse of her sari. Her whole frail being is folded into a meek bundle of cloth, the long, thin arms sticking out like two unconnected appendages. Only her head is held proud and erect.

The sweet tea is delicious. While I sip on it a little awkwardly, my generous host is still busy with the fire. She gestures to her pots, and then at me. She is inviting me for dinner. With many difficulties, I excuse myself. I tell her that it is getting dark outside, and that I really should return home. Dhan Maya will have none of that. With a smile, she starts preparing some potatoes. I shake my head guiltily. How can I accept food from her when I know that she cannot feed her family? Determined, I get up and gently tap her on the shoulder. I try my old excuse.

'Pholang ngamla.' She does not understand, but her son does. He translates, and by the pitying look she sends to my stomach, I know that an aching belly is something that she is more than familiar with.

Nodding, she puts the potatoes aside, but then she obviously reconsiders or thinks of something else.

Expertly, she rekindles the fire. Again, she opens her treasure chest. This time, she pulls out two eggs. There is simply no stopping her. I accept the hard-boiled eggs with a humble gesture of gratitude. Dhan Maya watches happily while I eat the offered fare. Unsure of the proper etiquette, I peel my eggs and then dip them into the coarse salt on a side plate.

When I finally get up, Dhan Maya understands that I have to go. Outside, darkness is about to swallow the ragged outline of the rough shantytown. Candlelight seeps through the many cracks and holes in the walls and plays in ghostly shadows on the ground. A few women gather outside Dhan Maya's hut, and a gentle commotion stirs. I wait. Through the whispering voices, Dhan Maya's son approaches from the neighbour's hut. He carries a flashlight, the heavy duty indestructible kind that you find all over India. Touched by their kindness, I bid my Indian friends goodbye. With her gentle voice, Dhan Maya thanks me for coming. In her chapped, hardworking hands, two white eggs reflect the light of the moon. Timidly she offers me the gift. I am humbled and ashamed that I have nothing to give to her. Desperately I hope that she understands how grateful I am. '*Kadinche la, Ama, Kadinche la.*'

Her young son lights the path for me back to the road. Back to the construction site, back to their daily merciless labour. I turn down the trail to the hospital.

TWENTY-TWO

DHARMA OR DOLLARS

A Hole in the Sky

A patch of white cloud appeared
and drifted behind the mountain range
A lama turned the last page
of an ancient script.

Ten years, ten months, ten hours
and ten minutes inside a lhakhang.
And now, he was ready to read
the last page.

Down the valley,
somebody fired a bullet

And the sound echoed off the mountains.
The white cloud stopped drifting.

His eyes were sunken
and his skin was dry and wrinkled.
The ancient script dropped
as the old lama started to shiver.

'Om…?'

Annitt Kumar, 1997

At the end of November, our DMO moves to the large home of the previous hospital supervisor, vacating his house at the centre of the hospital campus. After some initial misgivings by the hospital's administration, I am offered the now empty Class A quarters. Delighted to leave the damp ground floor apartment, I decide to move my few belongings one more time.

'That's great!' Bikul is immediately enthusiastic. 'You will live next door to me. And the house is not bad – but it's all cement, of course, like the other staff quarters. We'll need to paint the walls.'

Next thing I know, he arrives with several buckets of light yellow paint and an assortment of brushes. Looking at the foreign labels, I start to feel guilty about how much these treasures must have cost.

Bikul frowns, astonished. 'I want to do this for you. You need a good home. Come!'

Heedless of all potential stares from the neighbours, he takes my hand and pulls me into my new abode. I laugh, thinking about Mongar's rumour mill that might get scandal-born indigestion at such an outrageous sight. Quickly I plant a kiss on his cheek. 'Let's start painting then.'

Together we attack the horribly stained pink walls. After each finished metre, we step back and survey our accomplishment.

'I never knew that I like painting,' Bikul declares when the kitchen gleams in a happy yellow. Affectionately, he smears a drop of paint all over my cheek. 'We'll do the rest tomorrow, let's go and celebrate now. I'll take you up to Pancholing, and we'll get more artistic inspiration.'

Happily, I lace my fingers into Bikul's, and only reluctantly let go of his hand once we step out into the bright sunshine of the afternoon. At this moment, the world seems like a perfect place.

Our walk through Mongar turns into a stroll through a picture book. Beyond every ridge another valley tempts the imagination, and civilisation seems to disappear in the magnificent jungles of the Himalaya. The day is quiet but for the splashing of creeks and rivers. Peaks stretch all around us, green mountains dropping in steady slopes to narrow river valleys. Bikul points out the villages he has been to in order to treat patients. To the west, Jeposing and Lingmithang, and faraway the hills of Kheng; to the south, Depong and Jungling. South-east lies Phosrang and beyond it Chaskhar. To the east lies Mongar town, on the opposite mountain Takchhu, and marking the horizon is Kori La.

At the top of the hill, we reach the Pancholing lhakhang. Though modest and greyed by age, this small temple is very important for the villagers of this area, Bikul explains. Here, a lopon of Shabdrung Ngawang Ngamgyel came nearly five hundred years ago. As on my previous visits, a heavy padlock secures this site of ancient wisdom.

'Bikul, does anyone ever come here?' I am curious what surprises the old temple might hold.

'Of course, but there is only one gomchen who has a key. He lives halfway down to Norbu's house. Do you want to go meet him?'

I think for a minute. Looking for this lama will mean first descending the hill, only to turn around and climb up again. I consult my legs and they advise against such follies. Still, curiosity wins the upper hand.

'OK, let's see if he's there.'

Bikul nods, then seems to think of something, pulls me aside and whispers: 'There are several very important statues inside the lhakhang and the chortens around it. Some years ago, many of the treasures were stolen, and now this gomchen is the only one who is allowed to have a key.'

'Who stole the statues?' I ask.

'Well, no one knows, of course, but at that time, a caretaker from over there,' Bikul points at a hill a few miles to the left, 'was in charge of this lhakhang plus a few other temples in the area. One night when he was sleeping in the little house beside Pancholing, someone broke open the chortens. A lot of valuable things, including gold and zee – you know, cat's eye? – they disappeared.

'The police immediately suspected the caretaker because he had been sleeping nearby, and they arrested him and his brother. The caretaker told the police that he knew nothing, and that he always spends the night in that little house after doing puja in the lhakhang, but they did not believe him. The dispute lasted several years. Finally it was resolved somehow, but then a few more years later, another important statue was stolen. The caretaker got really scared and no longer wanted to be responsible for all the temples. So he gave over the keys to this gomchen from Phosrang.'

We find the Phosrang gomchen outside his hut, together with his wife and granddaughter. All three are busy separating dried corn kernels from the cob, throwing the yellow grains onto a big tarp. Later they will grind them into kharang.

'*Kuzuzang po la, Meme! Kuzuzang po la, Ama!*' Bikul and the gomchen talk for a few minutes while Ama and the little girl continue to pick at the corn. The old man seems in a slightly sour mood but cheers greatly upon my asking if I might take a picture of them. More than willing, the family poses for the camera. Then, by now fully convinced of our friendly intentions, Phosrang gomchen gets up to fetch the lhakhang's key from his house.

'Bikul, what was this zee you talked about?' I ask while we climb back up to the temple.

'Don't you know cat's eye?' he asks in return.

I shake my head.

'Cat's eye is a stone found in the China Sea, I think. It is a kind of pearl. The Dzongkha name is zee. Bhutanese women wear zee for good luck. One zee will be passed on from generation to generation – mother to daughter, it goes like that. Your luck and worth depends on how many zees you have. Zees are also considered good for your health and longevity. But the stone is very popular in Taiwan. The price depends on the number of eyes. A zee with one eye might be 100,000 rupees, but one zee can contain many eyes. So you think about the price. That's why the chortens were robbed.'

Once the wooden temple doors creak open, I see that the lhakhang is as beautiful as it is old. Even in this seemingly forgotten place, fresh flowers decorate the altar, and a caring hand has dusted the many antique ornaments. The three main statues of the temple show Lord Buddha seated facing the room. A bright yellow and orange robe draped over the main statue is harmoniously mirrored in vases of flaming marigolds. From his seat of lotus flowers, Buddha's golden face smiles, serene and forgiving. Bikul points to the special hand positions of each of the three statues. The large central figure symbolises Buddha's moment of awakening, while the slightly smaller one on the right talks about the first doctrine of his teachings. The third image symbolises the defeat of the demon Mara and all earthly temptations.

Bikul and I prostrate ourselves three times and place an offering of a few ngultrums on the altar. Phosrang gomchen pours a little holy water into our palms. Sipping at it and spreading the rest over my head, out of the corner of my eye I notice a moth-eaten cloth covering the right wall of the temple. I ask the gomchen what is behind it. He only nods and pulls the cloth aside.

In the dim light that filters in through semi-covered windows, the wall appears black with golden dots and stripes randomly flung onto the background. I follow some of the shimmering streaks and allow my eyes to refocus. Suddenly, wrathful figures on black slate jump out from the mural. Life and energy flood the dark wall. Fierce eyes glare from terrifying grimaces. Hynotised, I stare at the aggressive stances and drawn weapons. Phosrang gomchen lets the fabric fall back – and the vision disappears into obscurity.

Back outside we are blinded by the daylight. Phosrang gomchen seems in a sudden hurry to return to his family, and Bikul and I thank him and wave goodbye. Alone again, we stand hand in hand, lost in our own thoughts.

'You know,' I quietly turn to Bikul, 'I have seen many statues and pictures of Buddha – they all look different. Some of them are beautiful and some of them are wrathful. Exactly how many Buddhas do we have?'

'What kind of answer do you want?' Bikul grins.

I raise my eyebrows. 'Meaning?'

'Well, I can give you kind of a hand-wash answer, simple. Or else I can give you the real answer.'

'The real one, please,' I answer. 'But let's keep walking back. Knowing you, the real answer could take some time.'

'How did you guess?' Bikul laughs and puts his hand around my shoulder, trying to navigate us down the path together. 'The word "God" has two very different meanings in the West and in India. In the West, God is all powerful, He created the human being, and He is directly involved in shaping the history of us. We should obey the command of God, and we must believe in Him and His powerful authority. God is merciful, compassionate; He is up there on the summit, always ready to help human beings to live peacefully on earth as well as in heaven.'

Bikul points at the clouds in a sweeping motion. 'In India, God is an intelligent force, a cosmic energy of intelligence, we call it Brahma-shakti or Buddha-shakti, all pervading in the universe, and neutral to human history. The living being, as a part of the cosmic energy, has a natural urge to merge with the Buddha-shakti and the experience of merging with the Buddha-shakti is called "enlightenment" or "nirvana".'

I look at Bikul, somewhat sceptical. 'Am I looking for enlightenment then?'

Bikul nods. 'In your own way. We experience our connection to Buddha-shakti through our day to day experience of compassion. For example, you have compassion for your patients, and helping them makes you feel great. This is natural for us, since we are the creatures of compassion. Of course, not all people feel the same. We all have different levels of compassion, different levels of intelligence and perception, and therefore, we all follow our individual paths to nirvana.'

'So,' I counter, 'these temple robbers you talked about earlier, they also strive for enlightenment?'

'They do. All human beings have deficiencies, and we often tend to forget the real goal of our life. Fortunately, we are blessed with Buddhas of various manifestations to help different individuals of different personalities.'

'So they choose to worship wrathful manifestations, I suppose?'

Bikul shakes his head. 'No, all manifestations, also the wrathful ones, try to destroy evil. They look angry or violent because they fight the wrathful power of evil.'

'Then how would a manisfestation help the robbers?'

'For example, the Buddha of Compassion is the force that operates within us to make us compassionate. A spiritual teacher could help the robbers find a compassionate life. This could help them make better choices and improve their karma.

I shake my head, wondering which manifestations would help me understand all these religious intricacies.

We continue along a winding trail which takes us to a congregation of chortens dotting the hilltop. One chorten leads to the next, and we follow them until the trail winds itself down the mountain. Wanting to engrave this perfect moment in my mind, I linger a bit, and walk around the last chorten. It is a skinny monument. Below its bulging dome, it wears a necklace of handmade miniature structures made of clay and ashes of the deceased. But the back of the chorten is facing the thick jungle, and there, parts of it have been hacked away, the remains of tumbled stones hidden beneath the moss. Like an oozing wound, lichens and ivy trail down from the ragged edge, their roots clutching the remains of broken sculptures.

Chorten robbery. So much for artistic inspiration for our decorative painting of my new home.

I look at this scar of an attack on faith and religion, the emptiness that remains after a hunger for money.

Who dared to defy the fear of his karma for money in the purse?

'Is this what you talked about before when you mentioned the stolen treasures?'

'Yes, this is one of the chortens.'

'But how can it all be covered in moss already?'

'It only takes a couple of monsoons,' Bikul answers and points at the thick jungle covering most of the slope below us.

Suddenly I feel tired and have the urgent desire to leave this hill with its unenlightened robbers and go back to the safety of my own unruffled world, with Spud guarding the house and yellow walls shining cheerfully. 'Let's go, OK?' I say and try to pull Bikul along the trail.

'OK,' Bikul agrees and wraps his arms around me. 'Let's go and paint our home. That'll be a good change in Mongar.'

TWENTY-THREE

KADAM GOEMBA

A few days later, the monsoon seems to have returned and winter is fast approaching. The day is dark and wet – and I am getting sick. In my little physio room the windows are shut, there are no lights, and the deafening growl of the OT generator vibrates through my body. My ears hurt, my throat is sore and chills make my body shiver. Someone is pounding against the wall next door and a jackhammer goes off inside my head.

I walk to the duty room to sit beside the nurses' lovely wood stove for a while. Brother Kumar comes in and makes a long face. Politely I enquire what the matter might be. His reply is sullen. 'No water at all. They broke the pipe.' As if to demonstrate his point, Sister Gita washes her hands with the leftover trickle coming out of the filter. How long will that last? Then Dr. Kalita enters, ranting and raving, but today with good reason. No water means no surgeries, not even putting on a plaster cast.

The day goes by without even a flicker of lights.

The prospect of another evening without electricity does nothing to improve my mood. After work, I stare at my own tube lights that hang idly in the middle of the room. Bikul, who accompanied me home, is just about to plop himself on my bed.

'Do you mind not sitting on my bed with your dirty hospital clothes!' I scold. 'Get off!'

Obviously confused, Bikul stares at me. I can see that his thoughts are still in the hospital, and my sudden exclamation has taken him by utter surprise. For a moment he continues to sit right smack on my pillow.

'Get up!'

I feel a desperate anger rising. Past images from the hospital flash before me. I think of Sonam's haunting face; the poor girl who was lying in A6. Her skin was peeling off in huge raw patches from an allergic reaction to an anti-tuberculosis drug. Dozens of flies were buzzing around her and feasting on the oozing liquid coming out of her wounds. Probably the same flies that were previously refreshing themselves in the urinal. Several times I swatted them away, trying to ignore the nauseating stench that arose from the body. Like a corpse, Sonam's mother later covered the poor girl under a sheet to protect her from the pesky insects.

'Don't you understand that I need to keep at least my bed clean,' I wail. With one quick stride I cross the room, and pull Bikul off. Tears are stinging in my eyes. I look at Bikul's stained lab coat and envision the wards at their worst, during cleaning time, when dirt and garbage float in a sea of murky water being swept into the drain.

'I am so sorry.' Bikul hugs me tightly and gently kisses my wet cheek. 'I will go to my house and change, OK?'

Sobbing noisily, I nod.

'I want to go home.' The words escape without my doing.

Bikul continues to hold me, and my unpredictable outburst again targets him. 'What would my parents think if they saw you? Look at you!'

I know that I am lashing out, but somehow I have lost control of myself. Bikul looks guiltily in the mirror. His lab coat is open, his stethoscope dangles out of one pocket, his shirt has a small hole in the front, his hair is dishevelled and day-old stubble is darkening his chin. Dismayed I imagine my dad's reaction. 'Who is this? Don't tell me that you are in love with him!'

Bikul smiles ruefully at me. 'I am so sorry. Don't be angry.'

Tenderly, he hugs me tighter, and with a sigh I lean against him.

In the end, I can't bear to let him go to his house at all. We heat a huge pot of water on the stove, and while the wood starts crackling, we take turns with a quick scoop bath.

Resolutely, I close the curtains to shut out the rest of the world. Then we wrap ourselves in my sleeping bag and huddle beside the *bukhari*, my metal woodstove.

'What will happen when your contract here in Bhutan is over?' Sitting together and holding Bikul close, it seems impossible that I could spend even another hour without this man.

'I have thought about that,' Bikul replies slowly. 'Maybe I could ask for an extension.' After a pause he adds, 'I am actually finished with my preparations for postgraduate school in India. I was thinking about applying in Chandigarh in January. But I would also like to stay at least until your year is finished. Perhaps we could go to India together after that.'

'Yes,' I reply quietly. 'I can't think of staying here without you.'

Slowly the tension of the day flows out of my body. I close my eyes, enjoying the scratchiness of Bikul's stubble, and the smoky scent coming from the wood stove.

'Will you call the night nurse and tell her, if there is an emergency, to call you here tonight?'

I hold my breath, waiting for an answer.

'You know they will call you Mrs. Das tomorrow,' Bikul teases, referring to his last name.

I have to smile. Yes, I know.

'That doesn't sound so bad,' I mumble, and crawl deeper under the sleeping bag. This seems right to me, whatever anyone else might think. This is where I belong. Beside Bikul, right here.

'Please stay,' I say, kissing Bikul tenderly. Tonight, I don't want to sleep alone.

The temperature continues to drop. Time is measured in armloads of wood for the fire; rekindling the flames interrupts the dark evening.

The next morning, we wake up to watch our breath in the air. Getting out of bed becomes a battle with will-power, but a little later, sipping some steaming coffee, I hold onto my cup as if my life depended on it. Slowly the hot porcelain defrosts my fingers.

In physiotherapy, an old abi with rheumatoid arthritis is my only patient. I struggle with my Sharchhopkha, and Saidon Abi muffles back in toothless sounds. I ask how old she is but the answer gets lost in moons and Bhutanese years. Most likely, Saidon Abi does not know. Most minakpas have no idea on which day they were born; many can only guess at their ages. Time matters little.

Saidon Abi mumbles that she is from Kadam, an old temple on the hill above Mongar. I nod in recognition. I know a schoolteacher, Kesang Choeki, who lives up there.

'*Kesang Choeki – Kadam?*' I ask, and Saidon Abi nods enthusiastically.

Abi shows me her hands. Her fingers are bent and disfigured by the advanced stages of her disease. '*Ngamla*,' she repeats a few times. I nod. Then she points to her elbows, her shoulders, her knees, and her feet. She wants me to know that it hurts everywhere. I nod again. Beside me, a cold wax bath and a lifeless infrared lamp look dolefully into the powerless darkness. Parts of the hospital have electricity today, but my physioroom certainly does not.

A thought strikes suddenly. The outpatient rooms have power. Therefore Bikul has light! If I cannot treat my patients here, we will go elsewhere.

Abi follows me to Bikul's OPD chamber, where I deposit my heat lamp beside his desk. Bikul looks at me questioningly.

'What are you doing?'

'Well, you have electricity and I don't. I thought maybe Saidon Abi can sit here under the heat lamp.'

Bikul agrees. We turn the extra chair to stand sideways along his desk and place a footstool in front. At first, Saidon Abi wants to offer me her seat, but when she finally puts her feet up, she purrs with contentment. Even Bikul's patient who is watching from the examination table has to grin.

By the red glow of the infrared lamp, we let the hours tick by. First we warm her feet, then her knees (while Saidon Abi obediently makes little circles with her ankles), next one shoulder after the other, then elbows, and lastly her hands. Bikul's patients come and go, but no one seems to mind the tiny old Abi in the OPD chamber.

While my delightful old patient stretches her legs out under the heat lamp, she and Bikul joke around in fast and, for me, complicated Sharchhopkha. I prod Bikul to tell me what they are talking about.

'You,' Bikul grins.

'I know that, but what about me?' I have never liked hearing my name without understanding the rest of the sentence.

'I am just asking Abi if she thinks you are beautiful.'

'What?'

Bikul turns back to Saidon Abi. They laugh.

'What else?'

'Abi is asking me if you are my wife.'

Now I have to grimace. In the Bhutanese way, Abi's question is only natural. Traditionally, if a young man does not leave a girl's room in the middle of the night but stays until morning, the couple is considered married. In the minakpa's eyes, we would therefore be a couple. I smile and for the second time try on my imaginary new name, 'Mrs. Das'.

When the day is nearly over, the Administrative Officer stops his dissatisfied pacing of the front of the hospital to look into matters in Chamber No. 4. I try to smile politely, but his haughty supervision makes me cringe. His disapproval of my appearance in the OPD room is hidden behind an expressionless mask. To demonstrate that I am here with a patient, I turn to my Saidon Abi. '*Dakpa mo, Abi?*' I ask. Are you better? Saidon Abi beams me a smile. She is loving every moment of the soothing heat. Without a word, the ADM turns around and with hands clasped behind his back, resumes his pace in front of the hospital.

Saidon Abi rubs the last one of her warmed joints and, grinning, points at her feet. 'Again?' she asks. I look at my watch. Nearly three o'clock, and I am ready to go home. Even by the moderate warmth of Bikul's electric coil heater, my cough has worsened. Helplessly I shake my head. With a smile, Saidon Abi bows slightly. Then she pulls a rosary from the fold in her kira and, murmuring a mantra, returns to her bed in the ward.

When the sporadic electricity supply to the physio room is restored the next day, I ask for a space heater. 'I will try, madam. Maybe tomorrow,' our electrician in charge promises. Despite his honest intentions, my heart sinks. Instinct tells me that his promise for 'tomorrow' will turn into the day after or next week, if at all. In partial surrender and partial defiance, I treat most of my patients in Bikul's OPD room by the warmth of his pathetic heater. The stares from administration continue but no one makes a comment.

One day, Sister Rupali rushes towards me, heaving her corpulent body along the hallway in excitement. 'Sister! We received telephone from Sister Pema.' Mongar does not receive many long distance calls, and when one arrives the entire hospital is informed within minutes.

'Oh, did she call from Vellore? How are they?'

'Yes, sister,' Rupali confirms. 'They are still in Vellore. I think they must be fine, but only worried about the expense of accommodation and food all the time.'

'Did she say anything about Nima?'

'She didn't say, sister. But they will not be coming back this year.'

Shocked, I stare at Sister Rupali. It is the end of November, and Pema has been gone for nearly two months. If she does not come back until January, she will have missed more than three months of her training. And I will continue to be cold and lonely in our physio room. Depressed and a little annoyed, I leave Sister Rupali standing in the hallway to continue spreading the news.

On one particularly dreary afternoon, when Bikul is busy with inpatients and my mood sinks to an all-time low, I decide to escape the hospital campus and make a 'home visit' to my Saidon Abi at Kadam. High on the hilltop, Kadam goemba is surrounded by dozens of little huts and buildings. Many of them are home to the monks, but also old men and women who want to spend their retirements in meditation and prayer.

The climb is long and slippery, and after every few steps I have to stop and wait while my chest is rattled with spasmodic coughing fits. Once, on a steep and muddy stretch, I consider turning around, but for some reason I push on regardless.

A middle-aged woman dressed in red robes meets me on the path. I ask if she knows where Saidon Abi lives. 'Eh?' is the only response. Obviously my Sharchhopkha is incomprehensible to her. I gesticulate wildly that I am looking for an Abi with pain in her arm – and finally the nun nods. In her bare feet and turning her rosary, she leads me to a wooden shack, no bigger than my bedroom.

Inside the dimly lit walls, I have to blink. An old woman sits in a corner on a mat of animal skin, cradling her right wrist in her lap. Her husband rises to welcome me.

'*Kuzuzang po la, doctor!*' the woman greets me with respect and gratefully holds her thin hand out to me.

'*Kuzuzang po la, Abi! Hang eh?*' Not wanting to disappoint the old lady who looks completely unfamiliar to me, I carefully examine the obviously broken wrist. The fracture must be severe and cause tremendous pain. Her hand is limp and hangs at an odd 90-degree angle from the rest of the arm, but it is warm and otherwise intact. I try to find out how old the injury is.

'*Hapta nigzing,*' her husband replies.

Two weeks? That cannot be, I think, but then consider otherwise. Yes, it can be. Judging from the look of her skinny calves, the old woman likely can no longer walk the path down to Mongar, and she avoids a trip to the hospital at all costs. Still, I try to convince them that she has to see a doctor. I mimic an X-ray. The old man nods in surprising comprehension. 'X-ray?' he asks.

'Yes! X-ray!' I repeat excitedly. Then I fall silent. Even with an X-ray, I am not sure that anything can be done for the old woman at this stage.

The couple tries to invite me for tea, but I excuse myself because I am looking for my Saidon Abi. Another old woman takes my hand. She seems to know Saidon Abi.

We pass the new building of the goemba to our right, and the woman leads me once around the temple, setting the long rows of prayer wheels in motion. Then we walk past Madam Kesang Choeki's house on the left and arrive at a small hut off on its own, nestled under the huge branches of an enormous evergreen.

The hut is filled with smoke from the fire, and a single faint light bulb illuminates black-stained wooden pillars and walls. A few whisky bottles filled with arra, the home-brewed alcoholic drink, and some dried chillies in a bamboo bangchung stand in the shelves. An old grandfather alarm clock ticks away the wrong time. Ancient-looking pots and pans hang from the wall, boasting a charcoaled bottom to the world. A variety of spoons and ladles are lined up neatly in a row. A number of empty bottles await filling. Above the fire, a bamboo grill, most likely for drying meat, is now used for the storage of some indefinable objects of antique value. Everything has its place, probably assigned years ago, and now lovingly returned there after every use. Around the corner stands a single bed with a collection of blankets and kiras, all looking as old and as worn as Saidon Abi herself.

A now familiar odour welcomes me at the door; it is that unmistakable smell of unwashed bodies, a smell that greets you miles before a smile can shine through, and leaves its traces on clothes, sheets and rugs. It is the smell of sweat and datsi (cheese), of chillies and arra, of fire smoke and slightly rancid butter; the smell of generations in wooden huts and houses without chimneys and with the windows closed.

Saidon Abi is pleased to see me and painfully unfolds herself from the seated position by the fire. Her husband, the caretaker monk of the old temple of Kadam Goemba, immediately takes over the supervision of their grandson, a tiny toddler whom Abi had been cradling. Meme puts the small boy in his lap and, holding his prayer wheel, murmurs a few mantras. The boy crows happily and grasps for the exciting toy. When he finds that he cannot reach it, he breaks into an angry howl. Meme laughs and folds the boy's fingers around the handle of the wheel. Immediately satisfied, they turn the prayer wheel together, the boy settling deeper into Meme's arms.

Saidon Abi pulls out a piece of bamboo and blows into the amber. Within moments, the flames lick happily at a small black pot with boiling water. The wind keeps blowing the smoke back in through the door, and Abi creates more by stirring the fire.

I present Saidon Abi with my gift: a woollen scarf which should help to keep her warm over the coming winter. With delight I notice that its green and red checkered design matches Saidon Abi's red dress perfectly. Saidon Abi's red robes are similar to those of a monk, although she is obviously not a nun; rather, she has earned them by having retreated into meditation for many years.

With a crinkled smile, Saidon Abi hands me a cup of buttertea in a chipped porcelain chalice and places a plate of fancy biscuits before me. With great difficulty, I try to convince her that I would be happy to share their thengma and popcorn kernels. She laughs at my absurd wishes and hands me a bangchung with sweet zao instead. After all, I am an honoured guest and must be served with only the finest she has to offer. Still she continually mumbles expressions of regret, apologising that she has nothing worthy to give. I, however, munch on the thengma most contentedly and decide that buttertea has never been so tasty.

After tea, Meme takes me to the ancient Kadam temple. To my surprise, I find a young monk seated in one of the temple's corners, poring over sacred books. He looks up, and I recognise Tashi, a monk whom I met a few days ago in Bikul's OPD chamber. I remember that he has come home to Mongar from his studies abroad. Meme leaves to continue his chores, and Tashi proudly shows me around the temple.

Though small, there is nothing simple or cheap about this lhakhang. The walls disclose intricately sketched motifs, while the ceiling and supporting pillars are richly decorated with ornaments and thangkas, canvas paintings surrounded by colourful brocade borders with a wooden stick on the top and the bottom for hanging. For protection and storage, these paintings can also be rolled up. Most thangkas show a main image of a Buddha or deity, or else a mandala, the wheel of life, or some other religious shape.

Time has faded the most glorious of colours and coated everything with the mysterious dusty haze of years gone by. There is much to look at, but even more to discover with the imagination. The moment I enter, I feel the need to simply let my thoughts wander to the world of religion outlined on the walls.

From the main shrine, the golden features of Guru Rinpoche look down on me, not gently as I expected, but rather questioningly stern. The dimness inside the temple intensifies the white of the Guru's eyes to a powerful light, drawing my gaze to the golden features. To the right of the main statue, the image of another Buddha is unfamiliar to me. 'The Buddha of Compassion' Tashi explains while pointing at the eleven heads and numerous sets of arms of the image. 'And this one is a protector of the Buddhist teachings.' This time he points to the red statue of a terrifyingly wrathful-looking deity.

Quietly I sit down beside Tashi. He is already busy writing into the book spread on his lap. What I had mistaken as a prayer book turns out to be his practice drawings of the face of a Buddha.

'We have to follow the old instructions precisely,' Tashi tells me. 'We are not allowed to change any of the features or even colours of a drawing. We must draw everything just the same.

'I am not very good,' he adds, trying to close his book. I appeal for another look. On a blank page, Tashi has drawn geometric shapes and lines and, within these, he is now sketching the features of a head. On the little wooden table in front of him, a printed book serves as his guide.

'Do you have a teacher who helps you with these drawings?' I ask.

'Yes, madam, at our college we study. I will take many years to draw well. Actually, we are supposed to draw these figures under a tree and not inside a lhakhang,' Tashi said. 'If you draw it in daylight, you have a better chance to match proper colour. In India, where I receive my training, we always draw outside. But here in Bhutan, it is cold and filled with clouds.' He makes a gesture which seems to express his relief that no teacher is watching him drawing the precious Buddha while sitting inside a lhakhang.

Fascinated, I watch the developing artist at work. Without much artistic talent of my own, I find it incredible that one day he will be able to reproduce the precise and colourful paintings of gods and deities that brighten all Bhutanese temples and decorations.

Tashi walks me back to Saidon Abi's house. Coming from the temple, I discover decorations on Abi's home that had escaped my eyes before. Two rusty bicycle frames are propped against the wall, and a large collection of empty bottles, some old oil drums, a few corrugated iron sheets and a worn out shoe protect the rear of the house. Some distance off to the side, a few children are standing beside a big wooden bowl, stomping long poles onto kernels of something resembling wheat. In perfect rhythm and incredible speed, they alternate their pounding.

'Making arra,' Tashi explains with a smile, but I am not sure if he is joking.

Inside Abi's house, the activities are no less bustling. An old woman with leathery hands is grinding corn in a huge wooden trough. The grain resembles popcorn kernels before popping, and in fascination I watch them disappear under a plate-like millstone. Slowly the old woman turns the wooden handle until fine flour appears in a bowl below the trough.

In the back of the hut, Saidon Abi's grandson is joined by his elder sister for a game of catch. Everyone breaks out into hearty laughter when the toddler slides his feet into Abi's slippers and shuffles around the room, half falling, half supporting himself on everything in reach. One stumble sends him within inches of the hot ashes of the fire, and I think of the terrible burns that I have seen in the hospital. Saidon Abi must have similar worries, for she determinedly pulls the little boy back into her lap.

When dusk bids me to return home, Saidon Abi pushes a big plastic bag of thengma and a few walnuts into my hands, all the while apologising that she has nothing to offer. She asks me to come again, and holding her tiny hand in both of mine, I promise another visit soon.

Hesitant to leave, I linger by the chorten in front of Saidon Abi's house. Below me lies the town of Mongar, so close that I can see the individual rooftops – and yet a world away. A couple of villagers bring in their cows for the night. At the communal water trough, a few women wash the day's laundry. In the surrounding huts, fires are lit to cook an evening meal. Birds twitter a goodnight song, accompanied by the echoes of a puja. From the mountain behind me sounds the chanting of prayers.

TWENTY-FOUR

THE DANCES OF LIGHT

I n a dark corner of the courtyard of Mongar dzong
sits a blind man. Every day from morning until
night, he turns a large prayer wheel, keeping the
huge drum in rotation and sending prayer after prayer
into the world. The man is quiet and inconspicuous,
and I would hardly know of his presence were it not
for the steady sound of a bell, which strikes on each
rotation of the wheel.

*His world consists of prayer. The wheel and a rosary are his
companions. He is oblivious to the daily comings and goings of
men in starched ghos with long white scarves draped over their
shoulders. The hustle of the administrative officers marks his day
only at 9 a.m. when they stroll into the dzong, and at 5 p.m.
when the government employees return home. The blind man's*

251

*work, though, remains until it is time to sleep, and starts again
when the first daylight illuminates a world, which for him has
turned into darkness.*

*Tobgay Dhendrup shifts his sightless gaze upwards, and a
smile plays around his murmuring lips. Unfaltering, he recites
an ancient Buddhist script, a prayer so pure it makes his heart
dance. Not a hint of disappointment or bitterness reflects in his
features. Forty-two years of age, he has attained wisdom, out of
reach for many who could grasp life with all of their senses.*

*Eight years ago, a viral infection of the optic nerves took
Tobgay's eyesight. Over the period of one long month, he marked
the days when he would last behold the sight of his lovely wife
and three children. Since then, their features live only in his
imagination. His busy life of a farmer ended when he could no
longer find the edge of his fields, and slowly he turned inwards,
to the world of Buddha's words. He searched for a meaningful
task in his darkened days, and found it in the honourable role of
turning the dzong's prayer wheel.*

*Tobgay feels deep gratitude that the disease attacked only his
eyes. Over the years in the dzong, he has found his hearing to be
his trusted ally, a window that has opened his mind to the sounds
of prayer. From his spot in the courtyard, he listens to the monks
chanting. He follows their recitations and rituals and embraces
each word in his memory.*

*Now, the blind man nods quietly in rhythm with the drums
that echo through the courtyard. Although he cannot see the
monks practising the intricate steps of ancient dances, he knows
each movement by heart, and in his mind, he sees their bare feet
leaping high through the air. Excited, he turns the prayer wheel
a little faster, matching the tempo of the dance.*

While in Canada Christmas is nearing, everywhere in the district of Mongar people are busy with the yearly preparations for *tshechu*, a lively four-day festival in honour of Guru Rinpoche. Tshechu is celebrated in the dzong with dances, performances and prayers, but it is also a popular social gathering, a time to chat, feast and show off the finest clothes.

Now, two days before the big event, preparations are in full swing. On the clay stoves in village homes, colourful dishes are spiced and seasoned, there are pots of simmering rice and boiling potatoes, and bags are filled with zao and thengma. From the road, you can hear the diligent knocking of looms as young women feverishly try to finish their new festival garments. Even the hospital is caught in the industrious calling of the upcoming celebration. Patients in the ward ask to be discharged, and the outpatient chambers remain empty. No one wants to miss the commemoration of the great master Guru Rinpoche.

From within the dzong's walls, I can hear the drums of dances. It is the last day for rehearsal of the religious performances of tshechu. Tomorrow the dancers will take a day of rest before the festival begins. Inside the lhakhang, there is much to do. Offerings are made and butterlamps filled for many hours of midnight prayers. Fruit and baked goods line the altar, packages of Dalda and sugar join a huge variety of fresh produce. Villagers offer even the most precious items for merit during this sacred festival of dance and prayer.

Although the rites of tshechu date back to the beginnings of tantric Buddhism, outside the white walls of the fortress, a new kind of fair is prepared. Blue tarps are spread over wooden poles to construct makeshift huts. Pickup trucks bearing tables and chairs sputter up the peaceful roads. Men carry boxes and crates full of beer and liquor to be placed behind temporary bars. Dice are unpacked and cards stacked on tables. Outside the dzong, a transient casino has been erected.

Tobgay's son Wangdi leads Bikul and me into the dochey, the inner courtyard of the dzong.

'Apa,' Wangdi gently puts his hand on the blind man's shoulder, 'I am back.'

Tobgay smiles and stretches a hand out towards his youngest son.

'Come sit,' he says, and shuffles aside to make a little room.

'Dr. Bikul is here, and Madam,' Wangdi explains.

Tobgay's smile broadens and, tentatively, he reaches out for us. Bikul takes his hand and holds it between both of his palms.

'How are you, Tobgay?'

The blind man nods and smiles. Bikul introduces me to Tobgay. Again, the blind man's face radiates honest joy.

'Will you come to join tshechu, doctor?' He points to the courtyard where several men are still prancing in swaggering steps, bowing deep, then twisting their bodies in a slow rolling motion.

'Yes, of course,' I answer.

Tobgay nods, and turns towards his son. 'Which dance are they practising, Wangdi?'

'They are all villagers, Apa, they must be finishing *Drametsi Ngacham*.'

Tobgay seems satisfied with his son's prompt answer. He takes pride in teaching his children the real importance of tshechu.

'Apa,' Wangdi adds quietly, 'I think those men had too much arra. Their steps are a little weird.'

'I know,' Tobgay replies with a shrug of his shoulders. 'Some of those villagers cannot dance without the help of arra. I think they are almost finished now?'

'Yes, Apa,' Wangdi confirms.

Tobgay addresses us with sorrow in his voice. 'Doctor, did you see the tarps outside? What do you think about this new generation?' he asks. Then without waiting for an answer, he continues. 'This modern youth, they believe only in drinking and gambling, but not in the truth of the sacred dances.'

The drums have silenced and the villagers have gathered in the far corner of the dzong. Jigme, Bikul's friend and the monks' second in charge, firmly leads them out of the courtyard. The monks want to get on with the preparations for tshechu. The dance rehearsals are over.

In the hospital, anticipation and excitement stir both staff and patients. Tshechu is a time to ask for blessings. Families, huddled on crowded beds, pull crumbly old ngultrum bills out of their hiding places within the folds of freshly washed kiras and ghos. Entrepreneurial vendors materialise overnight to offer their ware of bananas, packages of butter and incense sticks. In the evening, the wards turn into a temporary hostel, filled with caretaking family and friends.

Not many new patients are admitted, but a few familiar faces return just in time for tshechu. When the weekly bus from Trongsa is followed by a hospital vehicle from Thimphu, a small flock of former patients files into the festive town. Among them is a young lady standing upright between the bars of a walker.

'Lhamo, look at you!' With delight and surprise, I greet Lhamo, my little protégée with her injured knees.

'*Kuzuzang po la*, doctor.' Carefully placing her walker on the uneven ground, Lhamo approaches me.

At the sight of her slender figure which is standing nearly as tall as I, unable to contain my excitement, I rush to give Lhamo a hug. Forgotten are the weeks of frustrating exercises with a little whiny girl. Now I can only think of one thing: we did it! Lhamo is walking again!

Lhamo mumbles something and blushes deeply. Then her faces turns serious, and she looks at me expectantly, as if I would now pronounce the final verdict over the success of her operation.

'Wonderful, Lhamo. It's wonderful!'

In my mind, there can be no doubt over the success of her trip to Thimphu. The operation report had preceded Lhamo's arrival, and I know that the fusion of her left knee was a huge victory. The only complication resulting from the surgery was the injury of her common peroneal nerve, which has given Lhamo a drop foot. This new problem, however, can be corrected with an orthotic, and perhaps in time it will even improve further. What matters is that Lhamo is standing upright, supporting her weight on her own legs, even if the right knee is still somewhat contracted from the burn injuries.

Lhamo's mother seems as pleased as I am. Repeatedly she points to Lhamo's knee and tells me something in an excited torrent of words. I nod, then we both laugh. There is a lot of work left to do for Lhamo, but the worst is definitely over. No more wheelchairs and no more pressure sores! Over the course of a few weeks, Lhamo has grown into a beautiful young lady.

Three days later, on 7 December, the second day of tshechu, I suggest to Lhamo to accompany me to the dzong. Her response, however, is unintelligible to me, lost in the overwhelming speed of her chatter. When her excited gestures finally slow down, I realise that her jubilant attitude is laced with doubt. She thinks that it would be impossible to enter the dzong with her walker. And above all, she does not have a good kira. She would stick out terribly with her simple dress.

Annoyed with the little trivialities that dare to stand in the way of a great opportunity, I counter – perhaps a little roughly – that certainly Guru Rinpoche will not mind if she attends tshechu in the yellow and orange striped kira she is wearing. And as to the walker, she would have to get used to showing herself in public with it anyhow.

Her mother agrees immediately, but Lhamo remains unconvinced.

'I don't have a *rachu*,' she points out in a rather sulky voice.

Puzzled, I look at Lhamo, then turn to one of the nurses nearby. 'Is a rachu really needed?' I ask. Sister Gita nods. The rachu is a long red scarf, which the Bhutanese women have to wear over their left shoulder whenever they enter a dzong. It is part of the official attire, and just like the wearing of kira and gho, is enforced by the police.

Lhamo's mother admits that without a rachu, she will not be able to go to tshechu; however, Lhamo is only thirteen, and for children exceptions are always made. Determined that Lhamo should go and ask Guru Rinpoche for her blessings, the tiny resolute mother puts on her most adamant scowl. Lhamo has little choice but to relent.

An hour later, we arrive at the dzong and, to my greatest relief, Lhamo's worries prove to be completely unnecessary. Although she is subject to many curious stares, the faces of the other villagers mirror amazement and respect, nothing of the anticipated suspicion towards her strange walking contraption. After a few kind words from the patrolling police officers, this last imagined hurdle is cleared too, and Lhamo's face relaxes. Still self-conscious of her walker, she half-heartedly asks a few more times to turn around, but once she has spotted the first dancers through the wide gate of the dzong, her face shines with childish excitement.

The dzong is packed with people. The very centre of the courtyard is cleared for the spirited dancers, and row upon row of Bhutanese villagers are seated along the outside and fill doorways, balconies and windows. Everyone is dressed in his finest garments, the crowd turning into a sea of colourful toegos and kiras and meticulously starched ghos.

Jigme quickly ushers us to the main portal of the central tower which doubles as the monks' 'dressing room'. From there we will soon have an unobstructed view of the courtyard; for now, though, Lhamo and I find ourselves surrounded by a lively chattering group of monks getting ready for their great performance of the *Shaa Nga Cham*, dance of the black hats.

Open-mouthed, Lhamo and I admire the preparing dancers while sashes are tied, hats strapped to a layer of protective cloth over the shaven heads, felt boots pulled on and fittings double-checked. One of the young monks grins and shifts nervously from one foot to the other. His red silky brocade robe fluffs and falls elegantly as he practises a few steps and a spin. A wide fur-trimmed hat wearing a scornful face is securely tied to his head. It is topped by a tall spike of a collection of sacred items: the head of a grinning skeleton flanked by two flames and two horns on either side, the moon cradling the sun, and a crown of several peacock feathers. In his left hand he holds a long curved drumstick, and in the right, a big leather drum.

Jigme pushes the heavy curtain to the side and peers out into the courtyard. A few more monks line up on either side of the curtain and, to a secret sign, throw it wide open. With a graceful twirl, the costumed monk dashes out to join the dance.

Sitting beside Lhamo, I have to smile when I glance at the girl who is watching in awe as the black hat dancers twirl in the courtyard. '*Thump*' … Silence … '*Thump*' … Silence … '*Thump, thump, thump*' … The drum's steady beat measures the steps for each dancer. '*Thump*' – three wide steps… '*Thump*' – a sideways movement to either side… '*Thump*' – jump on one leg, a little shift of the body… '*Thump*' – incline towards the ground, jump and twist, resume stance on one leg.

Most of the ancient dances, called *cham*, are religious, telling through their actions and music the teaching of Buddha, the dharma, to a population that is largely illiterate and depends on the clergy for instructions in the spiritual path. The dances are extremely powerful and must be taken seriously. Cham calls on the Buddhist deities for protection from misfortune and to drive out evil spirits. The mere act of watching the cham allows the spectators to gain merit and receive a special blessing.

Before us, the colourful brocade dresses of the twelve monks lift into perfect circles as they turn in precisely measured steps. To the ringing of cymbals and the blowing of long horns, the black hat dancers purify the grounds of the dzong. Their footwork and their gestures have been practised over many years according to the exact methods of subduing evil. Many of the movements are danced on one foot alone, the other leg bent and held up in front with the sole of the foot pointing forward. They move in a large circle, and each monk rotates within his position, the fancy footwork crushing all evil, the sound of the great drums of Buddhism announcing the victory of religion over demons and evil spirits.

Across from us, in a corner of the crowd, I notice Tobgay and his son. Both are following the dancers' movements with rapt attention while Wangdi whispers to his father, probably describing the monks' appearances, costumes and masks. Tobgay sways his body to the rhythm of the music. I am sure that in his mind he can see the dance as clearly as I, even aware of the fine subtleties of steps and hand movements, which remain indistinct to my untrained eye. His contented smile tells me that the dances bring light into his darkness, and the colours of the festival shine brightly.

After the cham is completed, back in the dressing room sweaty boys are eager to unwind the hot cloths from their heads and take off the heavy dancing robes. There is a collective sigh of relief that the many months of rehearsals have paid off and the dance went flawlessly. One monk lost his hat once, but a nearby *atsara*, a clown, came running over to fix the costume.

To my great confusion, now an atsara bounces over to our seats. His face is well hidden behind a funny white mask, making it impossible for me to recognise him. He seems to know me, though, and asks Jigme to take a picture of us. Lhamo beside me starts giggling, and with much laughter and teasing, a photo is snapped. A little suspicious, I look for any sign of their party piece – a wooden penis. Atsaras mimic many of the dances and entertain the crowd to lighten the more serious moments of the tshechu. For me, though, the sight of them poking their wooden phalluses into the air makes me feel utterly uncomfortable. Not so my little companion Lhamo. She laughs and claps her hands at the atsaras' comic antics while other villagers are noisily encouraging.

In the courtyard, the first dancers now arrive for the *Raksha Mangcham*, the dance of the judgement of the dead. This dance is very special, and Guru Rinpoche in magnificent robes joins the earthlings. The cham begins with the rakshas, Buddha's helpers in the form of animals who separate a person's good actions from his bad deeds. In unison, they prance and hop, they strut and skip, they leap and cavort. Then, out of the interior of the temple, following the trail of heavy incense, a solemn group of monks carries the small seated statue of Amitabha or Oepame, the Buddha of infinite light. He is placed on a pedestal to the left of the tower's entrance, in front of the continuous row of prayer wheels. In a long procession headed by monks playing trumpets and cymbals, the huge puppet of Shinje, the Lord of Death, enters, followed by his two attendants, the white god and black demon who live with every being. With great ceremony, they seat themselves on the colourful throne of the court of justice.

The rakshas resume their dance, and old minakpas lean forward to catch a better view. The lessons of this dance will help the old people prepare for their own deaths. A single black-dressed dancer enters, representing the recently deceased sinner who wanders in the Bardo, a state that is reached immediately after death, where one meets the Court of Justice. While the rakshas weigh both his good and his bad deeds on a scale, the crowd hushes. A powerful warning silences the spectators when the sinner is sent to Hell, accompanied by the fearful-looking demon. The next dancer is more fortunate. He is a virtuous man who has followed the Buddhist doctrine, and as a reward for his piety, beautiful fairies accompany him to paradise. He makes his exit in a grandiose and delightful dance, and the subdued crowd relaxes. Across from me, an old abi pulls out a handkerchief and wipes her forehead. The rakshas conclude their dance by performing magnificent jumps and twirls, and then lining up in front of Shinje, the Lord of Death.

It is now up to the spectators to ask for good fortune, and from a huge crowd set into motion, we are reunited with

Lhamo's mother, who has successfully borrowed a rachu from one of the nurses. Together, mother and daughter join the long line forming to receive *wang*, a collective blessing. Men carry their toddlers on their shoulders, women help old abis with their canes. Everybody, one by one, bows to the Buddhas. A few monks have set up a *tashi gowang*, a miniature temple with many tiny doors into which the pious push a few ngultrums for future merits and good luck.

The crowd seems endless. Hundreds and hundreds of Bhutanese from all walks of life line up for their wang. I wave to Lhamo, then I search the masses for Tobgay and Wangdi, but the two have long since disappeared in the endless line approaching the altars. Judging from the number of people waiting their turns, the blessing ceremony will take several more hours, and I decide to head back to my quarters to fill my empty stomach.

At the gate to the dzong, leaning on a stone pillar so as not to get pushed over by the crowd pouring in for wang, Ugyen's little sister Karma Dema is playing with some friends. For a while, I stand on my tiptoes, trying to catch a glimpse of Ugyen's telltale wooden crutches, but there is no sign of them anywhere.

'Karma Dema! Where is Ugyen?' I call to her.

'Home,' Karma Dema answers with a shy smile.

'Ugyen did not want to come?'

'Ugyen busy cooking,' Karma Dema says.

'Are you having fun, Karma Dema?' I ask, trying to reassure the timid little girl.

'Yes, madam.'

Yes, madam. Karma Dema is having fun, but Ugyen is at home. Why is Ugyen not here to receive her blessing? Did she feel, like Lhamo, too shy to come to tshechu? Or is she afraid that she will get pushed over with her crutches? For a moment, I have the urge to walk over to Ugyen's house and bring her to the dzong too, but then I decide against it. Ugyen is a smart kid, and, unlike Lhamo, she is at home in Mongar. She will take care of herself. With the firm resolution not to meddle too much, I turn around to wave goodbye to Karma Dema, but she has already disappeared in the crowd.

'Madam! Oieehhh! Madam!' On my way home, someone roars loudly over the hubbub of the road lined with eating stalls and gambling huts. I cannot recognise the voice and continue marching past the flimsy tarpaulin booths filled with cheering and drinking people.

A girl in a yellow and orange kira pours drinks for a few men sitting around a table. Not much taller than Lhamo, the stubborn look in her eyes reminds me a lot of my little patient who is now standing inside the dzong waiting to receive her wang. At this very moment, I am filled with an immense satisfaction, I am so proud of Lhamo. After all, she found the courage to lumber past the hundreds of watching people, pulling her fused straight leg behind her. Despite her see-sawing gait and the cumbersome walker, she made her way to the courtyard where the dancers were twirling to receive her blessings and merit from the cham.

It could not have been easy for her, yet, to me, Lhamo's efforts represent hope for what Tobgay saw as a generation in moral and spiritual decline; the hope that even Bhutan's younger people – some of whom have been dazzled with pictures and ideas from the modern West – will continue to seek the light of the dances.

TWENTY-FIVE

A MIDNIGHT PRAYER

D octor, will you bring some blessings for Apa from tshechu?'

Norbu Ama looks with questioning eyes at Bikul who is feeling the pulse of a frail, dehydrated man lying with hepatic coma in the ICU room.

'How can I do that, Ama?' Bikul places the pale wasted hand of his patient onto the blanket and makes a note in his chart.

'We heard that you always go to the prayer early in the morning. Please ask Lam Neten for a blessing for my uncle.'

Bikul nods and turns to his patient. Behind protruding cheekbones, the man's eyes are closed and have sunk into the deep hollows of his skull. Months of struggle with a deadly disease have left a haunted expression on the high brows, and his skin is waxy and yellow.

Absent-mindedly, Bikul strokes a few limp hairs off the lifeless face. There is not much hope left for Tshering. Several weeks ago, the carpenter from Trashigang contracted hepatitis B, and now the virus is close to winning the fight over his weakened body. In Mongar, the doctors neither have the necessary equipment for analysing the biochemical parameters of the disease state nor the appropriate methods to keep the body fluid sufficiently balanced. Bikul knows that the man's chances of survival are slim.

'I will go to tshechu tonight, Tshering,' Bikul gently addresses the unconscious man. 'And I will bring blessings for you. Do not worry.'

As if he had heard him, the thin, chapped lips of the comatose patient seem drawn into the fine line of a smile.

'But, Ama, he still needs to take these, OK?' Bikul chides Norbu Ama who has taken it upon herself to wheel the hanging IV bottle away from the bed.

Smiling, Norbu Ama shakes her head. 'If he gets blessings from Guru Rinpoche, no medicine is needed. We will hold puja tonight.'

'Ama, please!' Bikul looks at Norbu Ama with pleading eyes. It is her turn to stay at Tshering's bedside today while Tshering's wife and children have gone to bring food and supplies from home. But Bikul worries that Norbu Ama will take things into her own hands. Today, any interference could push Tshering past any hope of recovery. Due to severe bacterial sepsis, Tshering needs at least the steady supply of fluids. With despair

Bikul reaches for a syringe containing the last dose of ampicillin. After he administers this dose, there will be no more left. The hospital has run out of the necessary antibiotic, and the bacteria invading Tshering's body have shown to be resistant to all other treatments. Sighing, Bikul starts to inject the remaining medication into the IV drip and watches while the transparent medicine slowly flows through the syringe. Then he holds the patient's cold hand and the room is silent but for Tshering's laboured breathing.

Norbu Ama hesitantly clears her throat. Her lips are quivering. 'Doctor, will you bring blessing from the dzong?'

Of course he will bring offerings from tshechu, but in Bikul's mind it is less for Tshering's recovery than to make it easier for the family. In truth, there is not much left to do for Tshering, but his wife and children will need strength to face life without him. Perhaps the Guru's blessings will help them to believe in the future.

'I will go tonight,' Bikul reassures Norbu Ama again while he uses a piece of cord to tie the IV bottle to the bed. Then he checks the flow of the liquid and counts out the seconds. Drip... drip... drip... one drop every two seconds, the medication enters Tshering's body, fighting against all odds for survival.

On the last day of tshechu, the clock shows 2 a.m. when, with chattering teeth and clumsy hands, Bikul and I peel ourselves out of bed and into kira and gho. Forty-five minutes later, we slowly climb up to the dzong. The night is clear and the faint light of the distant universe underlines the peaceful silence. We walk hand in hand, grateful for the night's shelter, content in each other's touch.

The dzong lies majestically before us, the whitewashed walls taking their solemn stance in the moonlight. No sound is heard until we reach the gate where dim lights humour the few drunken card players still trying their luck. Inside the courtyard, we hear the echo of drums and horns. Out of a few windows on the middle floor of the central tower shines a faint light.

The Guru Rinpoche lhakhang is filled with the sounds of prayer, the smell of incense, and colourful decorations honour the festivities. Brilliant banners and ornaments hang from the ceiling. The back of the shrine is hidden by fantastic buildings of coloured dough and butter, rich paintings and glowing butterlamps. Many offering bowls – the tallest ones filled with pineapples, bananas, guavas, oranges, sugarcane and packages of glucose – line the altar. Prayers are chanted. Music moves the air.

We are ushered to the far side of the room and settle beside the empty seat of honour. Lam Neten, the head monk, sits high on his throne, his long scarf wrapped loosely around him. Tshering, the umdze or 'choirmaster', is positioned a little lower to the left and holding a set of heavy cymbals. The other monks are seated on pillows on the floor in neat rows facing each other. On the other side of the room, in the far corner, I can recognise the faces of the dzong dancers and a few older minakpas.

It is the fourth day of tshechu, and the long preparations and nights of prayers and rituals are about to conclude.

Little monks, small boys in red robes, can hardly stay awake and sleepily follow their elders in prayer. Across from me, someone's eyes close tightly, a head slumps to the side and peaceful slumber takes over. A tiny neighbour tries to waken his friend by blowing into the dreamer's ear. Then the kudung, the 'master of discipline', swishes his rosary in reprimand.

Even Lam Neten's face disappears every few minutes behind a fold of his robe, seemingly asleep. Yet at a sign not visible to my eyes, he lifts his head and again his powerful voice leads the monks through rituals of devotion and sacred mantras.

The steady murmur of the prayer is mesmerising, at times ebbing to a low mumble, then rising to its overpowering crescendo. The soft singing of cymbals accompanies the verses. All of a sudden, the music swells. All instruments join force and the powerful blowing of the long horns, the melodic tune of trumpets, the quick tock-tock of the handheld, double-sided damaru drum and the urgent ringing of bells rise to an awesome fanfare – Guru Rinpoche is invited to join the puja. For a moment it strikes me that yes, certainly the noise is big enough to make even the furthest angels aware of the invitation.

Jigme, with a white scarf tied over his mouth and nose, fills a bowl on the altar with water, then holds a tiny ladle in his right; the other hand he lifts above and in front of him, as if greeting the Guru. Prayers quiet with that peculiar slowing of speech that reminds me of a gramophone playing at too slow a speed. To another 'chish' of the kudung 's rosary, little monks rush forward to serve tea and sweet rice. Three times everyone's cups are filled before the prayers resume.

From the altar, the glow of many rows of little butterlamps is reflected in the lustrous decorations, throwing fluttering shadows on the polished wooden floor. They sway with the draft of a breeze through the open windows and flicker with the deep intonations of prayer. And then, like a vision bestowed on dreamy sleepers, out of the mysteries of the back of the temple, a fairy springs. An angel dressed in blue and gold shimmering garments, a silver crown on the head, holding a damaru drum and a bell. Soon another fairy joins him, and together they prance and turn, jump and leap in a dance nothing short of magic. Their presence fills the room as they circle around each other, not once lingering to recover but proceeding in a breathtaking vision of beauty.

I feel uplifted, enchanted, in love with the delight of the moment, inexplicably bound to the wonders of the night. For a second, I am enwrapped by the mystery of the spirit that flees to where no human mind can grasp its essence. Faster and faster the fairies spin, boldly they leap, then their drums pause a moment. *Tock-tock… tock-tock…* and the dance goes on. Again they leap, they ring the bells, and, finally, they turn to face Lam Neten, bouncing high to touch both knees almost to their ears, and disappear. Their magic lingers on.

As dawn sends its first glitters of light through the lhakhang's windows, the puja ends. In the dim courtyard, a lantern-like vase pours out incense to purify the air. A procession of monks carries a long folded cloth

271

around the central tower. Bikul and I follow them. We circumambulate the building three times, setting many small prayer wheels in motion, before the huge cloth is pulled up to the top floor of the tower. Then, in front of the crowd of villagers watching in awe, the image of Guru Rinpoche unfolds.

The silence that follows is complete. Through the dim morning air, the Guru's face looks serenely down on us. We are encompassed by his view; we are enlightened by his sight. To the Bhutanese, the vision of this magnificent thangka is holy. Its name, *thondrol*, means 'liberation on sight'. With deep, zealous belief, sins are washed away by looking at the Guru's kind appearance.

On the stones of the courtyard, seated facing the thondrol as they would otherwise face a shrine, the monks begin their puja. Incense sticks waft heavy perfume in front of the silken image, and hundreds of butterlamps flicker in the light of dawn. Quietly, minakpas gather to witness the precious thondrol. The unshakeable belief in their religion is clearly written on their devout faces. Today is a day of forgiveness and a fresh beginning with a hope for the future. A pink sky in the east welcomes the new morning, and with the first rays of sunlight peaking over Kori La, Guru Rinpoche's image is withdrawn to the temple for another year.

'I have to find Lam Neten. Will you wait here for me?'

I nod and watch Bikul entering the dark rooms of the temple. I know that all night the thought of his patient has weighed heavily on his mind, and he is anxious to return to the hospital.

When the drums begin to accompany the last day's dances, Bikul returns with a relieved smile.

'Let's go,' he says and leads me out of the dzong. He is carrying a bag filled with food and flowers, a package of butter and a silken scarf. Everything has been blessed on this most auspicious of days, and Lam Neten himself chose each item carefully for the dying man. Now Bikul is eager to present Tshering's family with a little piece of hope.

When we arrive at the hospital, the puja in the ICU room is still underway. Butterlamps flicker around the bed and on a makeshift altar beside it. The scent of incense wafts through the door, and I can hear the murmur of a low voice, accompanied by the ringing of bells. Bikul quietly hands Tshering's wife the temple offerings and with a small bow towards the altar, retreats. Then we quickly leave for the certainty that right now, a medicus is neither needed nor wanted in the ICU.

A few days later, before the beginning of rounds in the wards, I accidentally bump into a noisy group of doctors arguing loudly.

'These villagers are so strong, they'll fight any disease!' Dr. Pradhan argues.

'The man was just lucky, I tell you!' Dr. Shetri counters.

'Of course he was lucky,' Dr. Pradhan agrees, 'but all the luck in the world wouldn't have saved me if I had been this weak.'

A little unbelieving, I open the door to peep into the ICU room. On the bedside table a butterlamp is flickering peacefully, and a tall vase containing holy water throws a long shadow over a glass with yellow and orange flowers. Beside it, on a grimy blue sheet, our patient's pale skin is flushed with the first feeble signs of life. Tshering has awakened. And with a trusting mind and perhaps the help of Buddha, he starts his difficult journey towards recovery.

TWENTY-SIX

WOES IN TRASHI YANGTSE

There, that's done!' With a lopsided grimace, I hand the envelope to the clerk in the post office. Here goes the last letter of 1997, probably the most important one I have ever written.

'I really hope that my parents won't have a heart attack. What do you think they will say?' Searching for some reassurance, I look at Bikul. In his unruffled way, he smiles at me.

'I don't know. I think they'll understand.'

His answer is not exactly calming me. 'When do you figure they will get it?' I ask even though I am fully aware that mail to Canada can take anywhere between two and eight weeks.

'Maybe just after New Year's?' Bikul seems a lot less concerned about the timing of our great announcement than I am. Exasperated, I give him a friendly nudge. This is important! Bikul applied for an extension of his contract in Bhutan, and we finally wrote a long letter to my parents confiding in them about our romance. To say that I am worried is an understatement. How will they react when they hear that their youngest daughter wants to stay with a man she met only a few months ago? And on top of that, he is Indian and not Canadian. Will they approve? I cannot imagine that they would be particularly pleased.

'Maybe they will get it while we are in Trashi Yangtse,' I suggest, hoping that our absence from the telephone will give my parents some time to think and get over the initial shock before they speak to us.

'Hmmm.' Now that the letter is on its way, Bikul is obviously no longer worried. Instead he is enquiring with the postmaster about the bus schedule to Trashigang.

Bikul and I decided to celebrate the New Year in Trashi Yangtse, the eastern-most district of Bhutan. Bikul is desperate to finally see the rare black neck cranes, a migratory species of birds that spend the winters in a few remote areas of Bhutan. Our plans seem perfect; the weather is brilliant.

Three days before New Year, at the break of dawn, we leave Mongar in the cab of a big Tata truck going towards Trashigang. From there, we catch a lift to Chorten Kora. Through narrow valleys and along steep inclines, the road bumps over gravel and stones into the remoteness of Eastern Bhutan.

Trashi Yangtse has not seen much development. The town is small and simple; there are a couple of stores selling the basic necessities and one 'hotel' that features five rooms without electricity or water. We visit a friend of Bikul, the Trashi Yangtse District Medical Officer, in his tiny office. The hospital is under construction and instead the DMO works out of a little three-room bungalow, rigged up with the most basic necessities. When we arrive, the doctor is just completing a vasectomy on one of the villagers, under the watchful eyes of the local veterinary assistant.

The DMO extends a warm welcome to us and immediately invites us for dinner.

'So you and the doctor are walking to Bumdeling to see the black neck cranes,' he smiles at me. 'Be careful that Dr. Bikul doesn't lead you into the mountains. He seems to have a particular liking for exploring our little country.'

The DMO's mother packs us a lunch for the coming day, and we are loaded with advice on the best walking route and overnight shelter. Immediately I feel comfortable in this tiny nest of a town just west of the Indian border of Arunachal Pradesh.

In the evening sunshine we walk along the Kulongchhu to Chorten Kora. Smaller chortens and mani walls lead up to the impressive white monument. Chorten Kora is a large Nepali style chorten that was built after the great Bodnath Stupa in Nepal. Surrounded by a low stone wall, Chorten Kora with its four step-like bases under a shimmering white dome and spire is more than 250 years old. For the people of Eastern Bhutan, this site is of great religious importance, and it shows in the many prayer flags fluttering along the riverside.

Through an open gate in the wall, Bikul and I enter the courtyard surrounding the chorten. The ground here is partially covered in rough stone plates between which mosses and weeds struggle to reclaim their territory. Slowly we walk around the chorten. For once not worried about what I should do or say to fit in, I let myself enjoy the soothing evening mood. Looking at the steep cliffs that rise on the other side of the river, I feel small and insignificant, and utterly at peace. My mind flits here and there, and no firm thoughts interrupt my contentment.

When the sun sinks behind the western peaks, Bikul and I leave Chorten Kora and for a while sit on a stone by the water. Rushing over big boulders, the river splashes us with an icy spray. In the evening shade, the temperature drops quickly and, shivering, we walk back to the guesthouse. That night, in our one-room hotel without toilet or water, my nightmare begins.

I feel the nausea rising from deep within my insides, pushing, tormenting, until I vomit. I scramble down steep steps into the cold night air – where I expel a reeking gush of diarrhoea.

I feel weak; I want to sleep, but vomit and diarrhoea alternate relentlessly all night.

I see Bikul's worried face as he touches my feverish forehead. He holds a cup of water to my lips; he tucks me tighter into the sleeping bag.

The next day, I feel lousy but stubbornly refuse to ruin our plans to see the cranes. Although I am weak and fatigued, I convince Bikul that we should still go. We pass hills of flowering bushes and rice paddies and, determined, I drag myself along the path. Bikul carries our bags. We manage to see the birds, and I even snap a few photos, but then I collapse. Bikul sets out to quickly find us some accommodation.

A few hours later, it is New Year's Eve, and instead of celebrating, we are lying in the only available lodging, an office of the forestry division. I still feel horribly sick, and Bikul cradles my head on his lap. Below us, a family is noisily playing dice. Pain shoots through my head every time I hear the thud of the bowl hitting its thick leather pad. I pray that they will stop soon. Bikul tries to distract me with a children's tale about a little elephant.

At midnight I wake up. My stomach seizes in cramps and I am drenched in sweat. Bikul examines me carefully, and now, he cannot control his own worries. The pain becomes worse, and convinced that I have appendicitis, I start crying. I imagine myself on the makeshift operating table of the Trashi Yangtse Basic Health Unit. Bikul tries to reassure me, but cannot find the words. Maybe it is appendicitis.

Clinging to Bikul, I spend the night in a mixture of agony and panic. The next day, when the pain does not subside, it becomes clear that we need to find proper medication. Somehow we struggle back to town and catch a ride in a vehicle heading to Mongar. My stomach cramps and at every pothole pain shoots through me like a knife. I vomit again.

When we finally reach our home, Bikul prepares my bed. Then he tries to start an IV, but of course, there is no electricity. By the light of a flashlight, he stabs at my arm trying to find my veins. His hands tremble and he too is close to tears. I am dehydrated and my blood vessels have shrivelled up. Finally Bikul calls a nurse and together they find a vein.

Later that night, Bikul's hand lies soothingly on my hot forehead. He sponges me with cold water, then tries to cook porridge.

Mongar Hospital is out of the necessary medication and, after conferring with the other doctors, Bikul decides to send me to Thimphu. Almost delirious with fear, I agree. A couple of days pass until the VSO vehicle comes to pick me up, and somehow Bikul manages to get leave to accompany me on the two-day drive to the capital.

We spend three weeks in Thimphu while the doctors try to come up with a diagnosis. My vomiting stops but I cannot eat. Friends take care of me; everyone tells me that I am getting thin. Medically, they fear it could be TB of the abdomen, or something could be wrong with my ovaries. Most likely, it is dysentery. At the end of three weeks, still without a diagnosis, VSO arranges for a flight to Bangkok for an endoscopy. Bikul's leave is finished and he returns to Mongar.

And yet, despite the most modern equipment and a myriad of tests, Bangkok does not provide a definite answer either.

'We are not certain what caused your disease, but you need to fly home, be surrounded by your family,' the Thai doctor explains. 'Eat regular food, that is the most important. Your intestines are extremely inflamed. They need to settle; you need to rest. I do not think that returning to Bhutan is a wise idea.' The doctor shakes my hand in farewell.

Exhausted from my rapid weight loss, I try to make a rational decision. I know that the doctor is right. I should fly home to Canada, of course, but it would mean an end to my life in Bhutan. I would have to quit my job with VSO; I would have to leave Bikul. The thought of losing him is unbearable, overshadowing *any sickness or weakness. I think about it long and hard. Then, against the doctor's advice, I return to Mongar.*

For two months I remain on sick leave and time passes in a complete blur. I know that somehow I have to put on weight, regain my strength, but I still cannot eat. All I can think of is how weak I feel. I am always tired.

'Can I make you some tea?' Bikul touches my forehead tenderly. His face is troubled, and he has dark rings under his eyes.

'What time is it?' I ask.

'It's almost nine o'clock. I have to go to the hospital now.' Bikul fusses with my pillow and I try to lift my head a little. Sleep is still dragging me down heavily, I feel drowsy and a little nauseous. I must have dozed off again.

'Britta?'

I know the voice, it is dear and familiar to me, but for a moment I cannot identify it. With great effort I open my eyes.

'Oh, what happened to you? You are looking so thin!' A petite young woman enters the room, frowning with concern. It is Pema.

'You are back!' I am so relieved to see her, I sit up too quickly. Dizziness blacks out my view and I sink back onto the pillow.

'Yes, and we heard you were taken to Thimphu. What happened?' In her composed and careful manner, Pema sits down on the bed beside me.

Still drowsy, I wave her question away.

'I'll be ok. But what about Nima? Did they find anything?'

At first, Pema seems reluctant to discuss their trip, but when I insist, the words start spilling from her lips.

For the first two weeks in Vellore, Nima underwent many tests, was sent from doctor to doctor, but no one told them any results. Finally, after Nima had a CAT scan, an EEG and several nerve conduction tests, he was given a temporary diagnosis of athetoid cerebral palsy with seizure activity.

When Pema pronounces the dreaded words, I can see her swallowing hard. Cerebral palsy – a neurological disease which is caused by brain damage around the time of birth. There is no cure for it, and the only chance for improvement involves continuous therapy and rehabilitation.

Trying to follow Pema's choppy story closely, my mind instantly becomes more alert. To encourage both her and me, I touch her elbow gently. Pema continues. After the diagnosis was made, for three months Pema and Karma stayed with Nima at the rehabilitation centre of Vellore and worked with therapists and doctors. Nima was given several long-term doses of medications, including anti-seizure drugs, and Pema was told to bring him back in six months' time. When Pema explained that it was unlikely that Bhutan would be able to refer him again within the next year, the doctors shrugged their shoulders. Unfortunately, there was nothing else they could do.

'Do you think it is cerebral palsy?' Pema turns to me with unspoken appeal. I know that she is still denying the diagnosis, that she cannot, simply cannot, come to terms with such a final blow. But it is not my place to sweeten the truth.

'I think the doctors are right, Pema,' I answer as gently as I can. 'But it looks as if it is a mild case. If you work with him every day, he should improve. Definitely.'

'In Vellore I saw so many equipments,' Pema sighs. 'But here we have nothing. So many exercises the therapists did with him there – but I see no improvement.'

Pema's eyes fill with tears, and I feel a burning lump in my throat. I cannot think of anything that I can say to lessen her pain. I know that she wanted a diagnosis so very urgently, but now, I worry how she will deal with the verdict.

Yet Pema is always stronger than I think and, as so many times before, she amazes me with her positive attitude. Within a few minutes she has recomposed herself and starts cleaning up scattered clothes and empty glasses from the room. Then, standing tall, she smiles at me.

'Now you have to get better. You must eat something. I will cook you some rice.'

Accepting no protests and sweet talking, Pema marches off into the kitchen, and within no time I hear pots clanking and water running. Half an hour later, she serves me a bowl of soft rice and a milky white soup. Then she returns to her duty in the hospital.

Determined to start making myself useful, I swing my legs out of bed and walk a little unsteadily to the window. Outside my doorstep, the peach and plum trees have come into blossom. It is the end of February, and spring is painting the land in lovely shades of soft pink and green.

Next week I will have to return to my job. It is high time to continue teaching Pema. If only I did not feel so weak. I glance in the mirror and then quickly turn away. My face looks thin and sickly; everything about me appears tired. Two months of hardly eating have left their marks.

At lunchtime, Bikul comes running to distract me from my untouched plate of food. 'I got the extension. I can work here for another year.' Excitedly chattering, he shows me the official letter from the Ministry of Health. We hug in joy. Now, at last, I know that we can stay together.

But can we? If my health does not improve, I will have to return to Canada for at least a few months. The doctor in Bangkok had cautioned me not to go back to Mongar.

A bout of nausea sends me scrambling for the toilet, and I start shaking with the effort of staying upright. I refuse to pack up all together but I know that something will have to give.

On Monday, I return to work. It must be the first rainy day of 1998. My reappearance in the hospital is hailed by clouds and fog; wet weather that creeps into your underwear and refuses to leave. No lights, no heater, unpleasant as could be. Only Pema's presence cheers the dreary day. I visit the office and get a frosty smile from the ADM. When I sit down, the DMO gets up and leaves without a word.

I try my best to be useful in our physiotherapy room, but over the next few days, I cannot manage to teach Pema. I hardly find the energy to watch her assess and treat the patients. Giving in to my weak body which refuses to recover, at the beginning of March, only three weeks after my return to work, I resign from my duty.

When I tell Pema about my decision, I feel as if I had sentenced myself to eviction. My days in Bhutan are numbered. I will not be able to complete my placement, I will not even be able to wrap up all my charts properly. And Mongar will continue to be an unexplored mystery. All those walks and visits which I had promised to do now will remain excursions in my imagination. Those early morning hours that Bikul and I wanted to spend at the dzong I will soon be spending alone without the sound of prayer and drums to waken a new day.

My return to Canada looms too close, but I see no other way. My weak body is beginning to frighten me, but I am equally terrified of the uncertainty of the future beyond Paro airport and the mountains of the Himalaya. Yet I have to go home. With a bleeding heart, I accept that choice, not knowing if and how Bikul and I will ever be able to stay together again.

For many hours and days I cry while trying to come to terms with my pending departure. Then one day, when the first rhododendrons outside my house come into bloom, I realise that I am just wasting precious time. Mustering all my courage, I promise myself to make the most of my three remaining weeks in Mongar.

TWENTY-SEVEN

LOSAR NEW YEAR

The twenty-seventh of February is a warm day, and I am feeling somewhat refreshed and a little adventurous. The sun is teasing tender new buds, and the fields are sprinkled with a hint of green. Fire-red rhododendrons paint patches of colour into the otherwise still drab landscape. The jovial shouts of minakpas enjoying a game of archery echo across the valley. Old men, young men, small boys, all are out to take part in a bit of friendly competition as a celebration of Losar.

Walking on this merry day turns out to be more than just a little dangerous. Over the next hill, Bikul and I meet a group of minakpas who are blasting their arrows across our path. Howling and yelling ensues when the players spot us. 'Oieehh, *o dele*?' 'Doctor! *Kuzuzang po la!*' The cheerful tongues are unmistakably slurred by the heaviness of arra.

'*Kuzuzang po la! Kuzuzang po la!*'

We return the welcoming greeting and join the merry group of players. From there we watch their arrows fly across a field and over a narrow creek. On the other side of the watershed, the target is barely visible and must be more than a hundred metres away. Players on one team are already on the way to cross over to the other side.

Beside me, a tall thin man with a scraggly beard laughs and clowns around the next archer, obviously trying to distract the opposition from their aim. The shooting archer, however, a short, sturdy man holding a long bamboo bow almost as tall as himself does not appear in the least disturbed. He draws the bow tightly, and before I can manage to focus on the target, the arrow flies across bushes and shrubs. Accompanied by the triumphant cries of his teammates, the little man runs a few steps forward and then breaks into a joyous dance. He must have hit the target. The other men on our side join in, jumping up and down on one foot and chanting victoriously from the bottom of their lungs. In unison, happily cajoling, the group runs to the other side, joining their opponents in a companionable rummage through the foliage in search of the lost arrows.

Further up the hill, we watch a few more games. The aim of all teams is astounding, their precision quite flawless, and the arra seems to heighten their abilities. Bikul tries his skills once but is outshot by a group of small boys, imitating their elders in the game. Then we are nearly run over by two 'cars' booming along the path. Each is steered by a tiny boy, hardly taller than my knees, crashing down the slope on three wheels and a wooden slab. Losar festivities are in full swing.

Losar, the Bhutanese New Year, is celebrated according to the lunar calendar and generally falls somewhere around February. The Bhutanese name their years with a combination of the twelve animals of the zodiac and the five cosmic elements fire, earth, iron, water and wood. Today marks the end of the 360 days of Fire Ox, celebrating the beginning of the Earth Tiger year.

When we reach Norbu's house, Ama is outside, naked down to the waist, taking a bath from their large wooden trough. Her short wet hair stands in spikes at right angles to her head; she smiles hello.

Meme Monk sits outside the house on a bench, his large body leaning against the wall. His eyes seem closed, but when we approach, his face lights in recognition. Slowly and deliberately he rises from his seat and directs us to the house.

After we cross the three wooden poles that constitute the gates of the yard, skinny old Abi waves to us. Bent over at the waist, walking in a permanent sitting posture, she can barely look up, but still her smile beams in her leathery face.

Pema welcomes us with the familiar apology: 'We are poor and our house is dirty. Nothing to offer for Losar. Please sit down.' I hesitate to stay inside the altar room, but Bikul convinces me that it is necessary to follow the tradition. So we seat ourselves on an old mattress by the window and wait for someone to join us.

As always, my eyes are drawn to the altar across from us. The big oak table is heavily decorated with butterlamps and offerings. Behind it, Buddha sits in deep meditation. Once Ama tiptoes in to light a butterlamp and to start a fresh incense stick. Meme Monk enters and lowers himself onto the floor; enthroned behind a small table, he starts the ritual prayer.

Soon the entire family gathers: Pema brings a big pot of *thukpa* (noodle soup) followed by Ama, who is carrying Nima on her back; Chimmi; Abi; Karma; Ama's brother Larjap Lopon and his wife; Kinley, Ama's monk son; and her youngest daughter Rinzin Tshering.

Pema offers a cup of thukpa to Meme Monk and then to the guests. Thukpa is followed by arra, again prayer and offerings, then a meal.

Bikul and I are served a huge plate of rice, fried pork and fried datsi.

'*Zhe*, doctor, *zhe!*' Pema smiles and winks at me. Soon I know why. The food is delicious, but the chilli on the meat makes my eyes water and my nose run, and with a few prickly stings, it instantaneously clears my sinuses.

'You are still not used to chilli, isn't it?' Pema says and grins. 'You see, Nima and Chimmi have no problems.'

And it is true. Chimmi is happily devouring her meal heaped with meat and garnished with a few raw green chillies, while Nima most contentedly sucks on Norbu Ama's finger, which she keeps dipping into the red-brown sauce. Neither one shows even the slightest signs of culinary displeasure.

'Will you be getting chilli in Canada?' Pema enquires with mischief in her eyes. I shake my head emphatically. No chilli – and perhaps I will skip the rice for a while as well.

Pema misinterprets my rueful smile. 'Don't worry. We will send you some,' she comforts me, then loads another spoonful of sauce and meat onto my plate.

After the meal, we drink cup after cup of buttertea, accompanied by zao and thengma. Abi puts Nima on her lap, takes a little arra into her bowl, and splashes a few drops on her left side as an offering to the earth deity. Then Larjap Lopon's wife dishes out the strong alcohol with a big ladle. Bikul is the first to get his bowl filled with steaming hot arra mixed with eggs, and he has to drink and receive his refills until the ladle is empty. Everyone else joins in. Abi contents herself by feeding the home brew to Nima, who sucks the warm liquor with obvious pleasure. Since I firmly resist all offers of arra, my buttertea is generously refilled after every sip.

After a while the arra takes effect, loosens the tongue and chases away all shyness. Bikul strikes up the notes to his favourite song, 'Etho Metho'. The lyrics are for both a boy and a girl and, with a shy smile, Pema joins in.

'*Lay-la gooh-cho au-san bo-rang ga,*
Etho metho leg-pu pho-g pa la,
Metho photnee nan gaa tsham thong gaa,
Leg-pu chot-pay mi wa cha…'

Everyone listens intently, their faces expressing the popular lines. At first, a boy asks his sweetheart to look at a flower: 'This rhododendron, I want to put it in your hair. You would be so pretty.' The girl answers: 'No, I do not need this flower. Please do not pluck it; let it bloom. It looks much more beautiful in the forest.' The boy again praises his love: 'You are the most beautiful amongst all the girls. Let me take you to my home and give you a nice kira.' Again, the girl pleads for him to listen: 'I have many kiras, there is no need. If you want to give me something, please give me your love.'

Bikul finishes and looks at me with a broad smile until I feel myself blush. Luckily, at this moment, Ama and her daughters join to sing another love song. Ama's face crinkles into many fine lines while the arra heats her cheeks. At the end of the song, the girls are overcome by happy giggling.

Meme Monk takes out his little bamboo flute and toots a few notes. The instrument squeaks and squeals in protest. The old man nods in sympathy, picks up his bowl, and starts feeding the flute hot liquor. With a twinkle in his eyes, he tells us the secret to good music. 'You've got to take care of your friend. He might be hungry too.'

When Meme has quenched both his and the flute's thirst, Bikul takes the cymbals off the wall, and together, he and Meme make noise as well as they can.

The children are sent to fetch the real trumpets and horns, and when the orchestra assembles it is an impressive one. Meme is on his flute, Bikul alternates between the cymbals and another long bamboo flute while Larjap lopon and Kinley play the trumpets and Karma a long horn. There seems to be only one common goal in the merriness: to be heard as far and wide as possible, in tune or out. The noise they produce is awesome. Ama laughs and claps her hands; Chimmi bounces excitedly up and down; Nima, holding Abi's hands, sways his body either to dance or due to mild intoxication. And Meme monk interrupts his playing a few times to refresh both him and the flute with a wet little something.

Leaning towards me in order to make herself heard over the enthusiastic orchestra, Pema asks 'When you reach Canada, you will be coming back again?'

Surprised, I look at my friend. Although her body is rocking in rhythm to the music, her eyes are downcast and perhaps even a little sad.

'I hope so, Pema.' My answer is honest, but at the same time, I cannot help but wonder how long it will be.

'Please write to us.' Now Pema's voice is urgent.

'I promise.'

I meet Pema's suddenly anxious eyes. 'And will you send some information for Nima?'

Again I nod, and we both look at the little boy whose body still sways gently back and forth while his fingers roll his lower lips in tiny circles.

Then Bikul sets down his cymbals. 'Why are you two looking so sad over there? Why don't you sing with us?' Once more, he launches into his favourite Sharchhop song, completely out of tune with the orchestra. Pema grins. 'You are singing very nice, Dr. Bikul. I think you are feeling in love!' And satisfied to see Bikul blushing deeply, she turns to me and says, 'You must also learn the words. I will teach you before you go.'

Hours later, we reluctantly bid our friends farewell. In front of the old farmhouse everyone gathers for a picture, and the goodbyes are long and heartfelt. Larjap lopon invites us to visit him at his monastery. Abi holds my hands for a long, long time, and Meme Monk calls me for a picture of the two of us. Chimmi shouts loudly 'Goodbye Auntie!' while Pema takes Nima's hand and together they wave.

The two younger monks, Kinley and Larjap lopon, lead us in a small procession to the chorten at the village entrance. Ama and her sister-in-law follow us with buttertea and arra. On the chorten's base, we sit down one last time to drink, eat and play music. Finally, when the sky darkens and the rain sets in, the horns accompany our descent. Shouts hail through the air. Losar farewell.

TWENTY-EIGHT

THE SOUND OF A CONCH

A s my departure date nears, I start to count the days with a sinking heart. Every encounter becomes like another goodbye. Phuntshok shows up on our doorstep and decides to stay until I leave. He too seems to feel the enormity of my decision. Through Phuntshok, we ask Lam Neten if Bikul and I may offer a puja at the dzong, a way to wish farewell to Mongar. Lam Neten immediately agrees. He is happy about our timing. He himself will leave Mongar in a few weeks in order to return to his meditation at Sangpu Gompa, a remote monastery where he will spend the next few years in retreat. Tomorrow, he tells us, is one of the most auspicious days in the Bhutanese calendar, tomorrow would be a good day for us to hold a puja. Tomorrow, on

Friday the thirteenth of March, the monks will gather to perform the Sangay puja, a prayer to Lord Buddha.

Lam Neten smiles throughout our unofficial preparations for a farewell. He confidently reassures us that we will meet again, if not in this life, then sometime in another reincarnation. I so much want to believe that he is right.

In the late afternoon, Sangay, one of Bikul's monk friends, accompanies us to town to buy food for the puja. We pay for the rice, butter, biscuits, some vegetables, milk powder, sugar and tea, all of which Sangay takes back to the dzong. Meanwhile Bikul and I add a few more items to our shopping bag: incense sticks, Dalda for the butterlamps, two white ceremonial scarves, and a yellow fleece sweater as a present for Lam Neten.

'Let's bake chocolate cakes for the monks!' We are in high spirits, and it is out of our overboiling excitement that this ridiculous idea is born. Bikul makes the suggestion and promises to help. 'How many monks are there?' I ask. 'Oh, maybe seventy-five.' That means eight cakes! Bikul reassures me that it will be no problem.

By the time we reach home, it is past 7 p.m.; there is no electricity, only candlelight, and then, of course, no oven, only my doddering woodstove bukhari. I take out my big aluminium pot, which is lined with stones, and measure the diameter. Only one smaller pot containing the cake dough will fit into the interior. The whole construction will then have to heat up on top of the bukhari until the stones inside the large pot create enough heat to bake my cake. The whole procedure can take over an hour, so somehow I have to manage to construct two ovens and bake two cakes at once.

My kitchen turns into an assembly line of wet dough, aluminium pots and Bikul scuttling back and forth between the bukhari and the sink. The first two cakes burn and refuse to come out of the pots. Though my baking crew of Bikul, Phuntshok and his friend is eager and willing, they are quite useless. They do not even smell the charcoal when smoke starts rising from the bukhari!

It is madness. Bikul is sent to the kitchen to scrub pots while I stand at the dining table trying to peel burned paper off the bottom of the next two cakes. More and more cakes follow the fate of the first two, ending up in larger and smaller chunks with crusty bottoms. By midnight, when we shove the last two cakes onto the bukhari, Phuntshok and his friend are fast asleep, and I collapse on the bed. Bikul reassures me that he will manage the rest.

Nothing can go wrong now, I think to myself before sleep overtakes me.

I was mistaken. The clock shows 3.45 a.m. when Bikul finally comes to bed. 'What took you so long?' I ask drowsily. Bikul does not answer, he has already passed out beside me. We are supposed to be at the temple by 5 a.m., but Bikul is sound asleep.

Finally, at 5.30 a.m., still drowsy, we stumble up to the dzong carrying huge pots of what should have been chocolate cake. At the entrance to the Sangay lhakhang, by the light of my head-torch, I try my best to cut my work of wonder and package it into individual papers. At first, I am told that there is no rush, but then all of a sudden, it cannot go fast enough. Consequently, Lam Neten does end up with the biggest piece, but also with the only one that still has paper stuck to its bottom.

I join the puja and take my seat of honour beside Bikul and Phuntshok. After a while, though, our motionless position proves to be more painful than I had anticipated. As the minutes pass, my hips start to burn as if they will fall out of joint, and the hard wooden floor seems to push my anklebones deep into my tender flesh. My back starts aching, and leaning against the wall behind me, I can feel every single one of my vertebrae outlined against the wooden pillars.

Even the prayer starts to sound somewhat disjointed. Although I know that all the monks are praying the same words, I cannot shake the impression that everyone is doing his own thing. Some speak loudly, some low, some deep, others high. And many a time, a little monk will join in way off cue and quickly stutter his lines to catch up with the others.

Yet, listening to the enthusiastic voices of the small monks, I travel back to my own childhood, baffled at how different my upbringing was to theirs. For better or for worse, these little fellows are beginning a life of prayer and ritual. Not just today, not just this night, but for years and a lifetime to come. They will chant sacred words; they will devote their days to the Buddha's teachings. They will meditate in seclusion; some of them might achieve great skills and become honoured masters. Their world lies within the walls of a monastery, though their minds might yearn to travel. They will learn about truth and suffering, about abstinence and desire. And some day, ordinary folks will come to them to seek their blessings.

Today, however, the naughty little boys in them are not quite subdued yet, and daringly they make balls out of the cake paper and throw them at each other. Jokes are whispered at the chance of being discovered by the kudung, the temptation proving just too delicious.

At about 6.30 a.m. we all get up for a break. The only girl amongst the red robes, I have to trudge all the way up the Mongar's guesthouse to find a private spot. Although I run, my trip takes a long time. Back in the temple, Jigme ushers me past a group of monks into the lhakhang. There, before Lam Neten's quiet eyes, Jigme asks Bikul and me to light the butterlamps.

'This is a really great honour,' Bikul whispers excitedly, and I realise that all of the monks have filed into the doorframe, watching us and smiling. The lhakhang is still empty, only Lam Neten, Jigme and the two of us. When the last wick has been lit, I look at the sea of lamps, and I wish that there were more lamps to light, a longer time to stand beside Bikul and take part in this time-old tradition.

Phuntshok joins us, and together we return to our seats. The monks stream in and within moments, the puja is underway again. The low drone of the long horns and the thumping of metal rods on leather drums gently lead my mind to places and times centuries ago, to the ancient rituals of pure belief, of enlightened beings and wrathful deities, and of the power to rise beyond our mortal understanding. Time ceases to exist, loses itself in the steady drums of history.

Finally even the horns hush and the voices of the monks slow down and become quiet.

An expectant silence settles. Phuntshok pokes me gently in the side. 'You go to Lam Neten,' he whispers and we walk with bowed heads past the altar to the middle of the room.

'What is happening?' I ask Bikul, but he only shrugs his shoulders. The monks are all grinning. Standing with our backs to the altar, we prostrate to Lam Neten. Jigme pours a little holy water on our right palm and we sip at it before spreading it over our heads. Then we present Lam Neten with our white ceremonial scarves. Jigme motions us to sit, and we kneel facing the great lama, while the room becomes so quiet, you could hear a pin drop.

His gaze fixed upon us, Lam Neten starts to speak. I have never heard him by himself, quietly intoning the powerful words of a sermon. Still my mind flits to somewhere else. How should I kneel? If I copy Bikul, I will be taller than Bikul, which is what I would like to avoid, but surely it cannot be appropriate to sit back comfortably on my heels. Thankful that my long skirt is hiding my legs, I remain half kneeling, half leaning forward, until my thighs start screaming. I want to concentrate on Lam Neten's words, but I am too aware of the fifty pairs of eyes watching us closely. Lam Neten continues to speak, and now at regular intervals all of the monks join him for a single word spoken in unison. It sounds like an agreement, as if they are reinforcing the lama's words.

Then Jigme asks Bikul to get up and walk over to Lam Neten's seat. I follow close behind. Still speaking softly,

Lam Neten lays the ceremonial scarves around our neck and shoulders, as if presenting us with a medal. I am so nervous I can feel my hands shake, but Lam Neten's warm smile reassures me. I still do not know what is happening, and I am perplexed by the grin in the faces of dozens of monks.

Confused and delirious, we walk back to our seats. Phuntshok too is grinning. The monks' chants now rise in volume, and the words seem spoken faster and faster. There is no music, and then all becomes quiet, only Lam Neten's voice murmurs deeply. The others join in again, and their words are now accompanied by the ringing of bells, the horns, the low 'om' of the conch, and finally the sound of cymbals. Then the instruments hush, and only the horn introduces another thump of the big drums.

Everything feels a little unreal; perhaps a lack of sleep and the smoke of heavy incense have tricked my mind. Phuntshok whispers to us, and after a slight pause, Bikul turns to me.

'Lam Neten just gave us his blessings for a long life and many children.'

For a moment, I think my heartbeat stops.

'You mean…?'

Bikul nods and grins. Then he reaches for my hand and squeezes it gently. Our fingers remain locked.

Desperately, I try to focus my mind, but it seems that all thoughts have begun to bounce around in complete chaos. I want to picture the moment again. We prostrated, there was a prayer, Lam Neten presented the scarves to us – and all the monks were grinning. Suddenly I feel jubilant and victorious. At last, Mongar has accepted our love! In front of Buddha and some of his faithful disciples, we have just been married.

After the puja, Bikul and I linger for a while in the silent room. Outside the window, the deep call of a conch echoes through the valley. The soothing stillness of the mountains awake in me a sense of peace and contentment. Around me lives history, and yet this is the reality too. Somewhere another bell is ringing for prayer. It reminds me that it is time to let go. I know that I am saying goodbye to Bhutan; it is time to move on.

I look at Bikul and see the tiny reflections of candles in his eyes. I have to smile. My goodbyes are not for Bikul. The world is a big place. Somehow, somewhere, we will find a spot for both of us.

No, today, I am quietly thanking Bhutan. Over the last year, this tiny Himalayan kingdom has been my home. For one year, I have worked, fought and wept here, and I have dreamed, laughed and loved. I have come to appreciate the kingdom's struggle for survival and the King's quest to preserve its unique and ancient culture. There are many things about Bhutan, which to this day, I do not understand. It is no Shangri-La, and yet it is a special place that casts a spell on most who have entered.

As I listen for the echo of the conch calling through the valley, I know that a small part of me will always long for Bhutan, for the mountains, the trees and the prayer flags. I am sure that even if far away, I will reach out for the simplicity of this life that measures time in moons and counts the years with animals and elements.

There are people here who have touched my heart and moved my soul more than I ever thought possible. They are our friends in the villages, the minakpas and the monks, and a few kind spirits in the hospital. I know that I will miss them, their gentleness, their generosity and smiles, and their peaceful religion, which is so much part of this life in the mountains. And with all of my heart, I hope that some day we will meet again.

Yet I wonder what I will find if I return. Will I look back on this past year as my only true glimpse of a secluded Himalayan kingdom and a religion that has carried man through the centuries of change? I worry about the destructive nearness of technology. I am scared that the charm and innocence of the villages will soon be lost. How far will development spread? Is there hope that this ancient kingdom will survive its launch into the modern times? So many questions left – and only a few vivid images to guide my answers.

Perhaps one day, time will spread its lazy haze over my memories. Details will lose their shapes, and fantasy will dress the remaining pictures. Maybe one day, I will question the reality of those special nights, hidden behind the walls of a fortress, in a small country which is bowing to change. And still, I believe that the dream will remain. It is a dream of ancient times, of harmony and traditions. A dream filled with the hope that the voice of Buddhism will survive, here in the mountains of everlasting snow, where it is carried to heaven by the chanting of a mantra and the song of the prayer flags in the wind.

EPILOGUE

From the state of Assam in India, Bhutan is no more than a day's drive, and from a hill high above the banks of the river Brahmaputra, I can see the Himalayan foothills shimmering blue in the rising heat.

'Look! Beyond those mountains lies Mongar! Can you believe that my home is so close to Bhutan?' Excited, Bikul points towards the north.

'Yes, but what a long road it was for us,' I reply, thinking about a journey that spanned two years – from the isolated valley of Mongar to the comforts of my home in Canada, and finally back across the Pacific to the wide floodplains of Assam.

Beside me, in a white dhoti and looking more handsome than ever, Bikul – my courageous friend, my husband and my true love – nods seriously.

'It seems like a long time ago, doesn't it?'

I squeeze Bikul's hand lightly.

Yes, it seems like forever since the day Bikul gave up his job in Mongar and his plans for postgraduate studies in India, to follow me to Canada, where, while my stomach recovered, we fought our battle with bureaucracy for eighteen months. We were ready to start a new life together, but where and how proved to be more difficult than we had expected. Our first hurdle was Canadian immigration who doubted Bikul's intentions of staying with me and the sincerity of our love. My poor health did not allow me to return to India, and to avoid a lengthy and uncertain separation, we quickly married in a court of justice near my home town. An Indian wedding ceremony as we both had wished was out of the question for the time being. Still, the immigration officials were not convinced, and after a year without permission to leave and reenter Canada, by default, we began to settle in Toronto.

Unfortunately, Canada also forced Bikul to change his career. Not only would he not be able to continue his postgraduate oncology courses, his Indian medical education and licence were not recognised in Canada, effectively annulling his position as a doctor. Still, my health left us no choice. While Bikul waited for his Canadian residency papers, he continued to study at our home, trying to find an alternative path that would allow him to work in the field of cancer research. Finally, when his papers cleared, he started work on a PhD at the University of Toronto, while working in the pathology laboratory of the Hospital of Sick Children.

I returned to work at a small physiotherapy clinic and while, slowly, my stomach settled and my strength returned, I began writing about my impressions of Bhutan, which would later turn into the pages of this book.

Things had not turned out the way we had expected, but despite all odds, we managed to stay together. During this time of readjustment and healing while Bikul and I started anew, Bhutan withdrew into a bittersweet nostalgia. Letters, though lovingly written, were often lost on their journey across the Pacific, and only Pema, my trusted friend, has managed to keep in touch. Yet her words often saddened and worried me, and one of her letters has remained deeply etched in my mind.

Dearest Britta and Bikul,

I was very happy to see your letter and photo you had sent, but when the reply was delayed, I thought you both had forgotten me. But I am very happy that my love and remembrance are still in your heart. Chimmi always talks about you two. She took one of your photo. Nima is almost same, he understands us little only. I am worried only for Nima. Day and night, I am thinking only of Nima, my tears fell when I think of more... About here, both the roads are blocked from landslides, no way to escape from Mongar. These days I am not going anywhere, staying only in physio. I feel like crying when I think of the past days with you... Ugyen is in class II but her teacher says that she is very poor in studies. Every time I met her, I am telling her to come for dressing but she never comes... What about your stomach now? Are you getting better? Do take care of it because you have to be a mom soon. If it is so, please inform me. I am very eager to hear the news for both of you... If you come to India, phone me so that we can meet each other...

Your friend always,

Pema

When we finally planned our Indian wedding in Assam, we invited Pema to join us in the celebration, but sadly, she could not make it. From Dr. Pradhan we heard that Nima is not improving and the trips to Vellore have only resulted in more bad news, more prescription drugs and insurmountable expenses. In some ways, I share Pema's helplessness; perhaps if Pema and Nima stayed in North America, Nima could receive better rehabilitation, better equipment, and Pema would get more support – but I do not know if it would be worth the cost of tearing them from their familiar environment and family. So all I could do was to send Pema some educational books and videos, but even then, I wonder if the pictures of fancy equipment and descriptions of modern rehabilitation tools would not add to Pema's frustration, knowing how such treatments are out of reach for her son.

As to my other little patients, time and distance have severed the already tenuous connection with the villages of Bhutan, and I can only hope that the absence of bad news heralds success.

In the meantime, Bhutan has taken its own huge step towards modernisation, and through the weekly newspaper, the *Kuensel*, I have been following Bhutan's developments with mixed emotions.

On 1 June 1999, with the help of foreign funding and a brave look towards the new millennium, Bhutan opened its doors to the media by hooking into the Internet and for the first time ever legalising television and satellite dishes. The floodgates to the dangers of a new generation of boredom and dissatisfaction have therewith been unbolted, and Hindi songs and Hollywood action will more easily dilute a precious but fragile heritage.

Friends who drove through Mongar a few weeks ago said that we would be hard pressed to recognise it. The new bypass road has been finished, the bazaar largely shifted, satellite dishes are sprouting like mushrooms even from remote hillsides, and the continuing works on the Kuruchu hydro project keep flooding the little town with Indian labourers, foreign rupees and industriousness.

In many ways, I wish that I could remember Bhutan the way that it used to be, and yet the no longer spoken words in Sharchhopkha are already fading from my memory. As Bhutan is moving towards a new era of cyberlinks and CNN news, and evening gatherings worship the television screen instead of an altar with flickering butterlamps, I guess that I too will move forward, embracing change as a survival technique.

I am an Indian bride now, adorned with fine jewellery and wearing my red bindhi and sindhoor. In a formal, three-day ceremony, Bikul and I have been married in front of my parents, who travelled with us, Bikul's family and hundreds of Assamese friends and neighbours, some cheerfully, some sceptically welcoming me into their community. I have changed from a Bhutanese kira into a delicate silk sari, shyness overcoming me as the elegant folds of my dress rustle while I rise to greet my new family. Quietly I whisper 'Namaskar' instead of 'Kuzuzang po la', and the altar with statues of Buddha and Guru Rinpoche has been replaced by a simple book of prayer on a bronzen offering bowl.

And yet – the conch in the Hindu holy man's hand makes the same sound I first heard in a small Himalayan kingdom: *Om*… it is the sound of a new beginning.

GLOSSARY OF FREQUENTLY USED BHUTANESE TERMS

Abi a term to address an older woman

ADM Administrative Officer

Ama a term to address an adult woman

Apa a term to address an adult man

arra an alcoholic beverage locally prepared from rice, corn or other grains

atsara a clown at the Bhutanese dzong festivals called tshechu

bukhari a metal woodburning stove used for heating and cooking

butterlamp a candle made out of hardened butter or vegetable oil in a solid dish

buttertea ('seudja' in Dzongkha or Sharchhopkha) – the local tea made from dark tea leaves boiled and enriched with butter and salt

cham	religious dance
chorten	a Buddhist stone monument containing sacred relics and treasures
damaru	a handheld double-sided drum for religious ceremonies
dharma	the teachings of Buddha
DMO	District Medical Officer; the medical supervisor of a district hospital
dzong	a fortress-monastery which today houses the government offices and the national monk body
Dzongkha	Bhutan's national language
gelong	an ordained monk
gho	the national dress for Bhutanese men
goemba	Buddhist monastery
gomchen	a spiritual villager who has received religious training
Guru Rinpoche	also referred to as Padmasambhava, a missionary often considered the 'Second Buddha' who introduced tantric Buddhism to Bhutan
kharang	coarsely ground dried corn
kira	the national dress for Bhutanese women

Lam Neten	the head abbot of the monk body in a dzong
lama	religious master
Lhakhang	temple
Lopon	Buddhist scholar or teacher
Losar	Bhutanese New Year
mantra	a prayer which is repeated over and over; a chant
Meme	title for an older man
minakpa	villager
ngultrum	Bhutanese currency
prayer wheel	a cylindrical 'wheel' containing prayers
prayer flag	long pieces of cloth printed with religious texts and symbols
puja	a Buddhist or Hindu religious ceremony
rachu	a long scarf worn over the left shoulder by women on formal occasions
seudja	buttertea
Sharchhop(kha)	language of Eastern Bhutan
Tata	Indian manufacturer of trucks

thangka	religious picture
thengma	dried and beaten corn
thondrol	a huge banner with the image of Guru Rinpoche
toego	a jacket that is worn with the kira, the Bhutanese women's national dress
Trulku	a reincarnated lama
tshechu	a yearly religious dance festival held at the dzong
wang	a collective religious blessing
zao	toasted rice

Britta Das was born in Germany in 1971, and at the age of thirteen she moved with her family to Canada. In 1994 she completed a Bachelor of Science in Physiotherapy in London, Ontario, then worked and travelled around Australia and South-east Asia. She volunteered with VSO to work in Bhutan after becoming enchanted by this rarely visited kingdom on a short trip there. During her volunteer year she met her future husband Bikul, and they now live in Canada with their two young daughters. Buttertea at Sunrise is Britta Das's first book and has also been published in Germany and the Netherlands.

For more information on Bhutan, or to view photographs from Britta's year in Mongar, please visit www.brittadas.com

Other titles from Summersdale

HEARTLANDS
TRAVELS IN THE TIBETAN WORLD

CHINA
(TIBET)

MICHAEL BUCKLEY

summersdale *travel*

Heartlands

Travels in the Tibetan World

Michael Buckley

1 84024 209 4

A glimpse into the troubled soul of hidden Tibet.

Reaching Lhasa is the dream of all Tibetan pilgrims, but China's brutal occupation has reduced this ancient civilisation to a shadow of its former self. If you want to discover real Tibetan culture, you have to go elsewhere on the plateau – to Ladakh, Bhutan or Mongolia.

Exploring these remote regions in a series of trips, Michael Buckley embarks on a quest to come to grips with Tibetan ways, from the celebrated spirituality to the downright bizarre, and finds himself balanced somewhere in between magic and reality. In a fascinating and personal journey of discovery, Buckley rubs shoulders with hardy nomads, encounters giant phalluses and stuffed kangaroos, cycles snowbound passes, chats with the Dalai Lama and survives interrogation by Chinese police.

Darkly funny, informative and inspired, Buckley's account of these amazing lands makes invaluable reading.

Michael Buckley was born in London, immigrated to Australia at an early age and has travelled extensively since. He currently lives in Vancouver, Canada, but is equally at home in the Himalayas and South-East Asia.

'... should become compulsory reading before any visit to Tibet or Dharamsala, or Ladakh or the Himalayas or Mongolia or Bhutan and if, like me you missed this book before you went, then it needs to be read on your return'

Isobel Losada

THE HOTEL ON THE
ROOF OF THE WORLD

FIVE YEARS IN TIBET

ALEC LE SUEUR

The Hotel on the Roof of the World

Five Years in Tibet

Alec Le Sueur

1 84024 199 3

Few foreigners are lucky enough to set foot on Tibetan soil, but Alec Le Sueur spent five extraordinary years there, working in the unlikeliest Holiday Inn in the world. Against the breathtaking beauty of the Himalayas unfolds a highly amusing and enlightening account of his experiences.

Fly infestations at state banquets, unexpected deliveries of live snakes, a predominance of yaks and everything yak-related, the unbelievable Miss Tibet competition, insurmountable communication problems and a dead guest are just some of the entertainments to be found at the 'Fawlty Towers' of Lhasa.

Daily challenges are increased by the fragile political situation. Le Sueur, the only westerner since the days of Heinrich Harrer to spend so long in Tibet, examines its intriguing cultural background, providing a fascinating insight into a country that was only just opening up to the outside world.

'Le Sueur... provides us with the means of improving our knowledge of a far away country about which we know little. Fawlty Towers goes to Tibet'

The Guardian

'... offers lucid details about living in a place that Westerners tend to misunderstand'

Time Magazine

'Hysterically funny, laugh a minute'

Adventure-mag.com

www.summersdale.com